FOOD STANDARDS REGULATION
THE NEW LAW

Iain MacDonald
Barrister

and

Amanda Hulme
Barrister

JORDANS
2000

Published by
Jordan Publishing Limited
21 St Thomas Street
Bristol BS1 6JS

British Library Cataloguing-in-Publication Data
A catalogue record for this book is available from the British Library.

ISBN 0 85308 649 4 ✓

Typeset by Mendip Communications Ltd, Frome, Somerset
Printed in Great Britain by MPG Books Ltd, Bodmin, Cornwall

FOOD STANDARDS REGULATION
THE NEW LAW

Preface

The Food Standards Agency has the potential to radically alter the way in which the regulation of food is dealt with in the UK. Its powers range from formulating policy to monitoring and setting standards for enforcement of food legislation. In order to understand how the Agency fits into the complex structure of food regulation, it is necessary to have an understanding of how regulation of this area has developed and the status quo prior to the introduction of the Agency. This book attempts to set the Agency in context, dealing with its powers and functions and how they can be exercised, in addition to highlighting areas of potential controversy and challenge.

The Agency is intended to cover the whole range of food issues, 'from plough to plate' (the European Commission, where the inclusion of matters equine in the food chain presumably raises fewer eyebrows, uses the phrase 'from stable to table'). The Agency will, for example, be concerned with animal feed, an area which is perhaps belatedly now receiving the consideration which it warrants.

To a certain extent, this book may be considered a little premature, since the importance of the Agency will depend on the way in which it chooses to exercise its powers. It certainly has the tools to deal with some of the many criticisms faced by those involved in the regulation of food. As far as the people involved in food production and retailing are concerned, they have the right to expect the Agency to exercise its powers to bring enforcement policy throughout the UK onto a more consistent footing. Consumers (in addition to benefiting from more uniform enforcement) can expect clearer advice from the Agency on food matters, such as nutrition or food safety, than they have been used to in the past. The Agency has been trumpeted as a body independent of central government, and there can be little doubt that the de-politicisation of food regulation can only benefit both government and members of the public. Of course, the government cannot abdicate all responsibility in this area and hard decisions, such as the banning of beef on the bone, for example, will of course remain the province of central government, albeit with advice and assistance provided by the Agency. The manner in which the Agency deals with controversial issues such as BSE will be an important test of its true independence.

We would like to thank our colleagues in chambers for their assistance throughout the writing of the book, in particular Fred Philpott and Claire Andrews, whose experience in the area has been a great help. We would also like to thank the staff at Jordans, who have maintained their enthusiasm for the book in spite of many shifts in the timetable. Last but not least, we would like to acknowledge the support and tolerance shown by Faye and Paul to the respective authors.

IAIN MACDONALD
AMANDA HULME
Gough Square Chambers
August 2000

Contents

Table of Cases

References are to paragraph numbers.

Table of Statutes

References are to paragraph numbers. References in *italics* are to Appendix page numbers.

Table of Statutory Instruments

References are to paragraph numbers. References in *italics* are to Appendix page numbers.

Table of EC and European Material

References are to paragraph numbers.

Table of Directions and Guidance

References are to paragraph numbers.

Table of Abbreviations

ACMSF	Advisory Committee on the Microbiology Safety of Food
ACNFP	Advisory Committee on Novel Foods and Processes
ACP	Advisory Committee on Pesticides
BSE	bovine spongiform encephalopathy
CAP	Common Agricultural Policy
CFI	Court of First Instance
COMA	Committee on the Medical Aspects of Food and Nutrition Policy
COT	Committee on Toxicity of Chemicals in Food, Consumer Products and the Environment
DoH	Department of Health
ECHR	European Court of Human Rights
ECJ	European Court of Justice
EEA	European Economic Area
EPA 1990	Environmental Protection Act 1990
EU	European Union
FAC	Food Advisory Committee
FAO	Food and Agriculture Organisation (UN)
FDA	Food and Drug Administration (US)
FEPA 1985	Food and Environment Protection Act 1985
FSPB	Food Safety Promotion Board
GMOs	genetically modified organisms
HACCP	Hazard Analysis and Critical Control Points
HAP	Home Authority Principle
JFSSG	Joint Food Safety and Standards Group
LACOTS	Local Authorities Coordinating Body on Food and Trading Standards
MAFF	Ministry of Agriculture, Fisheries and Food
MHS	Meat Hygiene Service
PACE	Police and Criminal Evidence Act 1984
SEAC	Spongiform Encephalopathy Advisory Committee
SPS Agreement	Agreement on the Application of Sanitary and Phytosanitary Measures
TBT Agreement	Agreement on Technical Barriers to Trade
WHO	World Health Organisation
the 1860 Act	Food and Drink Act 1860
the 1938 Act	Food and Drugs Act 1938
the 1955 Act	Food and Drugs Act 1955
the 1984 Act	Food Act 1984
the 1990 Act	Food Safety Act 1990

the 1999 Act	Food Standards Act 1999
the Agency	Food Standards Agency
the Convention	Convention for the Protection of Human Rights and Fundamental Freedoms
the EC Treaty	Treaty establishing the European Economic Community
the Maastricht Treaty	Treaty on European Union
1995 Regulations	Food Safety (General Hygiene) Regulations 1995
1996 Regulations	Food Labelling Regulations 1996
2000 Regulations	Genetically Modified and Novel Foods (Labelling) (England) Regulations 2000

Chapter 1
Historical Development of Food Law
and the Food Standards Agency

THE NEED FOR A FOOD STANDARDS AGENCY

1.1 It is apparent to anyone who reads a newspaper that, over the last decade or more, food has increasingly become a major public issue. Whether this is a result of greater media attention or whether it points to a genuine deterioration in standards is a matter of conjecture, but consumer interest in the topic is strong and cannot be ignored. When one compares, for example, the risk of dying as a result of contracting Creutzfeld-Jacob disease and the risk of death in a motor accident with the relative publicity the two topics receive, the extent to which food safety has become an area of concern is obvious. Salmonella in eggs, the Scottish E-coli outbreak, genetically modified foods and beef on the bone are all issues which have raised public awareness of food safety and standards.

1.2 The regulation of food is an extraordinarily complex undertaking. The plethora of advisory committees and public interest groups provide a bewildering array of advice, both to government and the consumer. The Ministry of Agriculture, Fisheries and Food (MAFF), the predecessor to the new Food Standards Agency (the Agency), enjoyed the role of both regulator and promoter of British food interests, hence unsurprisingly it was an easy target for criticism whatever decisions were taken, a factor central to the plans for setting up the new Agency:

> 'We must not lose sight of the ball itself: why the Agency is needed. It was proposed by both Government and Opposition Members before the general election, to overcome the perceived contradiction of the Ministry of Agriculture, Fisheries and Food, as the sponsoring department of agriculture and the food industry, being the guardian of food standards and safety. We could not carry the public perception. That is why the Agency is being set up.'[1]

The public has become disillusioned with the system of food regulation and sceptical over government health advice, and conflicting views on the benefits of red wine, or the problems of high cholesterol, for example.

1.3 The need for a clean start has been apparent for some time. It is possible to view the Agency as a cynical attempt to deflect potential criticism of the handling of sensitive food matters away from the government onto yet another quango but, as will be seen, the Agency has powers which could create greater embarrassment for the government if matters are mishandled.

---

1   Minister of State at MAFF in the Commons Second Reading, *Hansard*, vol 333, no 107, col 856.

1.4   One of the watchwords of the Agency is openness. The Agency has power to publish, subject to certain restrictions, all of its findings: research, results of observations and so on, including the advice it gives to Ministers. The significance of this openness was stressed by the Minister at MAFF in his evidence to the Food Standards Committee:

> 'If Ministers do not agree with the Food Standards Agency advice, everyone will know about it because the Food Standards Agency advice will be in the public domain and if Ministers choose to take a different approach, which may be in some cases even more precautionary, then it is the ministers' job to go to the floor of the House of Commons and defend their position.'[1]

1.5   A key issue therefore is the degree of independence which the Agency will have from ministerial direction. The extent to which Ministers are able to influence the composition of the Agency, the direction it takes on potentially controversial issues, and, crucially, the assumption of the powers of the Agency, will all be examined later in this book.

THE HISTORY OF FOOD STANDARDS REGULATION IN THE UK

1.6   The need to regulate the food industry can be traced as far back as the commencement of commercial food trade, when the adulteration of food was regarded as an easy way for dishonest traders to increase their profits. Consequently, traders saw the marketing advantages in promoting the idea that, as honest traders, they were trading only in pure foodstuffs. Therefore, although the introduction of food regulation was heralded as protecting the welfare of consumers, in reality, the impetus to regulate food standards was to protect the honest trader from the undercutting of prices by dishonest traders.

1.7   The initial approach towards regulating the industry was to promote self-regulation. As a result, even though a vast amount of legislation now exists, the system still relies to a large extent on informal methods, with a significant amount of guidance being contained in Codes of Practice and other guidance materials. Later, as legislation was introduced to set standards for specific foodstuffs such as tea, coffee and bread, it developed in a piecemeal fashion. However, the early legislation lacked efficiency because of unsophisticated systems of communication and underdeveloped scientific knowledge which meant that food was crudely tested.

1.8   Sporadic legislation continued to be implemented until the Food and Drink Act 1860 (the 1860 Act) was enacted, which attempted to provide a more general approach to food standards. This Act introduced offences of knowingly selling food containing an injurious ingredient and selling food, which was adulterated and not pure. This Act also created local food and drugs authorities which could

---

1   *Minutes of Evidence to the Food Standards Committee*, p 8.

appoint an analyst and could order food samples to be analysed. However, these public authorities were not obliged either to enforce the criminal provisions or to appoint an analyst, and sampling officers had no enforcement powers.

1.9 Powers of enforcement were strengthened some years later with the introduction of the Adulteration of Food and Drugs Act 1872. This Act made the appointment of a public analyst obligatory and sampling officers (called 'inspectors of nuisance', later to become the current 'environmental health officers', 'inspectors of weights and measures', now 'trading standards officers' and 'inspectors of markets') were given more power.

1.10 The 1860 Act did not extend to drugs, which were regulated separately by legislation introduced 8 years later. Food and drugs were finally combined in the Sale of Food and Drugs Act 1875. This Act is generally regarded as the forerunner to the present regulatory system.

1.11 However, following the Sale of Food and Drugs Act of 1875, there was a return to specific legislation which regulated the standard of individual foods. Thereafter, the history of food legislation was one of a multitude of specific pieces of legislation followed by consolidating Acts. In 1938, the Food and Drugs Act (the 1938 Act) repealed all the current food and medicines statutes and consolidated them into a single Act. The 1938 Act, which now covered important matters such as quality, composition, labelling and safety issues, also made important amendments to the legislation.

1.12 During this period of legislation and consolidation, many of the principles of the modern regulatory system were established, including local authority enforcement, analysis by a public analyst and the creation of the types of criminal offences which still exist today. More specific and detailed legislation set down standards for the quality and labelling of food. This trend became more predominant in the 1940s, when the composition of essential foods was prescribed. Again, this was not so much out of a desire to protect consumers, but as a result of the limited availability of foods during the Second World War with the consequential introduction of cheaper, poor-quality substitutes and rationing and a desire to prevent soldiers' ill-health caused by eating adulterated food.

1.13 This process finally culminated in the Food and Drugs Act 1955 (the 1955 Act), which regulated the preparation, advertising and sale of food for human consumption. This Act remained in force until 1984, which was, in the history of food legislation, a considerable amount of time. Unsurprisingly, following this Act, there were a number of additional statutes enacted, which supplemented food regulation (eg milk was regulated in separate legislation) and the UK's accession into Europe, with the consequential enactment of the European Communities Act 1972, resulted in a number of amendments to the 1955 Act. However, by the 1980s, it was becoming apparent that the current system of food regulation was unable to deal with the problems associated with modern production methods. In 1982, higher sentences were prescribed for food offences and legislation was enacted to make some offences indictable and, therefore, triable in a Crown Court.

1.14 By 1984, it was again decided to consolidate the regime and to implement fully the effects of entering into Europe.

1.15 It is apparent from this brief explanation of the history of food legislation that, certainly, until 1984, its roots were firmly established in a system dating back to the mid-nineteenth century. At no point had a radical new approach been applied. However, by 1984, the inadequacies were becoming apparent and the calls for a more efficient system were becoming stronger.

1.16 The Food Act 1984 (the 1984 Act) was general in nature and the detailed provisions were contained in regulations. This regime had a wide interpretation of food, which included ingredients in food but excluded water and, in certain circumstances, there was a presumption that food was intended for human consumption. Requirements as to the composition and labelling were strengthened. The offences under the 1984 Act, which are substantially reproduced in the current legislation, continued to be similar to the earlier offences and remained of strict liability, a finding confirmed back in 1888 in relation to the 1875 Act.[1] The 1984 Act also allowed for regulations to be made to set the standards required of food premises. Many of these features remain apparent in the current legislation.

1.17 The 1984 legislation contained a defence of warranty and the 'third party procedure', both of which had been contained in previous legislation and which are now both replaced by a general due diligence defence under the Food Safety Act 1990 (the 1990 Act). By virtue of s 100 of the 1984 Act, a person prosecuted for an offence could be acquitted by blaming a third party. However, in order to avail itself of this defence, the identity of the third party had to be notified to the prosecution 3 clear days before the hearing and that person then had to be brought before the court. The original defendant had to prove that the contravention was caused by the third party and that the defendant had used all due diligence to secure compliance with the provisions. This procedure was particularly burdensome.

1.18 The defence of warranty was contained in s 102 of the 1984 Act and provided that it was a defence for a person charged with an offence to prove that he was in possession of a warranty, which would be to the effect that the food complied with the statutory provisions. If a person possessed such a warranty, it was then only necessary to prove that he had no reason to believe that the food was anything other than as warranted and that the food was still in the same state as when it was supplied. A warranty could be given to a UK business by an overseas importer and this would provide a defence to the UK importer. As a result of this defence, it was often impossible for enforcement officers to control the importation of illegal products because the person who had provided the warranty was outside the country.

1.19 Enforcement powers were provided in the form of closure and emergency orders. These powers were brought within the food legislation, although they

---

1   *Betts v Armstead* (1888) 20 QBD 771.

had previously existed under environmental law provisions. These powers allowed local authorities to apply to the magistrates when they considered there to be a danger to health. However, a closure order could be made only on 14 days notice and when the business had already been found guilty of an offence, and an emergency order could be invoked only where there was an imminent danger to health and these had to be made on 3 clear days notice. Furthermore, the 1984 Act provided for compensation to be awarded to a food business if a closure order was granted in respect of premises which were later not considered to be an imminent risk. Compensation was paid from the local authorities' budgets.

1.20   These controls remained only a consolidation of previous legislation, which had itself derived from old, unsophisticated and outdated principles. Premises which were clearly a dangerous health hazard were allowed to continue to trade for at least 3 days before any effective action could be taken to stop them and the provision of compensation to defendants deterred effective enforcement as local authorities were often reluctant to risk their limited budgets.

1.21   Even before the 1984 Act was enacted, the government had announced plans for the review of the system and, in December 1984, shortly after the 1984 Act was passed, a consultation paper was released entitled *The Review of Food Legislation*. A number of proposals for reform were suggested, including the strengthening of controls over the sale of unfit food, a stricter approach to the sale of novel foods and the implementation of a new defence which required offenders to show that they had taken all due diligence to prevent the commission of the offence. In addition, it recommended the increased use of Codes of Practice to ensure that individual aspects of the food industry could also be regulated. However, these proposals were not embraced immediately.

1.22   At this time, issues of concern relating to food continued to grow. Against the backdrop of recent nuclear disaster and the resulting nuclear contamination of food, there was increased concern over the use of pesticides. Reported incidents of food poisoning increased sharply as did the number of interested pressure groups, and media attention grew. In 1988, media attention was at its peak when Edwina Currie made her infamous accouncement that all egg production in the UK was contaminated with salmonella. The years between 1986 and 1990 have been regarded as a time of 'food crisis', although it has been suggested that such criticism is unduly harsh.[1] None the less, in 1989, from the resultant political crisis emerged a White Paper entitled *Food Safety – Protecting the Consumer*.[2] This document proposed a major overhaul of food regulation.

1.23   The Food Safety Bill was published in November 1989 and was given the Royal Assent on 29 June 1990. The Food Safety Act 1990 (the 1990 Act) is the statute which regulates the food industry in the UK today. It is widely considered that this Act implemented a more efficient regulatory system, with stringent controls on food manufacture, processing and distribution. However,

---

1   See the Introduction to *Butterworths' Law of Food and Drugs* (Butterworths, 1997).
2   27 July 1989 Cmnd 732.

during its passage through Parliament, there were a number of criticisms of the proposed new Act but most significantly, there were calls for the establishment of an independent food standards agency. Those calls have only now been answered with the passing of the Food Standards Act 1999 (the 1999 Act).

HOW THE PROPOSALS DEVELOPED

1.24   The Food Standards Act 1999 came about after an extremely lengthy consultation process. The various stages are set out in brief here. Detailed analysis of relevant points arising from such consultation and scrutiny will be found within the relevant sections of this book which deal with the specific provisions of the 1999 Act.

Professor James' Report

1.25   Commissioned by the present Labour government when in opposition, Professor Phillip James of the Rowett Research Institute produced his Report on 30 April 1997. The Report was the foundation for the Agency, making the following key findings and recommendations.

- The public has lost confidence in the safety of British food, with secrecy in decision-making and the perceived conflict between political and industrial interests on one hand and issues of public health and consumer interests on the other being identified as significant factors contributing to this. The lack of coordination between the various experts and advisory bodies, together with the fragmented nature of the system of dealing with food standards are also significant problems.

- A Food Standards Agency should be established as a non-departmental public body, with a structure based loosely on that of the Health & Safety Executive.

- Funding should be the responsibility of Health Ministers, and the Agency should be accountable to Parliament through the Secretary of State for Health.

- The Agency should have a remit to assure public health in all matters of national food policy including the microbiological, chemical and nutritional aspects of food, and novel food and processes, such as genetic modification. The remit should also cover food standards and labelling and the Agency's role should include developing policy, proposing and drafting legislation and responsibility for public education and information. It should have powers of access for auditing, surveillance and enforcement 'from plough to plate' and work with local authorities to produce a cohesive structure.

- The Agency should have responsibility for law enforcement, in the sense of coordinating, monitoring, setting standards for and auditing local authority food law enforcement activities. It should have enforcement powers of its own and be able to assist local authorities if necessary. It should have an effective regional presence to support local authorities.

- The Agency would have to take over all of MAFF's responsibilities in respect of food standards and safety, including policy-making, expert scientific assessment, technical negotiation with the EU, food research, public education and food surveillance. The analogous responsibilities of the Department of Health would also be taken over by the Agency.

- The Agency should have a structure comprising a Commission of about 10 members appointed by the Prime Minister or Ministerial Council, which should include people with a background in industry but public and consumer interests should be in the majority. Representatives from Scotland, Wales and Northern Ireland should be included and there should be a full-time Commissioner, with members working at least 3–4 days per month.

- There must be high-quality administrative and scientific staff and a Chief Executive, with staff transferring from existing government departments acquiring a culture where public health and consumer interests dominate whilst proper account is taken of economic and business interests.

- Account has to be taken of the different surveillance and enforcement structures in the constituent parts of the UK and, in the event of devolution, the Agency would advise the devolved Parliament in the same way as it advises Westminster.

- An appropriate name for the Agency, to portray its focus effectively, would be 'The Food and Health Commission'.

- Costs arising from food-related disease are extremely high, whereas the direct costs of introducing effective food safety measures are relatively low. The proposals would reorganise a large number of public bodies into a more cohesive structure.

1.26 Responses to the report indicated, according to MAFF, 'widespread public support' for the Agency. Consequently, the Joint Food Safety and Standards Group, a body consisting of officials from MAFF and the Department of Health, was set up. It is this body which has been carrying out much of the work which is expected to become solely the province of the Agency and from whom a significant proportion of staff for the Agency will be drawn.

The White Paper: *The Food Standards Agency – A Force for Change*

1.27 This document was published in January 1998, following the consultation process, and inviting further responses from interested parties. It set out 'Guiding principles' for the proposed Agency, which are reproduced here.

- The essential aim of the Agency is the protection of public health in relation to food.

- The Agency's assessments of food standards and safety will be unbiased and based on the best available scientific advice, provided by experts invited in their own right to give independent advice.

- The Agency will make decisions and take action on the basis that:
  (i)   the Agency's decisions and actions should be proportionate to the risk;
  (ii)   the Agency pays due regard to costs as well as benefits to those affected by them, and avoids over-regulation;
  (iii) the Agency should act independently of specific sectoral interests.

- The Agency will strive to ensure that the general public has adequate, clearly presented information in order to allow it to make informed choices. In doing this, the Agency will aim to avoid raising unjustified alarm.

- The Agency's decision-making processes will be open, transparent and consultative, including representatives of those who would be affected, unless the need for urgent action to protect public health makes this impossible.

- In its decisions and actions, the Agency will aim to achieve clarity and consistency of approach.

- The Agency's decisions and actions will take full account of the obligations of the UK under domestic and international law.

- The Agency will aim for efficiency and economy in delivering an effective operation.

1.28   These principles are, unsurprisingly, not specifically reproduced in the Food Standards Act 1999, although there are provisions, which one can identify as an attempt to give such ideas a coherent legal form. They are, in some ways, self-evident, for example no sensible organisation would say anything other than it would act in a fashion so as 'to avoid raising unnecessary alarm'. None the less, the principles provide a backdrop of legislative intent and, therefore, are relevant to interpretation of the 1999 Act.

Consultation on draft legislation

1.29   A draft Food Standards Bill was published as part of a consultation document in January 1999, following responses to the White Paper. The draft Bill incorporated provision for the imposition of a levy on food premises, a recommendation made in the White Paper, to fund the Agency. There was widespread opposition to such a levy throughout the consultation process, not least because the proposal was for a 'flat-rate' charge on all premises, so that a small sandwich shop would pay as much as a large supermarket. When the Bill finally reached the House of Commons, the idea of a charge was dropped in favour of meeting the costs of the Agency from general taxation.

The Food Standards Committee

1.30   This Committee was set up to undertake 'pre-legislative scrutiny' of the draft Bill following a resolution of the House of Commons on 8 February 1999. The Committee called a number of witnesses to give evidence before it in February and March 1999 before producing a report on 24 March 1999. It made a number of recommendations, including the limitation and amendment of the flat-rate levy proposals, the most important of which are dealt with in the course of the commentary on the Act in Chapter 6.

1.31   This was the first committee of its type and, although the Bill was by no means in its final form at this stage, the fact that evidence was given by Ministers to the Committee gives its deliberations (and the evidence which was presented) particular value in interpretation of the Food Standards Act 1999.

Parliamentary scrutiny

1.32   The Bill was given its First Reading in the House of Commons on 10 June 1999 and had its Second Reading on 21 June 1999. This debate was 'guillotined', no doubt due to shortage of Parliamentary time. The Bill was subsequently considered in Standing Committee B in late June and July 1999. It received its First Reading in the House of Lords on 23 July 1999 and Second Reading on 30 July 1999. It was then considered in Committee in October. Royal Assent was granted on 11 November 1999. The relevant parts of the various debates are considered in the body of the commentary on the Act in Chapter 6.[1]

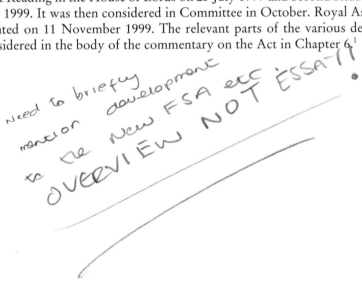

Chapter 2

European and International Regulation

THE ROLE OF EUROPE IN FOOD LEGISLATION

2.1 The UK became a Member State of the European Community on 1 January 1973 and, therefore, it was obliged to harmonise national law, including legislation relating to food, with that of the European Community. The principle source of community law is the Treaty establishing the European Economic Community (the EC Treaty), which is amended from time to time by later treaties.

2.2 On 1 February 1986, the Single European Act was signed, which had as its principal objective the completion of the internal market by the end of 1992. In February 1992, the Treaty on European Union was signed in Maastricht, which amended the EC Treaty and added new areas of competence to the Community, including substantive provisions concerning economic and monetary union. However, the Maastricht Treaty also introduced new provisions which have a direct effect on food legislation. The EC Treaty was further amended by the Treaty of Amsterdam, which came into force on 1 May 1999. As a result of the amendments made by the Treaty of Amsterdam, many of the Article numbers of the EC Treaty have now changed.

2.3 The important provisions in respect of food policy, introduced by the Maastricht Treaty include Art 129 (Title X) (now Art 152, Title XIII), entitled 'Public Health', which seeks to ensure 'a high level of human health protection by encouraging cooperation between the Member States and, if necessary, lending support to their action'. Community action is intended to be directed towards the prevention of diseases.

2.4 Article 129a (Title XI) (now Art 153, Title XIV), entitled 'Consumer Protection' seeks to protect consumers by taking specific action to support and supplement policies of Member States in order to protect, among other things, the health of consumers. This Article allows consumer protection also to be taken into account in other aspects of community policies. Finally, the Title dealing with the Environment was amended to include the pursuit of the objective of protecting human health (previously Art 130r, now Art 174 and Title XIX).

2.5 Although the Food Safety Act 1990 did not directly originate from EC legislation, it was compatible with all EC legislation existing at the time. In addition, s 17 gives Ministers the power to make orders implementing EC legislation.

2.6   In order to understand the role played by Europe in the regulation of food, it is necessary to have a basic understanding of the institutions and legislative framework of Europe.

The institutions of Europe

The European Council
2.7   This is made up of the Heads of State of Government of the Member States and its Presidency passes periodically to each Member State. It meets at least twice a year and is responsible for developing the general political agenda and policies of the EU.

The Commission
2.8   The Commission consists of 20 Commissioners, who are selected by the respective Member States. Some States have proportionately more representation than others. The UK has two Commissioners. The Commission's role is widely defined but, basically, it is responsible for initiating legislation and for formulating measures taken by Europe. It is often involved in extensive consultation and has a wide range of rule-making powers to ensure the proper implementation of European measures.

2.9   At the level below the Commissioners, there are the Directorate Generals, who are known by their number and who are headed by a Director General. For the purposes of food, the most important Directorate is DGXXIV on Health and Consumer Protection.[1] However, within Europe, food law policy does not come under any one body. Aspects of food law are also affected by Directorates dealing with Agriculture and Fisheries, the Common Agricultural Policy, the Environment and Competition and Markets. However, in January 2000, the Commission announced that all food safety issues would fall under the responsibility of Health and Consumer Protection.

The Council of Ministers
2.10   This is the main decision-making institution of the EU and is responsible for policy and legislative decisions. It is made up of a representative from each Member State at ministerial level and often the particular ministerial representative changes according to the particular issue to be considered. The Council meets on a regular basis. Its role is to coordinate economic policies and to pass legislation and therefore it is the legislature of the EU.

The European Parliament
2.11   This comprises Members of the European Parliament, who are elected directly by the Member States. The number of seats held by a Member State is roughly based upon its population. There are a number of different legislative procedures which involve the European Parliament in the legislative process.

---

1   See http://www.europa.eu.int/comm/dg24/.

In some cases, there is a mandatory requirement that the European Parliament is consulted in order for legislation to be enacted. On other occasions, the Council and Commission will voluntarily consult with the European Parliament. In addition to these powers, the European Parliament also has some economic control.

if problem art 234 ex 177 referral!

The European Court of Justice and the Court of First Instance

2.12 These are the judicial bodies of Europe. The European Court of Justice (ECJ) and the Court of First Instance (CFI) (a later creation) together ensure the uniform interpretation and application of EC law. National courts can refer to the ECJ for a ruling on a point of European law. This is known as a '177 reference', named after the Article number containing this power (now Art 234). In addition, actions can be brought against a Member State which has failed to implement Community law, by the Commission, another Member State, a Community institution or, in certain circumstances, individuals.

Sources of European law

MENTION BUT NO REAL detail!

2.13 The primary legislation of Europe is contained in the Treaties. Primary legislation usually provides the broad limits and the detail is often left to secondary legislation. Secondary legislation comprises Regulations, Directives and Decisions.

Regulations

2.14 These are binding in their entirety and are directly applicable in Member States, without the need for their implementation by national legislation. Regulations must not be altered in any way by national legislation and courts must apply them.

Directives

2.15 These are specifically addressed to Member States, which are free to implement them in whatever manner they choose, but which must ensure that the provisions of the Directives are fully implemented. There is usually a time-limit for implementation and a Member State which is in breach of its obligations in this regard can face action by the Commission. The UK will often implement such measures by means of a 'Regulation'. This should not be confused with a European Regulation.

Decisions

2.16 These are usually addressed to individual Member States and are binding on domestic bodies.

Recommendations

2.17 These can be issued by the Council or the Commission. They are not binding but should be taken into account when interpreting national legislation.

Judgments of the European Court of Justice and the Court of First Instance

2.18   These are binding on national courts which are interpreting European legislation.

2.19   In the field of food, European Regulations have been used to regulate foods such as milk, eggs, fruit, wines and spirits. However, Directives are the usual form of legislation. They regulate a wide range of matters, including labelling, advertising, additives, enforcement and hygiene.

THE EUROPEAN CONVENTION ON HUMAN RIGHTS

2.20   The UK was one of the first countries to sign the Convention for the Protection of Human Rights and Fundamental Freedoms (the Convention) on 4 November 1950. There are now 39 signatories to the Convention. However, unlike other nations, the UK did not incorporate the Convention into national law. This means that although its contents are recognised by the UK, an individual cannot argue infringements of the Convention in the national courts. Individuals have to petition the European Court of Human Rights (ECHR), which sits in Strasbourg, in order to rely upon the Convention.

2.21   The Human Rights Act 1998, which comes into force on 2 October 2000, will incorporate the Convention into UK law. Thereafter, it will be possible to rely upon Convention rights in domestic courts. Courts will not have the power to set aside conflicting domestic legislation, but will be required to give a declaration of incompatibility. Courts must also have regard to previous decisions of the ECHR.

2.22   Although the Human Rights Act 1998 does not have a direct impact on food law, its indirect effect will no doubt be significant. Certainly, a cause of action for breach of a Convention right lies against a local authority which infringes such a right. Individuals may argue that enforcement action infringes fundamental rights, such as the right to a fair trial under Art 6 of the Convention. There may be scope for arguing that a decision to revoke or suspend a licence may infringe the Act and the seizure of goods might be open to attack under Art 1 of the First Protocol which protects property rights. Certainly, enforcement action generally will be scrutinised more closely and it is anticipated that it will be challenged more frequently. All public bodies will be subject to the 1998 Act, including decisions taken by the new Food Standards Agency.

THE EFFECT OF THE INTERNAL MARKET ON FOOD REGULATION

2.23   The object of Europe was to establish a common market with no restrictions on trade between the Member States. The establishment of a single European market had a significant impact on the volume and content of national regulation of food. However, as EC food law was at an undeveloped stage in 1973, the UK played a significant role in its development.

2.24   Article 28 of the EC Treaty (formerly Art 30) prevents quantitative restrictions on imports between Member States. This has been interpreted very widely by the ECJ so that it is now established that it applies to forbid any trading rules capable of hindering, whether directly or indirectly, intra-community trade. The exception to this is contained in Art 30 (formerly Art 36) and permits Member States to place restrictions on trade where, among other things, it is justified on the ground of public policy, public security or for the protection of the health and life of humans, animals or plants. However, that Article also states that 'such prohibitions or restrictions shall not ... constitute a means of arbitrary discrimination or a disguised restriction on trade between Member States'.

2.25   The principle of mutual recognition of products between Member States was affirmed by the decision of the ECJ in the case known as '*Cassis de Dijon*' in 1979[1] and it has remained an entrenched principle in all similar decisions of the ECJ since then (for examples of cases in which the principle has been applied by the ECJ, see *Butterworths' Law of Food and Drugs* at Division E). Therefore, laws prescribing requirements for foodstuffs cannot prevent the lawful import-ation of a product that does not conform to a higher national standard, from being sold in that Member State. If the law were otherwise, it would be open to Member States to enact legislation, which, although not directly restricting imports from a different Member State, had that effect, and thereby to circumvent the operation of Art 28. This principle is applied and inconsistent compositional standards disallowed, regardless of the effect of such national legislation. It was argued by France in *EC Commission v France*[2] that, as there was little foie gras produced outside France, it was hypothetical whether there was an infringement of Art 30 (now Art 28). The ECJ did not agree. The appropriate test was whether the provisions were capable of hindering intra-Community trade.

2.26   However, a recent case of the ECJ demonstrates the limits of Art 28. In *Re Goerres*,[3] the defendant sold products in Germany, which were not labelled in German, but only in French, Italian or English, but he displayed a notice next to the products with a translation. He was prosecuted by the German authorities for an infringement of German labelling legislation, which implemented Council Directive 79/112/EEC. The German national legislation prescribed the use of German for the labelling of foodstuffs, but also allowed, as an alternative, the use of another language which was easily understood by purchasers. The ECJ considered that such legislation did not impose a stricter obligation than that of using a language which is easily understood and, therefore, there was no infringement of European law. It was a matter for the national courts to assess, in the light of the circumstances of each individual case, the ease with which the

1   *Rewe-Zentral AG v Bundesmonopolverwaltung für Branntwein* [1979] ECR 649.
2   NLD 22 October 1998.
3   C-385/96 (1998) *The Times*, 21 August.

information supplied could be understood. It was not sufficient under European law to display a notice next to the product.

2.27   It would seem from authorities dealing with an alleged breach of Art 28 that the majority of cases concern the adoption by a Member State of differing quality standards. These quality standards often seek to prohibit the marketing of a product (usually from a different Member State) on the basis that the product does not conform to the appropriate standard for that particular product.

2.28   In the main, these attempts have failed, but they have led to a European policy which attempted to unify quality standards between Member States. The Commission set down standards for various products, including chocolate, sausages and bananas, but became embroiled in debates over trivial matters such as the shape of bananas. This lost sight of the real issue, which was the safety of food. Therefore, the Commission has sought to move away from this 'recipe' approach and has adopted a policy that concentrates on the safety of food. This development is also apparent internationally in more recent policies of the Codex Alimentarius Commission (see **2.56** et seq below).

EUROPEAN INVOLVEMENT IN THE ENFORCEMENT OF FOOD LEGISLATION

2.29   Until Council Directive 89/397/EEC on the official control of foodstuffs of 14 June 1989, there was no formal system for food law administration in the EC. There was a certain level of cooperation between a number of the Member States, but enforcement procedures remained the remit of national governments. Council Directive 89/397/EEC recognises the need to harmonise and make more effective official control of foodstuffs. It lays down the basic Community requirements for the enforcement of food law and thereby provides some degree of coordination at the European level.

2.30   It establishes the standard expected of inspections, both in terms of how inspections should be conducted and what should be inspected. It provides for official laboratories to undertake the analysis of samples and makes provision for the future review of a coordinated programme.

2.31   In 1993, the Additional Food Control Measures Directive (93/99/EEC) was enacted in order to improve control procedures in the Community. This Directive lists the standards to be met in the qualification and training of enforcement officers. It also requires all official laboratories to meet and work to prescribed standards and it requires accreditation bodies to work to the same level of competence. Methods of sampling and analysis must also be harmonised.

2.32   Article 5 of Directive 93/99/EEC requires the Commission to monitor and evaluate the equivalence and effectiveness of official food control systems operated by the competent authorities of Member States, and it is to report to the Member States in this regard. Under this power, the Commission made an initial visit to the UK in January 1995 and a follow-up visit in February 1998. During these visits, the Commission examined and evaluated the systems in place and also focused on particular aspects of the UK's policies. In the follow-up visit, the Commission focused in particular on the system for the control of imported foods not of animal origin.

2.33   Article 6 of Directive 93/99/EEC requires the competent authorities of the Member States to offer each other administrative assistance in the enforcement of food legislation. It required each Member State to nominate a single liaison body. In 1996, the UK nominated the Local Authorities Coordinating Body on Food and Trading Standards (LACOTS) (see Chapter 4 below). Under Art 6, the liaison bodies are required to assist and coordinate communication, and transmit and receive requests for assistance. The role of LACOTS as a single liaison body has been set out in a Memorandum of Understanding with the government. LACOTS has published guidance on dealing with transborder disputes and publishes reports on its work as the single liaison body. The Food Standards Agency may impact on this work of LACOTS (for a discussion of this issue, see Chapter 6 below).

2.34   In addition to Directive 93/99/EEC, Europe has issued Directives which deal with more detailed matters such as sampling programmes and procedures. The Commission also operates further controls, for example the Rapid Alert System for Foodstuffs, which seeks to inform Member States swiftly about problems concerning food which does not meet food safety requirements or food which is improperly labelled so as to pose a risk to consumers. However, this system is limited to products that go beyond a single Member State.

RECENT EUROPEAN INITIATIVES ON FOOD

The Commission Green Paper

2.35   Following the Edinburgh Summit at the end of 1992, the Commission stated a commitment to reviewing and rationalising European food law.

2.36   Following the Commission's commitment to review, in July 1997, it published a Green Paper entitled *The General Principles of Food Law in the European Union*,[1] which sought views on: the development of European food law; the extent to which European legislation is meeting the needs and expectations of consumers, producers, manufacturers and traders; and how European provisions could be better enforced in order to ensure a wholesome food supply.

2.37   The Commission set out the aims of the Green Paper as:

'1. to examine the extent to which the legislation is meeting the needs and expectations of consumers, producers, manufacturers and traders;

---

1   COM(97)176 final.

2. to consider how the measures to reinforce the independence and objectivity, equivalence and effectiveness of the official control and inspection systems are meeting their basic objectives to ensure a safe and wholesome food supply and the protection of other interests of consumers;

3. to launch a public debate on our food legislation, and thereby,

4. to enable the Commission to propose appropriate measures for the future development of Community food law, where necessary.'

2.38   The basic 'goals' for community legislation were set out as:

'1. to ensure a high level of protection of public health, safety and the consumer;

2. to ensure the free movement of goods within the internal market;

3. to ensure that the legislation is primarily based on scientific evidence and risk assessment;

4. to ensure the competitiveness of European industry and enhance its export prospects;

5. to place the primary responsibility for safe food on industry, producers and suppliers, using hazard analysis and critical control points (HACCP) type systems, which must be backed up by effective official control and enforcement;

6. to ensure the legislation is coherent, rational and user friendly. In order to achieve these goals, it is necessary to ensure that our regulatory approach covers the whole food chain 'from the stable to the table'. This gives rise to two issues:

7. the extent to which primary agricultural production and the processed foodstuffs sector should be brought within the same set of general rules;

8. the principle of producers' liability for defective products to be made obligatory for primary agricultural production (see Directive 85/374/EEC).'

Although the Green Paper suggested that European legislation should be simplified, it recognised that this should not be at the expense of the protection of the consumer. It suggested a greater use of regulations in preference to Directives. This was considered particularly favourable in order to increase the transparency of legislation and to ensure timely and accurate implementation. However, the Green Paper favoured the use of Directives for framework legislation.

2.39   Responses to the Green Paper showed a general preference for the use of Regulations by both governmental and non-governmental bodies. However, there was some concern that it is often difficult to reach consensus in regulation-making. There was widespread support for the introduction of a framework directive, which would lay down the principles and definitions to be used as the framework for all EU provisions. Furthermore, there were calls for the review of the present system, which operates a General Hygiene Directive (93/43/EEC) alongside a number of veterinary hygiene Directives, such that a General Directive was created, providing the basis for all other hygiene regulation. There was a call for a general safety obligation and it was agreed that the provisions relating to product liability should be extended to primary agricultural products. In addition, the present labelling provisions were considered to be particularly problematic.

The Commission White Paper

2.40 On 12 January 2000, the European Commission launched its White Paper entitled *Food Safety*,[1] which set out proposals for a large-scale reform of current European food law and built upon the consultation arising from the Green Paper.

2.41 The Commission now intends to establish an independent European Food Authority. This Food Authority will essentially be responsible for risk assessment. It will advise on matters of food safety and, for this purpose, it will have access to scientific and analytical support. It will also be responsible for operating the current rapid alert system and, therefore, will have the responsibility of informing consumers of risks. However, it is currently envisaged that the Commission will continue to be responsible for the implementation of appropriate legislation, although the possibility that the Authority might have its powers extended at a later stage has not been ruled out. The White Paper suggests that a European Food Authority might be in place by the year 2002.

2.42 The White Paper *Food Safety* also sets out proposals for amending current European food legislation in order to make it more 'coherent' and to implement comprehensive legislation covering all aspects of food production from 'stable to table'. This is certainly in line with the policy of the UK government to implement a similar regime under the Food Standards Agency which will be responsible for food production from 'plough to plate'.

2.43 The European Commission has stated its intention to propose a new legal framework covering the entire food chain. It has emphasised the need for a more coherent and transparent approach to regulation and has stated that it intends to propose a new legal framework incorporating the common principles underlying food legislation and establishing food safety as the primary objective. Therefore, it is proposed that a 'General Food Law Directive' will be adopted to embody the principles of food safety and to act as the general framework for areas of food law not covered by harmonised rules.

2.44 Among other proposals, it is the Commission's intention to overhaul the regulation of animal feedstuffs, animal health and disease, hygiene, contaminants, additives, novel foods and labelling.

2.45 The Commission also intends to strengthen enforcement of European requirements. It points to significant variations in the implementation of European measures in individual Member States and suggests being involved in the development of national control systems. It also proposes the implemen-

---

1   COM(1999)719 final.

tation of new methods of enforcement in addition to simply taking cumbersome infringement procedures.

CONCLUSIONS

2.46   Overall, current European legislation is extensive and has developed in a piecemeal fashion. There are a huge number of Directives which often apply to specific products. Member States implementing these provisions do so in a similarly uncoordinated style. This renders food legislation particularly difficult to follow and apply. A more general approach to food law is sought which sets out and builds upon the foundations of a common regulatory system. It is widely considered that these foundations should take into account international standards and, some have suggested, the adoption of the Codex Alimentarius (see **2.65** below). Furthermore, a more transparent system should be developed, which would in turn provide more consistent and coordinated enforcement of European legislation. The White Paper goes a long way towards answering these calls for reform in its proposals. However, the suggested programme is, to say the least, ambitious. It remains to be seen whether Europe can deliver all that it promises. Certainly, the next few years are destined to witness large-scale reform of the current European legislative system.

2.47   The manner in which the Agency is expected to interact with the EU on food policy is set out in the government's White Paper at paras 3.11–3.13. Essentially, the Agency will be responsible for advising the government and for proposing and implementing legislation on the matters within its remit (and if it fails to ensure that the UK's European, or international, obligations in this regard are met, it may be directed to do so by the Secretary of State).[1] Staff of the Agency will represent the UK at 'working level' within the EU, with care being taken to ensure 'coordination of the UK line' in such matters through normal Cabinet Office machinery. It seems that the Agency is expected to be very much an organ of central government in this regard.

INTERNATIONAL ORGANISATIONS

2.48   In addition to European regulation of food, there are international bodies which operate in food-related areas. However, the difference between these bodies and Europe, so far as the UK is concerned, is that these organisations have no binding effect on UK legislation and their provisions can only provide guidance.

2.49   The Agency is to be the primary UK point of contact for the international bodies set out below. This is made plain in the White Paper at para. 3.14:

> 'The Agency will have responsibility in areas which are dealt with in other international fora such as the World Health Organisation, the Food and Agriculture

---

1   See s 24(4) of the Food Standards Act 1999 (and **6.141**).

Organisation and the Codex Alimentarius. The same basis principles of coordination, consultation and representation will apply in these fora as in EU negotiations.'

Food and Agriculture Organisation of the United Nations[1]

2.50   The Food and Agriculture Organisation (FAO) was founded in 1945 with a view to improving levels of nutrition, standards of living and agricultural productivity, and to improve conditions for rural populations. It is the largest autonomous agency within the United Nations and has a membership of 175 countries, plus the EU. More recently, it has moved towards decentralisation and now has almost half of its workforce employed at decentralised offices and field projects.

2.51   The FAO's attention is centred on alleviating poverty and hunger and promoting an environmentally friendly and sustainable agricultural development, particularly in developing countries. However, it does play a more general role in the field of food standards and, historically, has played a significant role in the development of food regulation. In November 1996, it hosted the World Food Summit.

2.52   The FAO has four major tasks:

– it carries out a major programme of technical assistance on behalf of governments and development funding agencies;
– it collects, analyses and disseminates information and seeks to encourage the sharing of resources and technical knowledge;
– it advises governments on policy and planning; and
– it provides opportunities for governments to meet and discuss food and agricultural problems and provides mediation at the international level with a view to reaching intergovernmental agreements.

The World Health Organisation[2]

2.53   The World Health Organisation (WHO) was founded in 1948 and is a specialised agency of the United Nations. Its aim is described in its constitution as 'the attainment by all peoples of the highest possible level of health'. It encourages technical cooperation between nations on health matters and carries out programmes to control and eradicate disease.

2.54   The WHO sets out its four main functions as:

– giving worldwide guidance in the field of health;
– setting global standards for health;
– cooperating with governments to strengthen national health programmes; and

---

1   http://www.fao.org.
2   http://www.who.org.

– developing and transferring appropriate health technology, information and standards.

2.55   The WHO's main concern is safeguarding and promoting the health of individuals. As such, it often concerns itself with issues relating to food and one of its functions is 'to develop international standards for food, biological and pharmaceutical products'.

The Codex Alimentarius Commission[1]

2.56   The FAO in 1961 and the WHO in 1963 both passed resolutions to establish the Codex Alimentarius Commission and adopted the Statutes and Rules of Procedure for its operation. It was intended to provide a forum where food standards could be examined in order to reach some global agreement over health and economic aspects of those standards. Article 1 of the Statutes sets out the purpose and objectives of the Commission. It states:

> 'The Codex Alimentarius Commission shall . . . be responsible for making proposals to, and shall be consulted by, the Directors General of the Food and Agriculture Organisation (FAO) and the World Health Organisation (WHO) on all matters pertaining to the implementation of the Joint FAO/WHO Food Standards Programme . . .'

2.57   Article 1 goes on to set out the purpose of the joint programme, which, alongside such aims as protecting the health of consumers, ensuring fair practices in food trade, promoting food standards and prioritising issues to be considered, also sought to set up finalised regional and/or international standards, which would be published as a 'Codex Alimentarius'.

2.58   In 1998, there were 163 Member States of the Commission, which represented 97 per cent of the world's population ('Understanding the Codex Alimentarius'), including the UK. Representatives of the different States are appointed by the government of each State. In addition, non-representatives of interested organisations often attend sessions as observers. They are often consulted and their views are considered, although they are not involved in making the final decision. The Commission meets every 2 years.

2.59   The Commission, in collaboration with national governments, has established country 'Codex Contact Points' and many Member States have 'National Codex Committees' to coordinate activities nationally.

2.60   It is anticipated that the Food Standards Agency will now provide the contact point for the UK.

2.61   The Commission is organised into two types of sub-committee, Codex Committees and Coordinating Committees. Codex Committees are hosted by Member States, which are also responsible for the cost of the administration and maintenance of the Committee. These committees are classified as either 'General Subject Committees' or 'horizontal committees', which are concerned

---

1   http://www.fao.org/WAICENT/FAOINFO/ECONOMIC/ESN/codex/Default.htm.

with work relating to general standards, or 'Commodity Committees' or 'vertical committees', which are concerned with particular foods and are established for as long as their work requires. It is notable that, more recently, the emphasis has been placed on the horizontal committees, with a reduction in the adoption of compositional standards. Coordinating Committees are divided into broad regional areas and are not hosted by one particular Member State, but meet on an ad hoc basis. They seek to ensure that the work of the Commission is responsive to countries' needs.

2.62   In order to adopt standards, the Commission follows a procedure, set out in the procedural manual. The Codex comprises 'commodity standards' and 'general standards'. Commodity standards apply to defined foods and regulate the content of those foods in terms of, for example, permitted additives or contaminants or its special requirements, such as labelling or analysis. There are more than 200 commodity standards. The general standards apply to all foods and deal with general requirements for matters, including labelling, additives, hygiene, nutrition and inspection systems. In addition, the Codex sets general principles, guidelines and codes of practice, for example the Recommended International Code of Practice – General Principles of Food Hygiene, which is supplemented by detailed codes of hygienic practice. Furthermore, the Commission has published a Code of Ethics for International Trade in Food, which encourages the voluntary adoption of ethical practices by the food industry.

2.63   The Commission distributes information and documents to the Codex Contact Points in Member States, which are expected to disseminate the information to the appropriate bodies and interested parties.

2.64   Codex standards are not mandatory and, in themselves, they cannot affect what is specifically provided in national legislation. However, Member States are encouraged to implement their standards as a product that complies is usually accepted or has free entry into the market of another Member State without more. In some countries, the Codex standards are the basis of national legislation or are influential in determining the final form of the legislation.

2.65   On a European level, the European Commission Green Paper outlined the need for European legislation to be compatible with international obligations. It suggested that the EU should be able to participate fully in international standardisation activities, negotiations and agreements. Responses to the Paper revealed a desire by the governments of Member States to play an active role in Codex Alimentarius negotiations. However, difficulties arise over whether and how membership of the EU should affect individual States' roles in the Codex. Furthermore, the Consumer Committee of the European Commission would seek to safeguard the sometimes stricter European measures from the adoption of the weaker Codex standards.

2.66   The Commission claims that its founders 'were first and foremost concerned with protecting the health of consumers and ensuring fair practices in the food trade'. Certainly, Art 1 reflects this purpose. However, it must not be forgotten that the Commission was and remains equally concerned with harmonising food law throughout the world in order to reduce barriers to trade and provide for the free movement of goods – an aim which also pervades European food policy.

2.67   Indeed, in 1995, following the Uruguay Round of multinational trade negotiations, both the Agreement on the Application of Sanitary and Phytosanitary Measures (SPS Agreement) and the Agreement on Technical Barriers to Trade (TBT Agreement) recommend the use of the Codex Alimentarius, among other standards, as a reference point for facilitating international trade. Both these Agreements recognised that measures apparently taken by domestic governments to protect consumer health could in fact be discriminatory and cloaked attempts to establish barriers to trade. It was decided that there must be a 'sufficient scientific justification' for protective measures and that the risk of standards becoming barriers to trade should be minimised.

2.68   The Codex Alimentarius Commission reconciles the aims of consumer protection and free trade by claiming that 'if all countries harmonised their food laws and adopted internationally agreed standards, such issues [protecting consumer health and ensuring fair trade practices] would be dealt with naturally' (see 'Understanding the Codex Alimentarius', at **2.58** above). However, consumer health can only be assured if the harmonised standards are set at a sufficiently high level. A harmonised standard of food law, set at a minimum level, would result in free trade, but it would not necessarily assist consumer health. These aims, therefore, do not necessarily follow naturally. While the Codex Alimentarius Commission has a defined purpose of facilitating free trade, consumers cannot be guaranteed full protection.

Chapter 3
The Statutory Control of Food

INTRODUCTION

3.1 The legislation affecting food is vast and it is outside the remit of this book to consider all of the provisions. Appendix 1 of the government White Paper *The Food Standards Agency – A Force for Change* gives a helpful summary of the range of primary legislation affecting food and it is reproduced here to provide an outline.

'Food Safety Act 1990
1. This Act is the main piece of primary food legislation in GB. The Act is principally an enabling piece of legislation but it also provides for offences and defences in law and defines food and the enforcement authorities and their responsibilities. It also provides Ministers with various powers. The main provisions of the Food Safety Act 1990 came into force on 1 January 1991. The Act covers Great Britain and provides the framework for all its food legislation. Northern Ireland has equivalent legislation, the Food Safety (Northern Ireland) Order 1991, which came into force on 21 May 1991.

The Food and Environment Protection Act 1985
2. Part I of the Act empowers Ministers to make Emergency Orders where they consider that the circumstances exist, or may exist, which are likely to create a hazard to human health through the consumption of contaminated food. Such Orders prohibit the distribution of affected produce from an area where foodstuffs have, or may have, been contaminated. In practice these powers are used only where there are no other statutory means of dealing with contaminated food (eg sector-specific legislation under the Food Safety Act 1990).

3. Part I of the Food and Environment Protection Act was amended by s 51 of the Food Safety Act 1990 ...

4. Part III of the Act governs control of pesticides, conferring on Ministers powers to control the importation, sale, supply, storage, use and advertisement of pesticides and to set maximum pesticide residue levels in food, crops and feedingstuffs, to make information on pesticides available to the public, and to enforce these provisions and to establish an Advisory Committee on pesticides.

The Weights and Measures Act 1985
5. Section 28 of the 1985 Act makes short weight an offence. Orders made under s 22 require prepacked food to carry on the container an indication of the net quantity of the contents. When sold other than prepacked, food is required either to be sold by quantity or, in certain circumstances, the seller has to make the quantity known to the customer. Orders also limit the quantities in which certain goods (the prescribed quantity goods) may be prepacked when offered for retail sale ...

The Trade Descriptions Act 1968
6. This Act makes it an offence for a person acting in the course of a trade or business to make false or misleading statements about the goods, or knowingly or recklessly

to make false or misleading statements about services, accommodation or facilities. It contains Order-making powers to require that goods bear, or be accompanied by specific information in the course of their supply, and to define terms for the purposes of the Act. The Act prohibits the unauthorised use of devices or emblems signifying Royal approval or award ...

The Consumer Protection Act 1987
7. Part I imposes civil liability for damage caused by defective products (including food other than game and agricultural produce which has not been subjected to an industrial process). Part II provides for secondary legislation on consumer safety, eg of materials in contact with food.

8. Part III makes it an offence for a consumer to be given a misleading indication, by any means, of the price at which goods are available. Guidance is contained in The Code of Practice for Traders on Price Indications. The Act also contains powers to regulate specific price indications practices ...

The Animal Health Act 1981
9. This Act confers on Ministers powers to control diseases of animals, including power to make Zoonoses Orders to reduce the risk to human health from any disease of, or organism carried in animals (eg brucellosis, salmonella and BSE), to control the use of animal waste and by-products in relation to animal feedingstuffs, and to enable surveillance of live animals on-farm.

The Agriculture Act 1970 (as amended)
10. Part IV governs fertilisers and animal feedingstuffs and requires that feedingstuffs when sold should be fit for their intended purpose and free from harmful ingredients. A statutory statement is required on the composition of the feed and other information ...

Agriculture and Horticulture Act 1964 (Chapter 28 Part III)
11. This Act provides for the application and enforcement in Great Britain of European Community Regulations specifying the grading, marketing and labelling requirements for certain fresh fruit and vegetables and makes certain acts or omissions that contravene those rules punishable offences ...

International Carriage of Perishable Foodstuffs Act 1976
12. This Act enables Regulations to be made governing the standards for transport equipment used for the international carriage of perishable foodstuffs.

Agricultural Produce (Grading and Marking) Acts 1928–31
13. This Act enables Regulations concerning the grading and marking of agricultural produce and the cold storage of eggs.

Radioactive Substances Act 1993
14. This Act controls the disposal of radioactive waste.

Environmental Protection Act 1990
15. Part VI of the Act aims to prevent or minimise damage to the environment caused by the release of genetically modified organisms, and imposes restrictions on the importation, acquisition, release or marketing of such organisms.

The Medicines Act 1968
16. This Act controls the manufacture and marketing of medicinal products for humans and animals. Enables Regulations to be made implementing European

Council Directive 90/167/EEC concerning the preparation, placing on the market and use of medicated animal feedingstuffs ...

The Prices Act 1974
17. This Act enables Regulations to be made requiring prices to be displayed on any premises where food and drink may be for sale for consumption by the public ...

Alcoholic Liquor Duties Act 1979
18. Section 71 prescribes a penalty for misdescribing liquor as spirits or as wine fortified with spirits. In practice, therefore, this section reinforces s 15 of the Food Safety Act 1990 as far as these products are concerned ...

Scotch Whisky Act 1988
19. The Scotch Whisky Act 1988 makes provision as to the definition of Scotch Whisky and production and sale of whisky ...

Public Health (Control of Disease) Act 1984
20. Regulations made under Part II (Control of Disease) enable local authorities to impose controls to prevent the spread of food poisoning and food-borne infections in persons involved in the food trade.

Public Health (Scotland) Acts 1897–1907
21. Sections 58–59 prohibit infected persons engaging in any occupation connected with food unless proper precautions have been taken against spreading disease or infection.

European Communities Act 1972
22. Section 2(2) of the European Communities Act makes provision for any designated Minister or Department to make Regulations for the purpose of implementing any European Community obligations of the United Kingdom.'

3.2 What is contained in the remainder of this chapter is a more detailed look at some of the most significant legislative provisions.

CONSEQUENCES OF NON-COMPLIANCE WITH THE LEGISLATION

3.3 The primary means by which businesses are compelled to comply is through the creation of offences in the event of non-compliance. The offences may be prescribed in the Acts or in Regulations created under the Act.

3.4 Where offences are created, whether in the Act or in Regulations, they are dealt with in the same way as all criminal offences. The prosecution is commenced by the laying of an information in a magistrates' court. The information is the formal document upon which the proceedings are based, but it can be laid verbally.

3.5 Once an information has been laid, a summons is served on the defendant, which informs him of the charges and requires him to attend court on a specified date.

3.6   The legislative provision creating the offence determines the type of offence and maximum penalty that can be imposed if committed. If an offence is summary only, then the case will be heard in the magistrates' court. This will normally be before three lay magistrates or a single stipendiary magistrate.

3.7   If an offence is triable either way, it can be tried either in the magistrates' court or in the Crown Court. In this case, once the defendant has entered a not guilty plea to the offence, the magistrates will go on to consider where the case should be tried ('Mode of Trial'). Following submissions by both the prosecutor and the defendant, the magistrates decide whether they should retain jurisdiction. This decision is based on factors such as the nature and complexity of the case, the proposed length of the trial and whether their sentencing powers would be sufficient if the defendant were to be found guilty. If the magistrates decide that the case must be heard in the Crown Court, then the defendant has no choice and has to be tried there. However, if the magistrates decide that they can hear the case, the final decision rests with the defendant and if he decides that he wishes to be tried in the Crown Court, the case must be heard there. Trial in a Crown Court is before a jury. It should be noted that the government is currently pressing to reduce the right of a defendant to elect jury trial. The first Criminal Justice (Mode of Trial) Bill was thrown out by the House of Lords. However, despite considerable opposition and criticism, the government is pressing ahead with its proposals and, on 22 February 1999, it introduced a second Bill into the Commons. At the time of writing, this Bill had received its second reading.

3.8   The majority of food offences are tried in the magistrates' court, not least because the expense involved in a Crown Court trial is significantly higher and burdensome for both local authorities and food businesses involved. Occasionally, a very serious case, for example, one involving a significant number of food poisonings, will be tried in the Crown Court.

3.9   The penalty imposed for the commission of the offence is prescribed by the legislation. For the purposes of most offences, the maximum fine that can be imposed by magistrates is set by reference to the 'Standard Scale', which is contained in s 37(2) of the Criminal Justice Act 1982, and is currently a maximum of £5,000 for each 'level 5' offence committed. For a number of food offences under the Food Safety Act 1990 (ss 7, 8 and 14), the sentencing powers of the magistrates are increased to a maximum fine of £20,000 per offence (s 35(3)). In most cases, there is also the possibility of imprisonment, but where a company commits the offence, imprisonment is not possible and the only penalty available is the fine. However, under s 36 of the Food Safety Act 1990, if the offence is committed by a company and it is proved that the offence is attributable to the neglect of, or is committed with the 'consent or connivance' of, the director, manager, secretary or other officer of the company (or someone purportedly acting in that capacity), then proceedings can be brought against those officers. It is also possible for individuals to be prosecuted where it is alleged that an offence was due to their act or default.[1]

---

1   See **3.74** et seq.

OFFENCES UNDER THE FOOD SAFETY ACT 1990

3.10 The most important Act regulating food is the Food Safety Act. The 1990 Act itself creates a number of offences, but a significant number of additional offences are created in individual Regulations made under the Act. The normal rule is that a prosecution of a summary offence must be commenced within 6 months of the commission of the offence, but there is no limit on the commencement of a prosecution of an indictable offence. However, under the 1990 Act, a prosecution must be brought (ie the information laid) within 3 years of the commission of the offence or 1 year from its discovery by the prosecutor, whichever is the sooner (s 34).

Rendering food injurious to health

3.11 Section 7 of the Food Safety Act 1990 makes it an offence for a person to add a substance to food, use a substance as an ingredient in food, remove a substance from food or treat the food in such a way that it is rendered injurious to health when that person intends that the food will be sold for human consumption. Food will be considered injurious to health if the probable effect on any consumer who eats the particular food, or the cumulative effect of eating similarly constituted food in ordinary quantities, would be to cause any permanent or temporary impairment. It should be noted that, in the case of incidents of food poisoning, the Public Health (Control of Disease) Act 1984 requires incidents discovered by medical practitioners to be reported by them to the local authority, which must then notify the local health authority.

3.12 Similar provisions to some of the additions made by the Food Safety Act 1990 were contained in previous legislation. Therefore, some of the authorities decided under the previous provisions can still be applied.

3.13 Most of the offences under food legislation are strict liability offences, which means that there is no requirement for the prosecution to prove a culpable mental state of the defendant, for example to prove that the prohibited act was intended to be committed. However, s 7 of the 1990 Act does require the prosecutor to prove an intention on the part of the defendant that the food would be sold for human consumption. The burden on the prosecutor, however, is relieved considerably by s 3. Section 3 contains a wide presumption that:

- food, commonly used for human consumption and sold, offered, exposed or kept for sale; or
- a substance, which is commonly used in the manufacture, composition or preparation of food;

is intended to be sold for human consumption or to be used in a food that will be sold for human consumption, unless the contrary is proved by the defendant. Therefore, in fact, it will normally be for a defendant to prove that he did not intend the food to be sold for human consumption.

3.14   In addition, although it is necessary for the prosecutor to prove that the prohibited act actually caused the food to be injurious to health,[1] the wording of s 7 of the Food Safety Act 1990 would appear to suggest that it is not necessary for the prosecutor to prove that there was an intention that the food would be rendered injurious to health.

3.15   Strictly, the wording of s 7 would appear to suggest that an offence could be committed even if only one consumer was injured by it. However, under similar provisions in earlier legislation, it was held that an offence would be committed where the food was found to be harmful to a substantial proportion of the community.[2]

3.16   Furthermore, it should be noted that an actual sale does not need to be proved and, under s 2 of the 1990 Act, there is an extended meaning given to the word 'sale', such that it includes food given away as a prize or reward as part of entertainment or an advertisement or for some other furtherance of a business and which is supplied in the course of a business or is exposed or deposited in premises in order that it will be used in this way.

3.17   Today, these provisions are not invoked as often as they were under previous legislation. This is largely as a result of the more specific Regulations, dealing with permitted additives and the use of the offences under ss 8 and 14 which are often easier to prove.

Selling food not complying with food safety requirements

3.18   Section 8 of the Food Safety Act 1990 applies to persons who:

–   sell;
–   offer, expose or advertise for sale;
–   possess for sale or for the preparation of a sale; or
–   deposit or consign to another person for the purposes of a sale or preparation of a sale;

food for human consumption. Even where the product supplied is intended to be food, but, unknown to both parties, a non-food substance is supplied instead, this will still be a supply of food.[3]

3.19   It is an offence to deal in any of the ways listed above with food which fails to comply with 'food safety requirements'. Food will fail to comply with food safety requirements if:

–   it is rendered injurious to health in any way provided for under s 7 of the 1990 Act;
–   it is unfit for human consumption; or
–   it is so contaminated that it would not be reasonable to expect it to be used for human consumption in that state.

---

1   *Hull v Horsnell* (1904) 68 JP 59.
2   *Cullen v McNair* (1908) 99 LT 358 – in this case to children and invalids.
3   *Meah v Roberts* [1978] 1 WLR 1187.

Under s 8 of the 1990 Act, the contamination does not have to be by extraneous matter.

3.20   Under s 8(3) of the 1990 Act, if any food that is part of a batch or consignment fails the food safety requirements, all of the batch is presumed to have failed to comply unless the contrary is proved by the defendant. Furthermore, products derived from animals slaughtered in a knacker's yard are deemed to be unfit for human consumption (s 8(4)).

3.21   The concept of food being unfit for human consumption has a long history in food legislation. However, the concept of food being 'so contaminated' is new and is intended to provide a middle ground between food which is unfit and food which is not of the nature, substance or quality demanded by the purchaser (see s 14 of the 1990 Act).

3.22   Whether food is 'unfit for human consumption' is a matter of fact to be determined in each case by the magistrates. However, there are a number of cases that provide some guidance:

- food that is going mouldy may well be unfit, even though it is not harmful;[1]
- something more than unsuitable is required;
- food containing a used bandage may be unfit;[2] and
- contamination with minor extraneous matter may not render food unfit (eg a small piece of metal in a cake or a piece of string in bread).[3]

3.23   However, many cases previously considered under unfit provisions will now be covered as being 'so contaminated'. For example, this would cover cases of mould or foreign body contamination. It should be noted that the Code of Practice No 1 made under s 40 of the 1990 Act recommends that prosecutions for contamination by micro-organisms or toxins should be brought under s 8 of the 1990 Act.

3.24   Section 8 of the 1990 Act is an offence of strict liability and, therefore, no *mens rea* is required and, strictly speaking, mistake is no defence. As a result, an employer is vicariously liable for the actions of its employees acting within the scope of their employment, even if an employee acts contrary to the employer's instructions, but within the scope of his authority. However, it may be possible to rely upon a due diligence defence in these circumstances (see **3.82** below).

Selling food not of the nature or substance or quality demanded

3.25   By virtue of s 14 of the 1990 Act, a person commits an offence if he sells for human consumption to the purchaser's prejudice any food which is not of the nature, substance or quality demanded. This is a strict liability offence and s 14(2) specifies that it will not be a defence for the person accused to show that there was no prejudice caused because the food was bought for analysis or examination.

---

1   *David Greig Ltd v Goldfinch* (1961) 105 Sol Jo 367.
2   *Chibnall's Bakeries v Cope Brown* [1956] Crim LR 263.
3   *J Miller Ltd v Battersea Borough Council* [1956] 1 QB 43 and *Turner & Son Ltd v Owen* [1956] 1 QB 48.

3.26   Sometimes offences under s 14 of the 1990 Act might also constitute offences under ss 7 or 8, and some previous decisions under provisions similar to this section would now be charged under the wider terms of s 8.

3.27   Whether a purchase is to a purchaser's prejudice is a question of fact in each case. Under a previous similar provision, there was a specific defence of bringing the fact that a food is substandard or defective to the attention of the consumer. This particular defence does not appear in the 1990 Act, but it is difficult to see that a consumer who is given notice of the defect and chooses to go ahead with the sale could be prejudiced. However, any specialist knowledge of the particular purchaser must be disregarded. The test is whether the sale would have been to the prejudice of an ordinary purchaser.[1]

3.28   The fact that an article must be sold to the prejudice of the purchaser means that an offence cannot be committed if a consumer got something better than expected. However, a prosecutor does not have to show that there have been consumer complaints or that a consumer was prejudiced[2] and there is no requirement to show an actual loss. 'Prejudice' simply means 'that which is suffered by anyone who pays for one thing and gets another of inferior quality'.[3]

3.29   A prosecutor must decide which offence is alleged and all three deficiencies cannot be alleged in the same information. An information that does not specify whether the offence is in relation to nature, substance or quality will be bad for duplicity[4] and the trial cannot proceed on the basis of it. If the error is discovered, even after the trial has commenced, the prosecution can be put to election. Once an election is made, the remainder of the information is struck out and the magistrates must try the information afresh. However, if there is any question of prejudice to the defendant, an adjournment will often be granted (see r. 12 of the Magistrates' Court Rules 1981). If an election is not made, it cannot be amended later.

3.30   The three concepts of nature, substance and quality clearly overlap and it may be possible that some offences will fall into more than one category. In this situation, it is for the prosecutor to decide which is the more suitable.[5]

3.31   In practice, 'nature' tends to be used when the food supplied is different than that which was described, for example frying steak is supplied instead of sirloin steak (this may also be an offence under s 15 of the 1990 Act, see **3.36** et seq below).

3.32   The term 'substance' normally describes situations in which there has been some adulteration of the food, for example by foreign bodies or by mould. However, a sterile foreign body that does not affect the food, might not affect the substance or quality of the food.[6] None the less, the Divisional Court in the case

---

1   *Pearks, Gunston and Tee Ltd v Ward* [1902] 2 KB 1.
2   *Webb v Jackson Wyness Ltd* [1948] 2 All ER 1054.
3   *Hoyle v Hitchman* (1879) 4 QBD 233.
4   *Bastin v Davies* [1950] 2 KB 579; *Moore v Ray* [1951] 1 KB 98.
5   *Preston v Greenclose* (1975) 139 JP Jo 245; *Shearer v Rowe* (1985) 149 JP 698.
6   *Edwards v Llaethdy Meirion Ltd* [1957] Crim LR 402.

of *Edwards*[1] emphasised that each case was a matter of fact for the magistrates. An offence of 'not of the substance' may also be employed where there is a quantitive standard for ingredients below which the food has fallen.

3.33 'Quality' is usually used when the quality of the product falls short of what would be expected, for example if low fat foods in fact contain a high level of fat, if lean minced beef is no leaner than normal minced beef, or if Diet Coke is in fact ordinary Coke.[2] There are a number of Regulations prescribing the required ingredients and/or their percentages and a failure to comply with them is normally an offence under the individual Regulations. However, an offence against quality may also be alleged in cases concerning adulteration, where the food has not been affected in any way, but where customers would not expect to find the article in the food in question.[3]

3.34 Where the prosecutor submits that there is a standard below which the food has fallen, these standards may be legally defined or may be commonly held practices of the trade. In both of these situations, if the food does not contain the necessary ingredients, an offence will have been committed. However, in other circumstances, there may be no common standard and experts may hold different views. None the less, magistrates may still convict if they consider that the standard of the food fell below a fair minimum standard put forward.

3.35 The offence also requires the product to be below a quality or standard *demanded by the purchaser*. What product is actually demanded by the purchaser is a question of fact in each case. Where there is no statutory standard, the magistrates must fix the standard that was demanded by referring to the evidence. In doing so, the court can take into account what the ordinary consumer would expect to receive. Therefore, the fact that the food was cheaper than it might normally be cannot be taken into account when determining whether prejudice has been caused to a consumer.[4] However, the magistrates may take into account the price of the food when determining the standard demanded by the purchaser. Therefore, the commission of an offence is not based solely on the evidence of experts as to the normal standard for a particular food.[5]

Falsely describing or presenting food

3.36 It is an offence for a person to falsely describe food or to give an indication which is likely to mislead as to the nature, substance or quality of food. Such an indication or description can be given when any food is sold or is offered, exposed or in a person's possession for the purposes of sale either:

---

1   *Edwards v Llaethdy Meirion Ltd* [1957] Crim LR 402.
2   *McDonald's Hamburgers Ltd v Windle* (1987) 151 JP 333.
3   *Barber v Cooperative Wholesale Society Ltd* (1983) 147 JP 296.
4   See *Heywood v Whitehead* (1897) 76 LT 781.
5   *Goldup v John Manson Ltd* [1982] QB 161; *T W Lawrence & Sons Ltd v Burleigh* (1981) 146 JP 134.

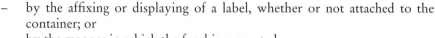

–   by the affixing or displaying of a label, whether or not attached to the container; or
–   by the manner in which the food is presented.

'Presentation' is defined by s 53 of the 1990 Act as including 'the shape, appearance and packaging of the food, the way in which food is arranged when it is exposed for sale; and the setting in which the food is displayed with a view to sale, but does not include any form of labelling or advertising'.

3.37   Under s 15(2) of the 1990 Act, it is also an offence to falsely or misleadingly describe food in an advertisement which is published or to be a party to the publication. Information is published when it is made public. However, s 22 of the 1990 Act makes it clear that a person who merely operates a publishing business and is ignorant of the fact that the material amounts to an offence will not commit an offence under the Act.

3.38   In order to commit an offence under s 15(2) of the 1990 Act, there must be a written misdescription on the label (or a physical misdescription in the packaging). An oral statement, which is not true, would not be caught by this section (although an offence may be committed under the Trade Descriptions Act 1968). Whether a description is false is a matter of fact for the magistrates.[1]

3.39   Generally, a description will be false where there is a statement of fact that is untrue. However, a description may still be false if it is literally true but there is an omission.[2] A description is normally alleged to be misleading where an ordinary consumer, with no special expertise, may draw a natural inference from that description which would be untrue. As a result, the wording may be strictly true, but as a whole the product may have a misleading appearance.[3]

3.40   The prosecutor does not have to show that a person has actually been misled[4] and the fact that the label or advertisement included an accurate statement of the composition of the food will not necessarily prevent the commission of an offence (s 15(4) of the 1990 Act).

Miscellaneous offences

3.41   In addition to the offences described above, there are a number of offences created by the Food Safety Act 1990 that are aimed at combatting non-compliance with procedural matters, such as the failure to implement or observe the terms of an enforcement notice or the obstruction of an officer acting in the execution of his duties (see Chapter 4).

---

1   A number of illustrative cases are listed in *Butterworths' Food and Drugs Law*, Division B.
2   For example *R v Lord Kylsant* [1932] 1 KB 442.
3   *Van den Berghs & Jurgens Ltd v Burleigh* (1987) unreported, Lewes Crown Court, which concerned a consideration of a cream-like product.
4   *R v Butcher* (1908) 72 JP 454.

OFFENCES PRESCRIBED BY REGULATIONS

3.42   There are so many Regulations dealing with the specific requirements of individual foods that it would be impossible to deal with all of these provisions in this book. For example, there are Regulations which have a more general application and which include the control of additives (colourings, flavourings and sweeteners) and contaminants (chemicals, pesticides and metals) and Regulations which regulate individual foods (bread, chocolate, eggs, fish, fruit juice, meat and, particularly in recent years, beef). Two of the most important and general sets of Regulations are dealt with below.

Food Safety (General Food Hygiene) Regulations 1995 (SI 1995/1763)

3.43   These Regulations (the 1995 Regulations) implement Council Directive 93/43/EEC on the hygiene of foodstuffs. In the main, they do not apply to primary production (including harvesting, slaughtering and milking) and those specific types of food production (egg, meat, dairy, wild game and fishery products) that have their own special rules. However, the EU is considering extending the remit of food regulation generally to primary products and, therefore, this exception may well change.

3.44   Regulation 4 places the obligations on proprietors of food businesses. Section 53 of the 1990 Act defines a proprietor as 'the person by whom that business is carried on'. In 1999, the Divisional Court considered that a person carrying on the business should be taken to mean the person who is taking a risk with a view to profit and, therefore, it held that an employee, however senior, would not come within this definition.[1] However, in the more recent decision of *Ahmed v Leicester City Council*,[2] the Divisional Court appears to have widened the definition. It considered that a proprietor does not have to be an owner nor does he have to be involved in the day-to-day running of the business. However, it is difficult to envisage a person who is neither an owner nor an employee, but who could still be considered to be a proprietor.

3.45   The obligations are imposed on proprietors during processing, manufacturing, packaging, storing, transportation, distribution, handling and offering for sale or supply in order that they are carried out in a hygienic way.

Hazard analysis and critical control points (HACCP)
3.46   The basis of the HACCP system is provided for in reg 4(3) of the Food Safety (General Food Hygiene) Regulations 1995, which requires a proprietor of a food business to 'identify any step in the activity of the food business which is critical to ensuring food safety and ensure that adequate safety procedures are identified, implemented, maintained and reviewed'. The food business must:

---

1   *Kol Curri v Westminster City Council* [2000] EHLR 16.
2   (2000) *The Times*, 29 March.

- analyse the potential food hazards which may exist in a food business operation;
- identify those points in the particular operation at which food hazards may occur;
- decide which of the points identified are critical to ensuring food safety;
- identify and implement effective procedures for controlling and monitoring food safety at the critical points; and
- review periodically the critical points and procedures in place.

3.47 As well as requiring businesses to implement HACCP, reg 4 of the 1995 Regulations also sets standards to be expected in food businesses, which are detailed in Sch 1 to the Regulations.

3.48 Guidance is given on the implementation and enforcement of HACCP systems in the Code of Practice No 9, Department of Health (DoH) guidance and LACOTS guidance on Food Hygiene Risk Assessment.

Food premises
3.49 The requirements for most food premises are set out in Chapter I of Sch 1 to the 1995 Regulations:

- premises must be kept clean and maintained in good repair and condition;
- the layout, design, construction and size of food premises must:
    (a) allow premises to be cleaned adequately,
    (b) prevent the accumulation of dirt, the possibility of food coming into contact with toxic materials, the shedding of particles onto food and the formation of condensation and undesirable mould on surfaces,
    (c) permit good food hygiene practices, which protect against cross-contamination by other foods, equipment or other sources, including pests, and
    (d) provide suitable temperature conditions for processing and storing food (specific requirements as to temperatures are set out in the Food Safety (Temperature Control) Regulations 1995, which also make it an offence to keep food in conditions which fail to ensure that foods are stored at the required prescribed temperatures, essentially below 8°C and above 63°C);
- an adequate number of wash hand basins must be suitably located and an adequate number of flush lavatories must be available, which must not lead directly into food handling rooms;
- wash hand basins must have hot and cold running water with materials for cleaning and hygienically drying hands and, where necessary, these should be separate from food wash sinks;
- premises must be equipped with suitable ventilation;
- sanitary conveniences must be adequately ventilated;
- there must be adequate lighting;
- drainage must be adequate; and
- changing facilities for personnel should be provided where necessary.

3.50 Chapter III of Sch 1 sets out the requirements for particular types of premises, namely moveable and temporary premises, those used occasionally for catering, those used normally as a dwelling house and vending machines. These requirements are obviously less stringent in view of the nature of the premises.

Food preparation rooms

3.51 The requirements for rooms where foodstuffs are prepared, treated or processed (except dining areas) are specified in Chapter II of Sch 1:

–   food rooms must contain:
   (a) floor surfaces which are maintained in a sound condition and which are easy to clean,
   (b) properly maintained wall surfaces, which are easy to clean,
   (c) ceiling and overhead fixtures which must not accumulate dirt, mould, condensation or shed particles,
   (d) windows constructed so as not to accumulate dirt and those which open onto the outside environment must be fitted with insect-proof screens or kept closed during production if this would cause a risk of contamination,
   (e) doors which must be easy to clean, and
   (f) surfaces that come into contact with food which are easy to clean and keep in good repair;
–   there must be adequate facilities for the cleaning and disinfecting of work tools and equipment; and
–   where necessary, adequate provision should be made for the washing of food in potable water (defined in reg 2(1) of the 1995 Regs).

3.52 The remaining Chapters of Sch 1 (IV–X) make further requirements of food businesses. Chapter IV sets out the standards expected of vehicles used for the transportation of food and the procedures that must be followed to reduce the risk of contamination. Chapter V requires that all articles, fittings and equipment that comes into contact with food be clean and properly maintained. Standards relating to the disposal of food waste and refuse are set out in Chapter VI, and Chapter VII sets out the standards required for the water supply to food businesses. Water has to be potable, and ice and steam coming into contact with food must be made from potable water. Chapters VIII and X are concerned with food handlers. They must ensure a high standard of personal hygiene, must wear clean and protective clothing and must not handle food if they are suspected to be suffering from any health condition that might be transmitted through food. Food handlers must be properly trained, instructed and supervised, although no specific qualification is prescribed. As a result, most food handlers are now required by their employers to obtain a 'Basic Food Hygiene Certificate'. Chapter IX sets out a number of standards to be met in relation to the use and storage of raw materials and the handling of food in order that it does not become contaminated or unfit for human consumption.

3.53   Each numbered or lettered paragraph within each Chapter creates a single offence and they should not be subdivided to create a multiplicity of offences.[1]

3.54   Regulation 2(3) of the 1995 Regulations states that measures should be 'necessary' or 'appropriate' for the purpose of ensuring the safety and wholesomeness (ie fitness for human consumption) of food. When executing and enforcing the Regulations, Environmental Health Officers should have regard to the risk associated with the premises when considering how frequently inspections should be required. In addition, they should consider to what extent a food business has complied with any guides to good practice. A number of these guides have been produced by organisations within the industry.

3.55   A person who contravenes a requirement of the 1995 Regulations commits an offence under reg 6. Like the offences under the 1990 Act, the offences under the 1995 Regulations are triable either way and are punishable with imprisonment. However, the higher sentencing powers of the magistrates do not apply to these offences and a person found guilty in the magistrates' court faces a maximum fine of £5,000 per offence.

3.56   The statutory defence of due diligence under s 21 of the 1990 Act is also a defence to an offence under the 1995 Regulations (see **3.72** et seq below).

Food Labelling Regulations 1996 (SI 1996/1499 as amended)

3.57   These Regulations are very complex and a detailed examination of their provisions is beyond the scope of this book. They apply to most foods, although certain foods are excluded from all of the provisions by reg 3, not least to ensure free trade in the European Economic Area (EEA) or from some of the provisions by regs 3 and 4. Detailed guidance on the requirements of the 1996 Regulations is provided by MAFF in its *Notes for Guidance* issued in February 1997. In addition, LACOTS food labelling panel has given more food specific guidance.

General labelling requirements
3.58   Part II of the 1996 Regulations sets out the labelling requirement for foods. The 'general labelling requirements' of foods are prescribed by reg 5. The following details are required to be marked or labelled with the food.

–   The name of the food – regs 6–11 provide more detailed provisions for determining the appropriate name of the product. In some cases, the name will be prescribed by law (see Sch 1) but, where it is not so prescribed, the factors in the Regulations must be applied, and it may be necessary to include a description of the process or treatment which the food has undergone (reg 11 and Sch 2).

---

1   *George v Kumar* (1982) 80 LGR 526.

- A list of ingredients – regard must be had to regs 12–18. The foods that are not required to carry a list of ingredients are set out in reg 18. The ingredients should be listed in descending order of weight and added water may have to be declared.

- The quantity of certain ingredients or categories of ingredients – these requirements are expanded in reg 19 and essentially require that an important ingredient of the product is quantified.

- The appropriate durability indication – these provisions require the insertion of 'best before' and 'use by' dates and the requirements are detailed in regs 20–22. Minimum durability indications are given by best before dates and it is not an offence to sell a product whose best before date has expired. Although the 1996 Regulations exclude certain products from the requirement to show a use by date, when a use by date is required to be shown on a product is not prescribed by the Regulations. MAFF guidance notes state that when considering whether to apply a use by date: 'the essential judgment is whether the food is microbiologically highly perishable *and*, in consequence likely, after a short period of time, to pose an immediate danger to human health. It is important to note that *both* criteria have to be satisfied.' It is an offence to sell a food beyond its use by date, and it would seem that an offence would be committed if a use by date were inserted on a product that did not need one (see the wording of reg 44(d) of the 1996 Regulations). However, it is doubtful whether any such prosecution would be in the public interest (see Chapter 4).

- Any special storage conditions or conditions of use – MAFF guidance notes expand on the type of information that might be required.

- The name or business name and address of the manufacturer, the packager or a seller within the EC (or all of them).[1]

- Details of the place of origin or provenance of the food if their omission might mislead a purchaser to a material degree – note that the addition of the phrase 'to a material degree' is similar to the provision in s 3 of the Trade Descriptions Act 1968. The offence of giving a misleading description under s 15 of the 1990 Act does not contain this additional element.

- Instructions for use if it would be difficult to use the food without any instruction.

Essentially, these are normally the minimum requirements for individual foods, but there are an array of other requirements imposed by more specific legislation.

3.59 'Labelling' is defined by reg 2(1) of the 1996 Regulations as including any words, trade marks, brand names, pictures or symbols which appear on any document, notice, label, ring or collar accompanying the food. In addition, reg 35 requires the information to be marked or labelled on the packaging, on a label

---

1   See also the ECJ decision in *Provincia Autonoma di Trento v Dega di Depretto Gino Snc* [1998] All ER (EC) 252.

attached to the packaging, or on a label that is clearly visible through the packaging where the product is sold to the ultimate consumer. Regulation 38 also requires the details to be easy to understand, clearly legible and indelible and in a conspicuous place where it is easily visible.

3.60   In the German case of *Goerres*,[1] a German shopkeeper sold products which were labelled in French, Italian and English. The ECJ considered that all of the compulsory particulars specified in Directive 79/112 must appear on the labelling either in a language easily understood by consumers of the State or the region in question, or by means of other measures such as designs, symbols or pictograms. However, it was a matter for national courts whether a label is easily understood. In the UK, the question of foreign language labels was considered by the Divisional Court in *Hackney London Borough v Cedar Trading Ltd*.[2] In that case, prosecutions were brought under the 1996 Regulations in respect of cans of Coca Cola and Sprite, which contained information only in Dutch. The Divisional Court considered that the label was not in a language easily understood by a purchaser and the trade mark or brand name could not be regarded as sufficient for the purposes of providing the name of the product.

3.61   LACOTS has issued a circular following the Divisional Court case,[3] which suggests that only English labelling will be considered 'easy to understand'. However, it is arguable that this policy may be in breach of the European Directive.

3.62   If a product is labelled in a foreign language, it is not sufficient simply to place a sign next to the product in the national language.[4]

Prohibited claims

3.63   Part III of the 1996 Regulations prevents certain claims or descriptions being applied to foods. Regulation 40 (which refers to Sch 6) prevents food claiming to have 'tonic' properties or having the ability to prevent, treat or cure a disease. It also restricts other types of nutritional claim (including low energy, protein, vitamin and cholesterol claims) and provides labelling requirements in circumstances where these claims are permitted.

3.64   Regulation 42 of the 1996 Regulations prevents certain descriptions being applied to food, such as the word 'milk', 'ice-cream' and 'low calorie'. The full list of the terms to which reg 42 applies is contained in Sch 8. In addition, reg 43 specifically prescribes the use of the word 'wine'.

3.65   Contravention of the 1996 Regulations results in the commission of an offence (reg 44). In contrast to the offences under the 1990 Act, these offences are summary only, and there is no possibility of imprisonment, but the maximum fine remains £5,000. A prosecution for an offence under the 1996 Regulations

---

1   See **2.26**.
2   (1999) 163 JP 749.
3   (LAC 12 99 8).
4   See *Goerres* C-385/96 (1998) *The Times*, 21 August, at **2.26**.

must be brought within 6 months of the commission of the offence – the normal time-limit for summary offences. In *Sandhu v Heirons*,[1] it was argued that the Food Safety Act 1990 time-limits should apply to these Regulations. The defendant in that case was convicted, but on appeal to the Divisional Court, the prosecution agreed with the defence that the 6-months limit was correct and withdrew its opposition to the appeal. The court therefore indicated that the appeal would be allowed without the need for a hearing.

3.66   The statutory defence of due diligence (s 21 of the 1990 Act) provides a defence to an offence under the 1996 Regulations, as does the defence of innocent publication (s 22 of the 1990 Act).

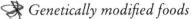

Genetically modified foods

3.67   The 1996 Regulations were recently amended by the Food Labelling (Amendment) Regulations 1999 (SI 1999/747). These were laid before Parliament on 18 March 1999 and came into force the following day, and implement EC Council Regulation 1139/98.

3.68   These amendments required the 'GMO particulars' to be added into the list of ingredients displayed on the outside of the food wrapping or, if there is no list, required a clear label to be displayed indicating that the food is produced from genetically modified soya or maize. There are particular requirements for foods pre-packaged for direct sale or those which are unpackaged. In addition, food premises, such as restaurants and food stands, are required to display labels or notices to indicate that some of the food sold at those premises contains genetically modified ingredients and that further information is available from staff. Staff are required to be sufficiently competent to be able to provide clarification as to whether the particular foods were produced in wholly or in part from a genetically modified product. A failure to comply with these requirements was made an offence.

3.69   These Regulations have been subject to further amendments by the Genetically Modified and Novel Foods (Labelling) (England) Regulations 2000 (SI 2000/768). These Regulations now draw together the requirements for genetically modified and novel foods in a single set of Regulations and, in so doing, remove them from the General Labelling Regulations.

3.70   The 2000 Regulations make one important change – they remove the exclusion for additives and flavourings that have been genetically modified or have been produced from genetically modified organisms, so that these too must now appear on the label. There remains an exemption from labelling in the case of small packages and certain indelibly marked glass bottles and the Regulations continue to allow alternative labelling arrangements in the case of sales to the final consumer by appropriate premises of food which is pre-packed for direct sale or unpackaged.

---

1   Unreported.

3.71   Offences and penalties for contraventions of these requirements are now prescribed in the 2000 Regulations.

✠ STATUTORY DEFENCE OF DUE DILIGENCE

3.72   As most food offences are of strict liability, once the prohibited act has taken place, defendants cannot rely upon the fact that they had not intended the act to have happened. Therefore, the only defence open to them will normally be the statutory due diligence defence in s 21 of the 1990 Act. This replaced the former defence of warranty (see Chapter 1).

The defence

3.73   Section 21 of the 1990 Act states that it will be a defence for a person 'to prove that he took all reasonable precautions and exercised all due diligence to avoid the commission of the offence by himself or by a person under his control'.

3.74   Where a person is charged with an offence under ss 8, 14 or 15 of the 1990 Act and that person did not prepare or import the offending food, he may be able to rely on a less strict due diligence defence. In this case, a defendant is required to prove that the commission of the offence was due either to an act or default of another person who was not under his control, or to his reliance on information supplied by such a person. In addition, if the defendant is selling own brand goods, the defence, prescribed by s 21(3), will be made out when the defendant proves:

–   that he carried out all such checks of the food in question as were reasonable in the circumstances or that it was reasonable for him to rely on checks carried out by the person who supplied the food to him; and
–   that he did not know and had no reason to suspect that an offence would be committed.

3.75   If the defendant is selling another person's branded goods, then the defence under s 21(4) of the 1990 Act is even less stringent than that under s 21(3), and simply requires a defendant to additionally prove:

–   that the sale or intended sale (which amounted to the commission of an offence) was not a sale under his name or mark; and
–   that he did not know and *could not reasonably have been expected to know* that an offence would be committed.

3.76   The onus is on the defendant to prove this defence, but the standard of proof required is the lesser civil standard of the balance of probabilities.[1]

3.77   Whether or not due diligence has been exercised by a defendant is a question of fact for the magistrates and, therefore, each case will depend on its own circumstances. However, the Divisional Court will interfere with a decision

---

1   *R v Carr-Briant* [1943] KB 607.

where there was no evidence to support it. The defence recognises that no system can ever be perfect and that defendants should not be penalised where the commission of the offence could not reasonably have been avoided. The due diligence defence only becomes relevant once there has been a contravention of the Act or Regulations and, therefore, it should not be a sign that the defendant has not exercised due diligence because the offence itself has occurred.[1]

Factors which should be taken into account when considering whether a defendant has taken all reasonable precautions include the size and resources of the defendant's business and the gravity of the injury which it is sought to prevent.[2]

3.78   In some circumstances, it may be reasonable to rely upon the quality systems in place at a reputable supplier's premises. However, a blanket assurance given by a supplier that all the goods it supplies comply with all statutory provisions will not be enough to satisfy the defence.[3] Equally, it may not be enough simply to rely upon the fact that goods are supplied with a British Standard. It may also be necessary to inspect to ensure that the requirements of the British Standard are being met.[4]

3.79   If a defendant simply relies on the systems of its supplier and takes no further steps, it will succeed only if there were no reasonable precautions that could have been taken. Where reasonable steps could have been taken (eg placing a purportedly waterproof watch in a bowl of water)[5] and they were not taken, the due diligence defence is not proved. Thus, if the company is a very large concern, the carrying out of random testing may be necessary to prove the defence.[6]

3.80   However, whether a defendant has exercised all due diligence must be decided in the context of the overall precautions and diligence that the defendant has exercised. The fact that there is some other precaution which might seem to be 'reasonable' for a person to have taken does not necessarily mean that the defendant cannot avail himself of the defence. The case of *William Frank Smith v T&S Stores plc*[7] concerned the prosecution for sale of cigarettes to an under-aged child. The prosecutor alleged that, in addition to the proper training which the staff had received, it would have been reasonable to have displayed a notice next to the till, to remind staff of their obligation to be vigilant. The Divisional Court considered that the fact that a further step could have been taken did not necessarily mean that reasonable precautions had not been taken and the due diligence defence was proved. However, Buxton J did suggest that he may not have reached the same conclusions as the magistrates on the facts.

---

1   *R v Bow Street Magistrates' Court, ex parte Cow and Gate Nutrition plc* (1995) 159 JP 120.
2   See Lord Diplock in the House of Lords' decision in *Tesco Supermarkets Ltd v Natrass* [1972] AC 153 at 194.
3   *Riley v Webb* (1987) 151 JP 372.
4   *Balding v Lew Ways Ltd* (1995) 159 JP 541.
5   *Sherratt v Geralds the American Jewellers* (1970) 114 Sol Jo 147.
6   *Garrett v Boots The Chemists Ltd* (1980) unreported.
7   (1995) 15 Tr LR 337.

3.81   In order to satisfy the due diligence defence, it is normally necessary to show documented procedures, recorded checks, proper selection of staff and adequate training and supervision.

3.82   A defendant may also rely upon a due diligence defence where offences are committed though the fault of its employees. This issue was considered by the House of Lords in *Tesco v Nattrass*,[1] which was a case considering the due diligence defence under s 24 of the Trade Descriptions Act 1968. It should be noted that the defence under the 1990 Act is slightly different. If a company is seeking to rely upon the less stringent tests laid down by s 21(3) and (4) of the 1990 Act, it could not rely upon omissions by its employees, as s 21 makes it clear that, in these circumstances, it must be a person not under its control.

3.83   However, a company relying upon the due diligence defence in s 21(1) of the 1990 Act can rely upon the defaults of its staff following *Tesco v Nattrass*. In that case, a shop assistant had acted contrary to the procedures laid down by the company and an offence had been committed. The manager was blamed by the company for his failure to supervise his staff properly. The House of Lords held that his act or default could provide a defence in circumstances where the magistrates were satisfied that the company had devised a proper system to ensure that the law was complied with and had set up good arrangements for ensuring that regular checks were carried out on that system. However, Lord Reid was clear that a 'paper scheme and perfunctory efforts to enforce it' would not be sufficient (at 174F).

3.84   In certain circumstances, it may also be possible for a defendant to rely upon advice given to it by enforcement officers. In *Taylor v Lawrence Fraser (Bristol) Ltd*,[2] it was held insufficient simply to regularly invite trading standards officers to inspect and test products the company was supplying. However, in *Carrick District Council v Taunton Vale Meat Traders Ltd*,[3] it was held possible for a trader to rely upon the certification by a meat inspector that meat was fit for human consumption, where the trader had a perfectly proper professional relationship with the inspector and had no reason to question his competence. In that case, the Divisional Court considered that there was nothing which required a due diligence defence to be based solely on the defendant and its employees. This defence has increasing potential where local authorities are being encouraged to give advice rather than take enforcement action and where the home authority principle and the Enforcement Concordat promote the vetting and monitoring of a company's due diligence procedures.

3.85   Section 20 of the 1990 Act makes it clear that proceedings may be brought against anyone whose action or default is alleged as being responsible for the commission of the offence, regardless of whether proceedings are commenced against the original person who actually committed the offence.

---

1   [1972] AC 153.
2   [1978] Crim LR 43.
3   (1994) 158 JP 347.

Notice

3.86   If a defendant wishes to rely upon the due diligence defence involving an allegation that the offence was due to the act or default of another, written notice of that fact, including the identification of those persons, must be given to the prosecutor at least 7 days before the trial and within 1 month of the first appearance in court. If a defendant fails to give such a notice, it cannot rely upon the defence without the leave of the court. A defendant must make all reasonable enquiries into the identity of any allegedly responsible persons.[1]

CONCLUSION

3.87   This is a relatively basic introduction to some of the most commonly encountered food standards prescribed by the legislation. The remainder of this book will concentrate on the enforcement of these standards by both central and local government and, most significantly, by the new Food Standards Agency.

---

1   *McGuire v Sittingborne Co-operative Society Ltd* (1976) 140 JP 306, a case decided under s 24 of the Trade Descriptions Act 1968.

Chapter 4
Central Government Regulation

4.1 Before the establishment of the Food Standards Agency, the responsibility for all food matters was divided between MAFF and the DoH. Of these two departments, MAFF was the most significant. However, with the introduction of the Agency, many of the responsibilities exercised by MAFF in relation to food have been removed and given to the Agency. The DoH has also had its powers increased in relation to food.

MAFF[1]

4.2 MAFF is the successor to the Board of Agriculture and Fisheries. The responsibility for food was transferred to the Ministry in 1955.

4.3 Until the establishment of the Food Standards Agency, MAFF was responsible for policies relating to agriculture, horticulture and fisheries in England and for policies relating to safety and quality of food in the UK, including composition, labelling, additives, contaminants and new production processes.[2] MAFF was also directly responsible for meat and milk hygiene.

4.4 Following the establishment of the Agency, responsibility for food safety has been removed from MAFF. The Meat Hygiene Service (MHS), which was formerly an executive agency of MAFF, has now been transferred to the Agency. This caused further controversy in an already politically sensitive area by virtue of the fact that the Agency will be responsible for setting standards for, and monitoring the performance of, its own activities in the regulation of meat hygiene. The Minister gave the following explanation of the interaction between the MHS and the Agency in Standing Committee:

> 'The MHS is operational only. The chief executive does not create policy; he receives policy instructions from MAFF. Likewise he will receive them from the FSA staff, who are not employees of the MHS but will probably be at the same civil service advisory level.... We want a management arrangement that deals with the relationship between the chief executives of the MHS and the FSA, but ... that is not a matter for the Bill. However, the chief executive of the MHS could be made accountable to a unit headed by the deputy chairman of the agency, with a membership separate from the main agency board. That break with the main board would result in more arm's length accountability.'[3]

---

1   At www.maff.gov.uk.
2   See 33rd *Civil Service Year Book 1999*.
3   Jeff Rooker, Standing Committee B, 13 July 1999, col 299/301.

4.5   The Ministry retains its powers and functions relating to agriculture, fisheries, the environment and rural issues. It also retains responsibility for the food industry. As such, MAFF remains a notable department in food issues.

4.6   Together with the Intervention Board (the body responsible for administering the European Common Agricultural Policy (CAP),[1] MAFF enjoys a significant role within the EU, being involved in the operation of the CAP and Fisheries Policy.

4.7   In relation to rural issues, including the environment, MAFF is the licensing authority for veterinary medicines and the registration authority for pesticides. It commissions research in order to assist in the development of policies.[2]

4.8   However, MAFF has a complicated structure and is assisted in its work by a number of specialised departments and advisory bodies. Even after the establishment of the Agency, many of these departments and advisory bodies remain. However, some of these bodies, particularly the advisory committees, now advise the Agency. The Food Standards Act 1999 provides for the transfer of existing non-statutory advisory committees to the Agency (which has power to set up advisory committees under s 5)[3] in para 7 of Sch 2. The provisions essentially allow the Secretary of State or Minister to direct that a committee shall be treated as if it had been established by the Agency and its members appointed in accordance with Sch 2. This applies only to existing committees, which are maintained for the purpose of giving advice to a public authority on matters connected with the Agency's functions (para 7(2)). One of the consequences of such a transfer is that the agency is responsible for the expenditure of the committee (para 6).

4.9   By far the most important division of MAFF, prior to 1 April 2000, in terms of food safety was the Food Safety and Environment Directorate. Its origin was the Food Safety Directorate which was established in 1989 to quell the calls for an independent regulatory body responsible for the safety of food and to respond to criticisms of MAFF's ability to perform its dual functions of protecting the industry and the consumer (see **4.19** et seq below). It was set up to report directly to the Permanent Secretary.

4.10   In 1997, the Food Safety Directorate became the Food Safety and Environment Directorate. This new Directorate continued to report directly to the Permanent Secretary and, for the purposes of food regulation, it was by far the most important department within MAFF.

4.11   The essential difference in its new formation was the inclusion of a new Environmental Group within the Directorate and the removal of Agricultural Inputs. Agricultural Inputs was responsible for plant health and variety, agricultural resources and emergencies and food protection. Following the

---

1   At http://www.ib-uk.gov.uk.
2   See 33rd *Civil Service Year Book 1999*.
3   See **6.9–6.10**.

changes, these responsibilities were distributed among other departments, largely within the Agricultural, Crops and Commodities Directorate.

4.12   There were several departments within the Food Safety and Environmental Directorate, including the Joint Food Safety and Standards Group (JFSSG). Before 1998, this department was known as the Food Safety and Science Group. In 1998, the JFSSG was set up as a jointly operated department by MAFF and the DoH. The JFSSG coordinated programmes of research and monitoring of the food supply and provide joint advice to the DoH and MAFF.

4.13   The work of the JFSSG covered a considerable range of food issues, including food additives, contact materials, novel foods, food contamination, animal feedstuffs, labelling, composition, enforcement, radioactivity, nutrition, meat hygiene, food hygiene, food poisoning, veterinary concerns and licensing of food premises.

4.14   Within its wide field of responsibility, the JFSSG provided the secretariat for a number of important advisory committees, including the Food Advisory Committee, the Advisory Committee on Novel Foods and Processes and the Consumer Panel. It played a significant role in topical food issues, including the setting up of the Food Standards Agency and the provision of information on BSE.

4.15   The JFSSG has laid the foundations for the work of the Agency and the majority of Agency staff have been sourced from it. The Minister, in Standing Committee, described it as *'the embryo of the Agency'*.[1]

THE DOH[2]

4.16   The other government department that plays a significant role in the regulation of food is the DoH. Unlike MAFF, its powers have been retained following the establishment of the Agency and it has been given additional responsibility, particularly in relation to the operation of the Agency.

4.17   Prior to 1 April 2000, the DoH was largely responsible for the health and hygiene aspects of food, including general food hygiene and microbiological food safety and nutrition. Like MAFF, the DoH receives advice and guidance from independent advisory committees, many of which are the same as those that advise the MAFF and the Agency.

4.18   In addition, the Health Education Authority, which was founded in 1987 as a special health authority and is largely funded by the DoH, plays a significant role in providing the public with nutritional information and advice. The division of responsibility between the DoH and the Agency in relation to matters of nutrition is discussed in Chapter 6.[3]

---

1   Jeff Rooker, 6 July 1999, col. 147.
2   At http://www.doh.gov.uk.
3   At **6.36–6.41**.

CRITICISMS OF CENTRAL GOVERNMENT REGULATION PRIOR TO 1 APRIL 2000

4.19   A number of criticisms were made about MAFF in relation to its regulation of food safety.

In his interim report, commissioned to propose the introduction of a Food Standards Agency (30 April 1997), Professor James pointed to three particular weaknesses in the current regulation of food. The first was a conflict of interest between economic and consumer interests.

4.20   The aims and objectives of MAFF were set out in the Public Service Agreement for MAFF and the Interventionist Board as follows:

'**Aim**
To ensure that consumers benefit from competitively priced food, produced to high standards of safety, environmental care and animal welfare and from a sustainable, efficient food chain, and to contribute to the well-being of rural and coastal communities.

Objectives
1. To provide public health in relation to food and to animal diseases transmissible to humans.

2. To sustain and enhance the rural and marine environment of the amenities they provide and to promote forestry.

3. To secure a more economically rational Common Agricultural Policy (CAP) which gives a better deal to consumers and taxpayers and pays due regard to the needs of the environment.

4. To assist the development of efficient markets in which internationally competitive food, fish and agricultural industries can thrive.

5. To enhance economic opportunity and social development in rural and coastal communities in a manner consistent with public enjoyment of the amenities which they offer.

6. To administer payments under the CAP fairly and in full accordance with EU requirements.

7. To conserve fish stocks for future generations and secure a sustainable future for the sea fishing industry.

8. To ensure that farmed animals and fish are protected by high welfare standards and do not suffer unnecessary pain or distress.

9. To reduce risks to people and the developed and natural environment from flooding and coastal erosion.

10. To safeguard the continuing availability to the consumer of adequate supplies of wholesome, varied and reasonably priced food and drink.'[1]

---

1   See Departmental Report 1999, above.

4.21   It can be seen from this list that the functions of MAFF were widespread and that its responsibilities included protecting industries, the environment and the public. It is also evident that MAFF's role was not primarily centred on the issue of food. Of the ten objectives listed in the Public Service Agreement, only two (numbers 1 and 10) directly concern food issues, with objective 4 relating to food, but being directly concerned with the interests of the industry and not food safety.

4.22   This varied programme laid MAFF open to further criticism concerning a perceived conflict of interest between the protection of farmers and the food industry and the protection of the consumer.

4.23   These criticisms were not new. On 2 November 1989, before the introduction of the Food Safety Bill, the Minister of Agriculture announced the establishment of the Food Safety Directorate within MAFF and the Consumer Panel, which was to act as an advisory committee. The Food Safety Directorate was to be charged with responsibility for government policy on food safety and the exercise of ministerial responsibility for statutory food controls and the Consumer Panel was intended to represent the interests of consumers.

4.24   Despite these introductions, the calls for an independent body continued. The critics were not convinced by the representation on the Directorate and proposed the appointment to that body of an independent chairman and representatives of professional bodies, including members of the Consumer Panel. However, the government did not accept these proposals.

4.25   Furthermore, during the passage of the Food Safety Bill through the House of Lords, an amendment was proposed which provided for the establishment of an independent Food Safety Agency. Despite some support for such a proposal, the amendment was rejected.[1]

4.26   Similar criticisms (ie about a conflict of interest) eventually led to the introduction of the independent Food Standards Agency. Professor James' report identified this duality of roles as a weakness in the system. He stated:

> 'MAFF has an important role to play in promoting the economic interests of the agriculture, fishing and food industries and this is particularly valuable in the international arena. Currently, however, MAFF is also responsible for promoting public health throughout the food chain by many different mechanisms, eg responsibility for many expert committees in the food safety area, veterinary monitoring, the Meat Hygiene Service, etc. Clearly, therefore, judgments have to be made in estimating the risks of a food-related health problem and in the rigour with which enforcement measures are developed and applied ... Inevitably at times there will be conflicts between concerns for food safety and the short-term economic needs of some industry sectors. These conflicts are currently handled within MAFF and it is not clear how they have been resolved ... it is now generally accepted that

---

1   See *Hansard* HL vol 515 at 1103–1114.

current arrangements have not been conductive to promoting national health or national wealth'.[1]

4.27 The research paper on the Food Standards Bill also identified as an issue 'the difficulties of achieving a balance in the dual roles of MAFF'.

4.28 The second criticism of MAFF centred on its complex constitution. Professor James stated that the problem was to be founded in the 'fragmentation and lack of coordination between the different bodies involved in food policy and in the monitoring and control of food safety'. He considered there to be 'considerable overlaps and gaps' between departments. The authors of *Butterworths' Law of Food and Drugs* suggest that this criticism is unfair and unfounded. However, what is clear is that the system was complex and carried a perception of inefficiency which did nothing to build consumer confidence in the system.

4.29 Furthermore, consultation on a Food Standards Bill revealed that people genuinely found the division of responsibility between different departments to be confusing. In its White Paper *The Food Standards Agency – A Force for Change* the government agreed that greater clarity was needed and stated that a 'better coordinated and more rational approach to food safety policy is essential'.

4.30 The creation of the Food Standards Agency will, it is hoped, alleviate some of this criticism.

TRANSFER OF FUNCTIONS FROM MINISTERS UNDER THE FOOD STANDARDS ACT 1999

4.31 Section 26(1) of the Foods Standards Act 1999 provides that certain functions of MAFF cease to be exercisable by it. These are functions contained under:

– Part I of the Food and Environment Protection Act 1985;

– the Food Safety Act 1990; and

– the Radioactive Substances Act 1993.

4.32 Certain functions exercisable by the Department of Agriculture for Northern Ireland cease to be exercisable by that Department under s 26(2), namely Part 1 of the Food and Environment Protection Act 1985 and certain parts of Part II of the Food Safety (Northern Ireland) Order 1991. The details of the transfer of these responsibilities to the Secretary of State for Health and the devolved authorities and to the Agency is set out in Sch 3 and Sch 5 to the 1999 Act. The most significant areas in which the Agency exercises powers are discussed in Chapter 6.

---

1   See **1.25**.

CENTRAL GOVERNMENT POWERS UNDER THE FOOD SAFETY ACT 1990

4.33   Before the Food Standards Act 1999, s 4 of the Food Safety Act 1990 (now repealed) defined which government departments were given responsibilities under that Act. By virtue of s 4, the powers and functions under the 1990 Act were essentially distributed between MAFF and the DoH, although certain powers could be exercised jointly. The Food Standards Act 1999 has changed the position to reflect the fact that a number of responsibilities previously exercised by MAFF have now been removed. Now, the functions listed in the 1990 Act are to be exercised by the 'Secretary of State', which is a reference to the Secretary of State for Health, and by the Agency (see Chapter 6), except in limited circumstances relating to enforcement functions being carried out by MAFF as a result of directions under s 6 of the 1990 Act. The amendments to the 1990 Act in this regard are dealt with in para 7 onwards of Sch 5 to the 1999 Act.

Enforcement of the Act

4.34   The Secretary of State may require any duty that is imposed on a local authority in relation to specific types of cases or a particular case to be discharged by the Minister rather than the local authority (s 6(3) of the 1990 Act). In addition, the Minister may take over the conduct of proceedings that have been commenced by somebody else (s 6(5)).

4.35   By virtue of s 42, if central government considers a local authority not to be properly fulfilling its duties and enforcing the 1990 Act, and considers such failures to affect the interests of consumers, it may require a different food authority to take over the functions of the local authority in default. In determining whether or not an authority is in default, the Secretary of State can order a local inquiry into the matter, but it is not required to do so. If it exercises these powers, it can require the defaulting authority to pay the expenses incurred. These powers have never been exercised.

4.36   The DoH may act as an 'enforcement authority', however, under normal circumstances, enforcement is usually left to local authorities (see the Food Safety (Enforcement Authority) (England and Wales) Order 1990 (SI 1990/ 2462); Statutory Code of Practice No 1: Responsibility for Enforcement of the Food Safety Act 1990 and Chapter 5).

4.37   For a more detailed discussion on how these powers will be exercised with the introduction of the Agency, see Chapter 6.

Emergency Orders

4.38   Section 13 of the 1990 Act gave new powers to MAFF in the event of emergencies relating to food, which had previously been operated on a voluntary basis. These powers are now exercisable by the Agency and the Secretary of State. The powers contained in s 13 are supplementary to those in ss 1 and 2 of the Food and Environment Protection Act 1985 which give powers to Ministers to make Emergency Prohibition Orders where there is a perceived hazard to human health, which may render food unsuitable for human health.

4.39   The powers in s 13 of the 1990 Act permit the making of an Emergency Control Order when Ministers consider a food product or producer to be posing an imminent risk of injury to health. These Orders can require the removal of contaminated foodstuffs from the market and the closure of premises where they are suspected of being the source of a food-borne infection.

4.40   Of course, local authorities have wide-ranging powers to issue notices prohibiting the production and sale of a particular food under s 9 of the 1990 Act when they obtain a court Order (see **5.82** below). However, unlike s 9, there is no provision under s 13 for the awarding of compensation in the event that the power is employed improperly.

4.41   It was anticipated that these powers would be exercised only in a contamination or food scare on a national basis where voluntary controls had not been applied uniformly in the first instance.[1] This appears to have been borne out.

4.42   The first order made under s 13 was the Food (Cheese) (Emergency Control) Order 1998 (SI 1998/1277) which prohibited the carrying out of commercial operations in relation to cheese manufactured by a Somerset farm called RA Duckett & Co. This Order was made as a result of a 12-year-old child contracting E. coli after eating cheese produced at that farm. A challenge was made to the Order, by way of judicial review, by Eastside Cheese Co, a customer of RA Duckett & Co which was supplied with 95 per cent of the cheese it sold by that firm.

4.43   Eastside Cheese Co argued that the Order made under s 13 of the 1990 Act was out of all proportion to the potential risk to health. The Divisional Court considered that the Order should not have been made.[2] It considered that the Secretary of State for Health could not take into account such matters as a fear of inconsistent decisions, lack of resources and administrative inconvenience incurred by enforcement by individual local authorities and, therefore, should not have made an Order under s 13 unless the powers of local authorities were considered to have been inadequate and the applicant had been given an opportunity to make representations before the Order was made.

4.44   However, the Court of Appeal allowed an appeal by the Secretary of State. It considered that the Secretary of State had not precipitately resorted to s 13 of the 1990 Act because of the scale of the potential problem and the gravity of the threat. The Secretary of State was entitled to a narrow margin of appreciation

---

1   See Baylis *Food Safety Law and Practice* (1994).
2   See *R v Secretary of State for Health, ex parte Eastside Cheese Co* [1999] EHLR 313.

appropriate in order to take decisions calling for the evaluation of scientific evidence.[1]

4.45 These powers can now be exercised by the Agency (see Chapter 6).

Powers to make Regulations

4.46 The Food Safety Act 1990 contains a large number of provisions that give Ministers the power to make Regulations regarding a variety of matters. The most significant matters are considered here.

4.47 Under s 16 of the 1990 Act, Ministers are empowered to make Regulations on the preparation, composition and distribution of food in order to ensure that it is healthy, safe and hygienic. Section 17 gives the power to make Regulations in order to implement EC legislation and s 18 gives the power to prohibit specified foods, novel foods and processes such as genetically modified foods.

4.48 Section 18 of the 1990 Act also allows Regulations to be made to license the producers and suppliers of milk and s 19 permits Regulations to be made to require the registration and licensing of premises used for food businesses. Further Regulations may prescribe what information is to be kept and under what conditions licences are given (s 26(2)).

4.49 Under s 26(1), Regulations may be made to prohibit the carrying out of any commercial operation in respect of a particular food. If offences are created by the Regulations, they may also provide for the mode of trial and penalties (s 26(3)).

4.50 Section 48 provides that the Secretary of State is required to consult those organisations representing interests which are likely to be substantially affected by proposed Regulations, except where the Regulations are to prohibit the importation of a particular food and are required to implement directly applicable European legislation (ie European Regulations). Under the amendments to s 48, Ministers are also required to have regard to any relevant advice of the Agency (s 48(4A)).

4.51 A huge number of Regulations have been made under these sections. Two of the most important and widely applicable Regulations are considered in Chapter 5.

Obtaining information

4.52 Under s 41 of the 1990 Act, as amended by para 18 of Sch 5 to the Food Standards Act 1999, the Secretary of State or the Agency can require food authorities to provide them with reports and information regarding the authorities' enforcement of the Act and local authorities are required to supply them with statistical information on inspections, prosecutions, official samples

---

1   *R v Secretary of State for Health, ex parte Eastside Cheese Co and Another* [1999] 3 CMLR 123.

and informal samples. These measures are now supplemented by the supervisory and monitoring functions of the Agency (see Chapter 6).

Training and qualifications

4.53 Under s 5(6) of the 1990 Act, Ministers may prescribe the qualifications that authorised officers are required to hold. These are prescribed by Code of Practice No 19.

4.54 In addition, Ministers may prescribe the qualifications that a public analyst (the principal scientific advisor to a food authority) is required to hold (s 27(2) of the 1990 Act). These qualifications have been set out in the Food Safety (Sampling and Qualifications) Regulations 1990 (SI 1990/2463).

Sampling and analysis

4.55 Under s 31 of the 1990 Act, the Secretary of State is empowered to make Regulations to prescribe the methods to be used when taking samples and analysing those samples. The detailed provisions relating to sampling are contained in the Food Safety (Sampling and Qualifications) Regulations 1990. These regulations must be followed when an enforcement authority exercises its powers to take samples and to submit them for analysis under ss 29 and 30.

Power to issue Codes of Practice

4.56 The Secretary of State may issue Codes of Practice under s 40 of the 1990 Act which are intended to be used as guidance for local authorities when using their powers and enforcing the Act. Before making any Code, there must be consultation with those interests which are likely to be substantially affected by the proposed Code. In addition, Ministers and now also the Agency may direct a food authority to comply with a Code. This direction must be complied with and, if not complied with, can be enforced in the courts by an Order of *mandamus*. These are also powers now exercisable by the Agency (see Chapter 6).

4.57 Twenty Codes of Practice have been made under the 1990 Act. These are all contained in *Butterworths' Law of Food and Drugs*, Division B.

4.58 Although central government clearly has a significant amount of power under the 1990 Act (indeed, it can itself act as an enforcement authority and, thus, be responsible for the exercise of all the powers and duties under the Act), in practice, the bodies responsible for the enforcement of food regulation are the local authorities.

NEW POWERS GRANTED TO MINISTERS BY THE FOOD STANDARDS ACT 1999

4.59 Section 25 of the 1999 Act confers the power on the Secretary of State (and on the other appropriate authorities in relation to their own sphere of competence) to modify by Order any enactment to remove or relax any provision in such an enactment which is (in s 25(5)) capable of either:

'(a) preventing the disclosure to the Agency of information that would facilitate the carrying out of the Agency's functions; or

(b) preventing the publication by the Agency of information in circumstances where the Agency's power to publish would otherwise be exercisable.'

4.60 Such an Order may (s 25(6)):

'(a) make provision as to circumstances in which information which is subject to the prohibition in question may, or may not, be disclosed by the Agency or, as the case may be, published by the Agency; and

(b) if it makes provision enabling the disclosure of information to the Agency, make provision restricting the purposes for which such information may be used (including restrictions on the subsequent disclosure of the information by the Agency).'

4.61 Thus, the Secretary of State may make provision for the Agency to have access to information which would otherwise be barred by statute and may render information which would otherwise not be in the public domain subject to the Agency's discretion to publish within s 19 of the 1990 Act, albeit with such restrictions as the Secretary of State thinks appropriate. The provisions apply to common law rules restricting publishing and/or the provision of information to the Agency as they do to statutory rules (s 25(7)). This power cannot be used to render publishable material that would not otherwise be publishable by the Agency in accordance with s 19 (s 25(5)(b)).

4.62 Section 27 of the 1999 Act enables the Secretary of State for Health and his equivalents in the devolved administrations (s 27(8)) to make Regulations to set up a notification scheme for the results of laboratory tests for food-borne organisms. This power can be used to help the Agency or any other public authority relating to the protection of public health to carry out its functions (s 27(3)). These Regulations are intended to enable the Agency to remain fully informed about incidents of food-borne disease and to better understand patterns of and prevalence of such disease. The organisms expected to be covered by such a notification scheme are salmonella, E. coli 0157 and campylobacter.[1]

4.63 Section 27(5) of the 1999 Act sets out the matters for which the Regulations may provide, such as the type and form of notification for each particular organism and the person who is to be notified. This can also include the creation of a summary offence of failure to notify with a penalty of a fine not exceeding level 5 on the Standard Scale. The authority making any Regulations

---

1   Explanatory Notes to s 27.

under s 27(5) is required to consult the Agency and any other organisations the authority believes represents interests likely to be substantially affected by the Regulations (s 25(6)). However, consultation undertaken before the commencement of that subsection is deemed to be as effective as later consultation by s 25(7).

4.64   Section 30 of the 1999 Act confers a new power on Ministers to establish by Order new provisions for the regulation of animal feedingstuffs based on the Food Safety Act 1990. This provision has little to do with the Agency itself other than that one of the functions of the Agency is the giving of advice in relation to animal feedingstuffs. An Order may be made under s 30 'with a view to protecting animal health, protecting human health or for any other purpose which appears to the Ministers to be appropriate' (s 30(4)). Before making any order under s 30, Ministers are required to consult with any organisations which appear to them to be representative of interests which are likely to be substantially affected by the Order and must have regard to any advice given by the Agency. As with s 27, prior consultation is deemed to be as effective as later consultation (s 30(7)). Section 31 deals with similar powers in relation to Northern Ireland.

4.65   The making of an Order under ss 25, 30 or 31 must be done using the 'affirmative resolution procedure' (s 37(3)), ie it will not be valid unless a draft of the Order has been laid before the relevant Parliament (in England and Wales, both Houses of Parliament, in Scotland, the Scottish Parliament and in Northern Ireland, the Northern Ireland Assembly) and approved.

DELEGATION OF MINISTERIAL POWERS

4.66   Section 17 of the 1999 Act contains provisions permitting the delegation of powers under certain enactments currently enjoyed by the Secretary of State to the Agency. These are, as listed in s 17(1)(a), the power to make Emergency Orders under s 1(1) of the Food and Environment Protection Act 1985 and, as listed in s 17(1)(b), the power to make Emergency Control Orders under s 13(1) of the Food Safety Act 1990. Where the Agency is authorised by the Secretary of State to exercise such powers, the authority given is subject to any limitations and conditions he may impose (s 17(2)). In exercising such power, the Agency is deemed to be acting as the Secretary of State (s 17(3)) who retains the power to act notwithstanding the making of such arrangements (s 17(4)). These provisions also apply, with the necessary modifications, to powers exercisable by the devolved Parliaments or the responsible Ministers therein within their own spheres of competence (s 17(5)).

4.67   The Explanatory Notes to s 17 of the 1999 Act states that 'in practice it is envisaged that the Agency will only make Orders in emergency situations where the Secretary of State is not available' and it is stressed that this power does not give the Agency power to make legislation itself in other areas. The fact that this power remains with the Secretary of State was stressed in Standing Committee:

'Under the well-established Carltona principle, the responsibility can, with agreement, be delegated to the Agency, but the presumption is that, because of their potential impact and seriousness, the Orders will continue to be signed by the Secretary of State.'[1]

4.68 In exercising this power on behalf of the Secretary of State, it may well be that the Agency's discretion is fettered to a greater extent than would be the case if the decision were to be taken directly by the Secretary of State. The reason for this is that in considering whether or not to exercise any power, or the manner in which to exercise any power, the Agency is required by s 23(2) of the 1999 Act (see below) to take into account a number of factors, including the likely costs and benefits of the exercise or non-exercise of that power.

4.69 However, according to s 23(3)(b) of the 1999 Act, the duty in s 23(2) 'does not affect the obligation of the Agency to discharge any other duties imposed on it'. Thus, if authorisation under s 17 can properly be seen as the 'imposition' of another duty on the Agency, it might be thought that the balancing process required by s 23(2) would not apply. That s 23(2) is intended to apply to this situation is clarified by the statement of the Minister for Public Health in Standing Committee:

'When responsibility is delegated, the Agency's actions will be required to be proportionate to the risks. The importance of the power being retained by the Secretary of State is that it is conceivable that he may want to take action that is more far-reaching, on the basis that evidence is provided to him. The safeguard in relation to the Secretary of State's actions is, as I have already said, that the decisions that he makes should be subject to judicial review.'[2]

4.70 The exercise of this power by the Secretary of State (concerning the making of the Food (Cheese) (Emergency Control) Order 1998 (SI 1998/1277) was examined by both the Divisional Court and the Court of Appeal in *R v Secretary of State for Health, ex parte Eastside Cheese Co and Another*.[3] For a detailed commentary on this case, see **4.43**. The discretion which the Court concluded the Secretary of State had in taking this decision may well be more limited in the case of the Agency by virtue of s 23(2) of the 1999 Act.

---

1   Tessa Jowell, Standing Committee B, 8/7/99, col 234.
2   Ibid.
3   [1999] 3 CMLR 123.

Chapter 5
Local Authority Enforcement

LOCAL AUTHORITY STRUCTURE

5.1 The Local Government Act 1972 created new structures for local government and allocated functions among the new authorities. Local government in London was not changed substantially by this Act – it had already been altered more substantially by the London Government Act 1963, and these changes were simply incorporated into the 1972 Act.

5.2 Under the Local Government Act 1972, Wales and England (other than Greater London) were divided into counties and districts. In England, certain counties were made metropolitan counties and the districts within these counties became metropolitan districts. Many districts in England were divided into parishes, and in Wales they were divided into communities.

5.3 The Local Government Act 1985 made changes to Greater London and the metropolitan counties. The Greater London Council and the metropolitan councils were abolished and their functions reallocated to the London borough councils and the metropolitan district councils.

5.4 The Local Government Act 1992 made further significant changes to local authority structure and particularly to the non-metropolitan counties. Under this Act, unitary authorities were established, although the county and district councils are retained in some counties. In 1994, Wales was completely restructured into 22 unitary authorities, being counties or county boroughs.

5.5 The term 'local authority' is used to describe any of these types of local government structures (ie counties, district, London boroughs, parish councils, counties, county boroughs and community councils). All of these bodies are corporate bodies and have the characteristics of corporations.[1]

LOCAL AUTHORITY ENFORCEMENT FUNCTIONS IN RELATION TO FOOD

5.6 The Local Government Act 1972 dramatically reduced the number of food authorities in England and Wales. This was seen as a positive move towards more consistent enforcement. However, the efficient enforcement of food law was hindered by the reorganisation under the Local Government Act 1985. Before the introduction of new structures under this Act, the responsibility of food enforcement had been exercised by the metropolitan county councils. Their

---

1   For a more detailed explanation of local authority structure, see SH Bailey *Cross on Principles of Local Government Law* 2nd edn (Sweet & Maxwell, 1997).

abolition and the consequent transfer of functions to the metropolitan districts destroyed the more developed enforcement authorities, but the transitional arrangements provided by coordinating committees did not fill this gap.[1] The Food Safety Act 1990 retains the local authority enforcement principle by virtue of s 5, which designates local authorities as food authorities and empowers them to enforce the Act.

5.7   The enforcement of the 1990 Act is the responsibility of a metropolitan district council. Where non-metropolitan authorities have not been unified, the county and district councils both have concurrent powers of enforcement. However, the Food Safety (Enforcement Authority) (England and Wales) Order 1990 (SI 1990/2462) specifies that non-metropolitan district councils shall be responsible for the enforcement of s 12 of the 1990 Act (emergency prohibition powers) and that county councils shall enforce s 15 (food falsely or misleadingly described). There are no statutory controls over the enforcement of the other provisions of the Act. However, Code of Practice No 1 (Responsibility for Enforcement of the Food Safety Act 1990) recommends that cases involving contamination by micro-organisms or their toxins (eg salmonella, listeria and botulism) should be dealt with by district councils and that county councils should deal with cases of chemical contamination and improper use of additives, posing no immediate risk to health, and compositional offences, adulteration and misleading claims.

5.8   The effect of these measures is that the enforcement functions have been defined and the county councils are responsible for enforcing legislation on food standards and the labelling of food, including the quality, composition, labelling, presentation and advertising of food and of food contamination. These matters are dealt with by trading standards departments within the county councils. The district councils, through their environmental health departments, are responsible for the enforcement of food safety and hygiene. Where non-metropolitan county and district councils have been unified, the unitary authority is responsible for all of the enforcement functions under the 1990 Act, but the unitary authorities, although operating a single department, often retain distinct functions for trading standards officers and environmental health officers, and their areas of responsibility often remain similar to their colleagues in those departments within non-unitary authorities. It should be noted that port authorities can also enforce food hygiene legislation.

5.9   Under s 27 of the 1990 Act, metropolitan councils, unitary authorities and non-metropolitan county councils must appoint at least one public analyst whom they are required to use for all compositional sampling work under the 1990 Act. Ministers have prescribed in Regulations the qualifications a public analyst must possess (see Chapter 3). Many local authorities have appointed privately owned public analysts, who carry out other work as well. The public analyst is the principal scientific advisor, providing an analytical service for local authorities. In order to ensure that there are no conflicts of interest, a public

---

1   See *Butterworths' Law of Food and Drugs*, Division A.

analyst must not be engaged, either directly or indirectly, in any food business in the area of the authority. The Regulations on qualifications have specified that this is to be interpreted to mean that a public analyst is prevented from being a director, owner or employee of a food business.

5.10 Under s 30 of the 1990 Act, when food is analysed by a public analyst, he will provide a certificate to the officer, which specifies the result of the analysis. This certificate is admissible as evidence in any legal proceedings and the public analyst need not attend to give evidence, unless required by the defendant.

5.11 Finally, the Laboratory of the Government Chemist acts as a reference laboratory when there are disputes between local authorities and food companies.

LACOTS[1]

5.12 Following the Second World War, the Ministry of Food provided guidance and advice on compliance with certain aspects of food regulation. However, in 1955, this service was abolished and a number of the more developed enforcement authorities took over the role and provided unofficial advice on the subject. None the less, conflicting advice continued. This led to the creation in 1959 of a Joint Advisory Committee, which was made up of enforcement authorities and public analysts and which continued to provide guidance on the interpretation of the law. This body later became the Local Authorities Joint Advisory Committee.

5.13 As regulation increased to cover more areas of consumer protection, it was considered necessary to have a broader advisory body. In 1976, the Association of County Councils and the Association of Metropolitan Authorities reached agreement to establish a new body, known as LACOTS. The role of this new body was to consult and negotiate with central government and trade and industry bodies with a view to establishing standards of quality. It now promotes and coordinates proper and consistent enforcement of environmental health and trading standards laws.

5.14 LACOTS is a company limited by guarantee and is constituted by and accountable to the Local Government Association for England and Wales, the Convention of Scottish Local Authorities and the Association of Local Authorities in Northern Ireland. It has a Board of Directors with five members and a Management Committee with 12 members. It also has an Executive Director and Secretariat of staff, who assist LACOTS to carry out its functions and who are accountable to the Board of Directors, the Management Committee and the Chief Executive of the Local Government Association for England and Wales.

---

1   At http://www.lacots.org.uk.

5.15   In 1999, the terms of reference for LACOTS were stated in the Scheme of Operation (1999) as follows:

'–   Promote quality regulation, coordinate enforcement and good practice.

–   Provide advice, guidance and codes for food safety and trading standards authorities.

–   Advise central government and European Union on relevant legislation.

–   Promote the Home Authority Principle as the key method of enforcement coordination.

–   Administer statutory arrangements as the UK's Single Liaison Body for transborder food problems.

–   Develop information and central record databases to assist practitioners.

–   Liaise with industry, trade and consumer organisations.

–   Collaborate with enforcement agencies overseas.'

5.16   As an advisory body, LACOTS publishes circulars and advice, which provide guidance on particular topics of concern. It also negotiates with central government on policies and their implementation.

5.17   As the Single Liaison Body for the UK in Europe (appointed under the terms of Article 6 of the Additional Food Control Measures Directive (93/99/EEC),[1] LACOTS is required to:

–   assist and coordinate communication between Member States on food issues;
–   forward complaints and requests for information to Member States;
–   receive incoming requests for assistance and direct these to the appropriate home authority; and
–   resolve difficulties in communication and liaison.

5.18   The more detailed arrangements for the operation of this system, in particular the procedures to be followed by LACOTS and local authorities in these situations, were outlined by the central government departments in Code of Practice No 20, made under s 40 of the 1990 Act. LACOTS has also set out the procedures to be followed when it is asked to perform a function in this capacity.[2] It also provides periodical reports on its work as the Single Liaison Body.

THE HOME AUTHORITY PRINCIPLE

5.19   The operation of a system similar to the Home Authority Principle (HAP) was initiated by a small group of chief trading standards officers in 1978. It was adopted and developed by LACOTS in 1980, with trading standards matters in

---

1   See Chapter 2.
2   In LAC 6(97) 1, 21 March 1997.

mind. From 1984, there were calls, particularly from environmental health officers, to extend the principle more generally and to apply it to food regulation. By early 1990, it was agreed that a system similar to HAP was required in food matters and, following a pilot scheme in 1994, LACOTS' guidance on HAP was revised in order to apply to food enforcement. In addition, a number of the Codes of Practice issued under s 40 of the 1990 Act were amended to include the recommendation of the operation of HAP. The current guidance was issued in January 1997.

5.20   The principle is widely supported by food and trading standards services throughout the UK, although a small number of enforcement officers have expressed criticisms, and it is seen by LACOTS as an essential part of modern enforcement coordination. The principle has also been recognised in Europe and adopted by the European Forum of Food Law Enforcement Practitioners in order to assist in the dissemination of information between Member States.

5.21   The principle involves the appointment of a local authority as the 'home authority' for a company or business. The home authority is selected in consultation with the business as the local authority in which the decision base of the business is situated. Therefore, it is usually the authority in which the head office or main operation is situated. If the business is decentralised, there may also be an 'originating authority', which is selected according to the area in which goods are produced or packaged. LACOTS keeps a database of home authorities and can help a business to find an appropriate authority.

5.22   The principle envisages that the home authority will pay particular attention to products originating in its area and will seek to prevent infringement by offering advice and guidance on compliance. In so doing, HAP aims to:

–   concentrate on goods originating in the home authority's area;
–   help businesses to comply at source;
–   promote coordination of enforcement by encouraging liaison between local authorities;
–   provide a means of resolving disputes, where appropriate; and
–   ultimately, reduce both public and business expenditure by increasing standards before distribution and minimising duplication of enforcement by individual enforcement authorities.

5.23   The home authority provides a regular point of contact for businesses and should be approached when the businesses have any queries. It also maintains records of incidents, enforcement action, due diligence procedures and relevant company policies. Its success, therefore, depends upon the home authority developing a good relationship and open dialogue with the businesses. The home authority should always be prepared to answer enquiries from local authorities that are considering enforcement action. Certainly, local authorities considering enforcement action should contact a business's home authority before the decision to prosecute is taken. In the event that agreement on the interpretation of the law cannot be reached, the issue should be referred, in the first instance, to a local liaison group or trade association. Only if disagreement persists, does

LACOTS consider providing assistance and guidance. However, HAP makes it clear that the appointment of a home authority and advice or guidance given by that home authority does not provide an absolute safeguard from prosecution by other local authorities.

5.24 In June 1999, LACOTS published a consultation paper on HAP, with a view to obtaining views on how the system could be improved. The paper considered a number of difficulties with the current operation of the principle. LACOTS recognised that it may need to provide more detailed guidance to local authorities on the extent of their obligations. As such, it suggested minimum service standards for home, originating and enforcement authorities. As part of these minimum standards, home authorities would be required to draw up written agreements with businesses, setting out the extent and limitations of the service provided by the home authority. In addition, home authorities would be expected to ensure, as far as possible, that a business would not be put at a disadvantage if it were given the wrong advice. This more detailed guidance would require home authorities to implement efficient procedures for communicating with other authorities. The guidance also expects a home authority to challenge enforcement authorities which are considering prosecuting, when it considers that a business has demonstrated good due diligence.

5.25 The proposed detailed guidance to enforcement authorities includes an underlining of the expectation that enforcement authorities should:

–   contact home or originating authorities at an early stage (preferably before contact with the business is made);
–   keep home and originating authorities informed of enforcement action; and
–   give proper consideration to the advice of home and originating authorities.

5.26 Some businesses, particularly multiple retailers, would like to see a more significant role played by HAP, with the home authority having better knowledge and greater analysis of the systems in place and coordination of local inspections and sampling.

5.27 Financial concerns have been expressed. The resources required to maintain a proper home authority relationship are significant and, in some cases, local authorities have complained that they are burdensome. There is particular concern over the financial resources required to operate as a home authority for large multiple traders. However, it is submitted that, although initial expenditure can be significant, a thorough implementation of HAP by local authorities would reduce expenditure on enforcement action substantially. Despite the fact that most local authorities appear to embrace HAP, there remains the view among a minority of local authorities and individual officers that their primary responsibility is to take enforcement action which results too often in prosecutions. In addition, LACOTS's view that only a minority of differences should be resolved by the court is not being borne out in practice.

5.28 Finally, the adoption of HAP by local authorities or businesses is not mandatory because LACOTS does not have the executive authority to require participation. The success of the principle clearly relies upon full participation. The government suggested in its White Paper for the establishment of the Food Standards Agency that HAP might be made mandatory, although to date such a course has not been implemented. In the meantime, the recognition of the HAP is strongly encouraged and local authorities are required to have regard to Codes of Practice recommending that authorities should operate a HAP when seeking to enforce food legislation.[1] In addition, LACOTS's guidance on the drawing up of enforcement policies encourages enforcement authorities to have contact with home authorities and describes this communication as essential when a company's due diligence system has been approved by a home authority but faces attack from a different enforcement authority.

5.29   The Food Standards Agency has also indicated its support for HAP in its consultation document on local authority enforcement and monitoring, which was issued in June 1999. This document sets out the proposed standards expected of local authorities in order to monitor enforcement performance. The proposed standards clearly endorse a strict adherence to HAP (see Chapter 6).

LOCAL AUTHORITY POWERS TO PROSECUTE

Who has the power to act within a local authority?

5.30   The procedure for the taking of decisions by local authorities is complex and can be determined largely by the specific council involved. All that is attempted here is a brief outline of some of the more general aspects of decision-making.[2]

5.31   Under s 5 of the 1990 Act, local authorities are designated as food authorities for the purpose of enforcing the Act. However, the designation is to the local authority as a whole and not to individuals. Therefore, food authorities are subject to the general rules on delegation of powers which apply in all respects to local authorities.

5.32   The general means by which local authorities discharge their functions is contained in s 101 of the Local Government Act 1972. This provision enables local authorities to authorise their functions to be performed by other local authorities, committees, sub-committees or officers of the council who may themselves be given a specific or general authority to delegate to other officers.[3]

5.33   However, the essential element in the performance of any function by any of these bodies is that the performance has been properly authorised by the

---

1   See Codes of Practice No 5 (Improvement Notices), No 8 (Food Standards Inspections), No 9 (Food Hygiene Inspections), No 17 (Meat Products) and No 18 (Dairy Products).
2   For a more detailed examination of this topic, see Claire Andrews, *The Enforcement of Regulatory Offences* (1998) ch 2.
3   See *Hilliers Ltd v Sefton Metropolitan Borough Council* 29 November 1996 (unreported).

council. Authorisation is given by resolution, Standing Order or specific delegation. A delegation to a council officer does not permit a member of the council to perform that task. Similarly, a delegation to a committee does not permit a single person rather than 'the committee' to perform the function.[1]

5.34 A delegation of powers can be specific, naming the particular function with which the committee or officer is charged, or it can be more general. An example of a more general delegation was examined in *James v Stein*.[2] In that case, the resolution of the council gave an officer the power to 'act as an officer within the said county for the carrying out ... of the Food Act ..., or any Act ... or any Orders made thereunder, and to prosecute before a court of summary jurisdiction or justices any information, complaint, or proceedings arising under the same discharge of his duties'. The Court considered that such wording also delegated to the officer the making of the decision about whom to prosecute.

5.35 Under s 5(6) of the 1990 Act, an authorised officer under the Act (whether or not an officer of the authority) must be authorised in writing, either generally or specifically, to act in matters arising under the Act. He must also possess qualifications prescribed by the Ministers (see Chapter 3).

5.36 In respect of criminal prosecutions, therefore, it is essential that the council authorise, whether specifically or by the delegation of general discretionary powers, the decision to prosecute, the commencement of proceedings and the trial. Courts are generally reluctant to hold that an act of the council has not been authorised. There are cases to suggest that the council need not give prior authority for the performance of the function, so long as the decision was later ratified[3], or there has been a fresh determination of the issue.[4] Although these cases involved civil proceedings, the courts have been prepared to take an equally flexible approach to authorisation when considering an authority to prosecute. In *MFI Furniture Centre Ltd v Hibbert*,[5] the Divisional Court was prepared to go to some lengths to construe the wording of the delegation in order to hold that there was an effective delegation. However, the court considered that even where an individual officer acts without authority, the proceedings will remain validly commenced by him personally, the only potential consequence relating to costs in the event that the prosecution is successfully defended.

5.37 The general power of local authorities to institute and conduct legal proceedings are contained in ss 222 and 223 of the Local Government Act 1972. Under s 222, a local authority can prosecute, defend or appear in any legal proceeding, provided it considers it to be in the interests of protecting or

---

1   *R v Secretary of State for the Environment, ex parte Hillingdon London Borough Council* [1986] 1 WLR 192.
2   (1946) 110 JP 279.
3   *Warwick Rural District Council v Miller-Mead* [1962] Ch 441; *Stoke-on-Trent City Council v B&Q Retail Ltd* [1984] Ch 1.
4   *Webb v Ipswich Borough Council* (1989) 21 HLR 325.
5   (1996) 160 JP 178.

promoting inhabitants of its area. However, in addition to the general power under s 222, the 1990 Act contains a similar power in s 6(5).

5.38 Section 223 of the Local Govenment Act 1972 permits any authorised member or officer of a local authority to prosecute, defend or appear on behalf of the authority in proceedings before a magistrates' court, regardless of whether he possesses the legal qualifications that are normally required.

5.39 Therefore, officers of the council who have been authorised by it as above can institute proceedings by the laying of the information and also appear on behalf of the council in the legal proceedings. The same authorised officer does not have to perform both roles,[1] but the officer does have to be properly authorised and such authorisation does not naturally follow from the position held by the officer.[2] Furthermore, under s 233, a local authority can only authorise an officer or member of the council to commence proceedings and not some other person.[3]

5.40 It should be noted that none of these provisions prevents an individual from commencing proceedings in a private prosecution[4] although, under s 6(5) of the 1990 Act, Ministers can take over conduct of these proceedings if they consider it necessary.

The decision to prosecute

5.41 The decision to prosecute is usually taken by the authority concerned, but the authority to make this decision is often delegated by the council to an officer, committee or sub-committee. Who has been given the authority to make the decision will vary from council to council. In larger local authorities, it is often the decision of the chief environmental health officer or trading standards officer. Where the decision is taken by a committee, these decisions are frequently taken in a public meeting. The authors of *Butterworths' Law of Food and Drugs* (Division A) comment that this can be an unfair procedure for a potential defendant, as these decisions are taken in public and can attract media attention.

5.42 Often, the actual consideration of whether to prosecute is forgotten in the investigation with the officers' anxiety to prepare the case for a prosecution. As Andrews comments,[5] this has led to ill-considered prosecutions which are not in the public interest. Just because it appears that an offence has been committed is not in itself justification for a decision to prosecute. In all cases, the council has discretion not to prosecute. As Lord Shawcross, in his role as Attorney-General, said during a House of Commons debate in 1951:

> 'It has never been the rule in this country – I hope it never will be – that suspected criminal offences must automatically be the subject of prosecution. Indeed the very

---

1   *R v Northumberland Justices, ex parte Thompson* (1923) JP 95.
2   *Bob Keats Ltd v Farrant* [1951] 1 All ER 899.
3   *Oberst v Coombs* (1955) 53 LGR 316.
4   *Snodgrass v Topping* (1952) 116 JP 332.
5   Claire Andrews, *The Enforcement of Regulatory Offences* (1998), p 19.

first regulations under which the Director of Public Prosecution worked provided that he should ... prosecute "wherever it appears that the offence or the circumstances of its commission is or are of such a character that a prosecution in respect thereof is required in the public interest". That is still the dominant consideration.'[1]

This view was endorsed by the House of Lords, and particularly Lord Diplock, in *Smedleys Ltd v Breed*.[2] In that case, the local authority was severely criticised for bringing a prosecution under the Food and Drugs Act 1955 against a company which canned peas and which supplied a retailer with a can of peas containing a caterpillar. The company's procedures were not criticised, but because there was no due diligence defence under the 1955 Act, the offence was proved. Lord Diplock could not see that the particular prosecution served the general interests of consumers and indicated that, in such circumstances, magistrates should consider imposing an absolute discharge.

Codes of Practice

5.43   Where local authorities are concerned with food offences, they must have regard to Code of Practice No 2 (Legal Matters), issued by MAFF under s 40 of the 1990 Act. Although the Code is not legally binding, a failure to observe its contents could result in MAFF issuing a direction that the authority must comply with its provisions.[3]

5.44   Part C of the Code of Practice No 2 deals with the taking of legal proceedings. So far as the decision to prosecute is concerned, the Code states that the food authority should have regard to:

- the seriousness of the alleged offence;
- the previous history of the party concerned;
- the likelihood of the defendant being able to establish a due diligence defence;
- the ability and willingness of any important witnesses to cooperate;
- the willingness of the party to prevent recurrence of the problem;
- the probable public benefit of a prosecution and the importance of the case (eg whether it might establish a precedent);
- whether other actions, such as issuing a formal caution or an improvement notice or imposing a prohibition, would be more appropriate or effective (it is also suggested that although it is possible to issue a notice and to prosecute, such action should only be taken in exceptional circumstances, for example where there had been a failure to comply with a notice'; and
- any explanation offered by the affected company.

5.45   The Code of Practice No 2 is only concerned with the prosecution of food offences under the 1990 Act. However, the more general Code of Practice

---

1   *House of Commons Debates*, vol 483, col 681, 29th January 1951.
2   [1974] AC 839.
3   This function has now passed to the Food Standards Agency; see Sch 3, para 4 to the 1990 Act.

followed in the majority of prosecutions of criminal offences is the Code for Crown Prosecutors. This was issued under s 10 of the Prosecution of Offences Act 1985. By virtue of s 6 of the 1985 Act, the guidelines contained in this Code do not apply to local authority prosecutors. However, para 19 of the Code of Practice No 2 states that the Code for Crown Prosecutors is a valuable reference for local authorities. LACOTS' *Guidance on Food Safety Enforcement Policies* (see below) also states that the Code provides guidance that should be considered. Therefore, local authorities should have regard to its contents when considering whether to prosecute.

5.46   The Code for Crown Prosecutors identifies two elements in the test for bringing a prosecution. The first is that there must be sufficient evidence to provide a 'realistic prospect of conviction'. The second is that the prosecution must be in the public interest.

5.47   In relation to the public interest element, the Code endorses the statement of Lord Shawcross in 1951 (see **5.42** above). The code gives indications of which factors may support a decision to prosecute, including, the likelihood of a significant sentence, the defendant's previous conviction record, and the fact that an offence is likely to be repeated or is widespread in the particular area. Factors which are said to make a prosecution less necessary include the likelihood of a small penalty, the fact that the offence was committed as a result of a genuine mistake or misunderstanding, the harm caused was minor, there was a long delay between the offence and trial, or that the defendant has put right the loss or harm caused. Alternatives to prosecution (eg a caution) should always be considered.

5.48   Furthermore, para 3 of the Code makes it clear that the review of whether a prosecution is in the public interest should not be something that is only considered as part of making the decision to prosecute. It is a continuing review and, therefore, if, after proceedings have been commenced, there has been a change of circumstances and it seems that it is no longer in the public interest to prosecute, a prosecutor should consider withdrawing the prosecution.

Local authority enforcement policies

5.49   In addition to the Codes of Practice, local authorities also draw up an enforcement policy for their officers to follow. These policies often set out the type of approach that local authorities should adopt when considering enforcement action. The guidance contained in these documents is not mandatory and the fact that a policy suggests a prosecution should not be brought in certain circumstances, does not necessarily prevent an authority from prosecuting. In fact, an overly prescriptive policy or a rigid application of a policy may be considered to be unlawful by the courts.[1]

5.50   Where the 'Enforcement Concordat' (see **5.59** et seq below) has been adopted by a local authority, local authority enforcement policies are still

---

1   *R v Commissioners of Inland Revenue, ex parte Mead* [1993] 1 All ER 772; *R v Chief Constable of Devon and Cornwall, ex parte Central Electricity Generating Board* [1982] QB 458).

permitted. However, these policies are often amended in order to implement the Concordat's contents.

LACOTS' guidelines on the drawing up of enforcement policies

5.51 LACOTS undertook detailed research into food safety enforcement policies of local authorities and in February 1994 produced a document called *Guidance on Food Safety Enforcement Policies*, offering guidelines to assist local authorities in drawing up appropriate enforcement policies. The Chairman of LACOTS stated that the guidelines 'promote greater consistency, balance and fairness in the enforcement of food safety legislation' without imposing 'undue prescription' by providing a 'systematic approach to policies' (the Foreword to the Guidance). The adoption of policies along the lines suggested is intended to ensure that enforcement action is 'focused on situations where the public is put at risk and on food businesses which are negligent of their obligations or are intentionally infringing the law'. The Food Safety (General Food Hygiene) Regulations 1995 require local authorities to adopt a risk-assessment-based approach to enforcement, particularly when carrying out inspections (see Chapter 3).

5.52 As far as the policy document is concerned, LACOTS recommend that:

– all authorities have a documented policy on food safety enforcement;
– enforcement policies should be reviewed in light of the recommendations in the Guidance;
– the policy should include a statement of its objectives;
– all enforcement action should be based on an assessment of risk to public health of non-compliance with food safety law (the Guidance states that enforcement action should not constitute a punitive response to minor technical contraventions of legislation);
– the enforcement policy should commit the local authority's support for the adherence to the Codes of Practice;
– any departure from the policy should be exceptional, capable of justification and be considered fully by relevant local managers before the decision is taken; and
– all officers should be acquainted with the policy and appropriate training should be given.

5.53 As far as the decision to prosecute is concerned, LACOTS states that it is necessary for enforcement policies to set out when a particular form of enforcement action is required. It identifies the following options as those a local authority should consider:

– taking no action;
– taking informal action;
– using statutory notices;
– issuing formal cautions; and
– prosecuting.

5.54   It suggests that there should be particular criteria applied to each of these possible enforcement procedures to determine if they are appropriate. These critiera would achieve consistency between authorities in the approach to enforcement action. It recommends that policies should endorse the HAP and should observe it in cases of differences of opinion between authorities.

5.55   The Guidance suggests that informal action would include offering advice, issuing verbal warnings and requests for action, the use of letters and issuing food hygiene inspection reports. However, if such action is taken, then the advice should always be clear and specific and should distinguish clearly between legal requirements and suggested best practice. LACOTS suggests that such an approach is suitable where:

–   the act or omission by the business is not serious enough to warrant formal action;
–   the past history of the business has shown that informal action will achieve compliance;
–   the authority has confidence in the management of the business; or
–   there is no significant risk to public health.

5.56   The Guidance states that a decision to prosecute is a very significant one and recommends that prosecutions be restricted to 'those persons who blatantly disregard the law, refuse to achieve even the basic minimum legal requirements, often following previous contact with the authority, and who put the public at risk. Such persons are, however, a minority'.

5.57   The suggested criteria for making the decision to prosecute are:

–   where there are flagrant breaches of the law such that public health, safety or well being is or has been put at risk;
–   where there has been a failure to correct an identified serious potential risk to food safety after having given the business a reasonable opportunity to take such corrective action;
–   where a business has failed to comply with a statutory notice; and
–   when there is a history of similar offences which have involved a risk to public health.

5.58   In addition, LACOTS proposes that all the circumstances should be taken into account and recommends that a policy be implemented to invite routinely suspected offenders to offer an explanation before a decision to prosecute is taken. The Guidance also states that an authority should be satisfied that there is sufficient evidence to give a realistic prospect of a conviction and that the prosecution is in the public interest. It recommends the observance of the indications on public interest given in the Code for Crown Prosecutors (see above). Finally, once the decision to prosecute is taken, the case should be passed to the solicitor or person responsible for conducting those proceedings without undue delay.

The Enforcement Concordat

5.59 Following the enactment of the Deregulation and Contracting Out Act 1994, there has been a move to reduce unnecessary and burdensome regulatory activity. This move eventually led in March 1998 to the Better Regulation Unit (now renamed the Regulatory Impact Unit) of the Cabinet Office issuing a policy document called the 'Enforcement Concordat', which is signed by both central and local government. It is hoped that all local authorities will sign up to and adopt the Concordat, although they cannot be forced to do so. This document applies not only to the regulation of food, but also generally to any regulatory activity of the local authority.

5.60 The Enforcement Concordat sets out what businesses can expect from enforcement officers. It recognises:

–   that the primary function of government enforcement work is to protect the public and consumers;
–   the need to carry out enforcement functions in a consistent and fair manner;
–   the fact that most businesses want to comply with the law and, therefore, that local authorities should seek to 'help' businesses meet the legal requirements without unnecessary expense; and
–   that firm action, such as prosecution, should be taken where appropriate.

Clearly, these factors should be considered in any decision to prosecute.

5.61 In addition, the policies and procedures that should be implemented include:

–   actively working with businesses to help them to comply by giving them advice and assistance;
–   minimising the costs to businesses in complying with the law;
–   ensuring that local authority action is proportionate to the risks associated with a failure to comply;
–   the authority taking into account the attitude of the business towards compliance;
–   the implementation of arrangements to promote consistency of enforcement between different authorities;[1] and
–   providing an opportunity for informal discussion before enforcement action is taken, where urgent action is not required, to try and resolve differences.

5.62 All of these factors should be taken into account by a local authority when considering whether a prosecution should be brought.

5.63 Clearly, the adoption of the Enforcement Concordat and a proper observance of enforcement policies that take into account Enforcement Concordat principles and LACOTS' guidelines should make the decision to

---

1   Although not referred to specifically, clearly the proper observance of the HAP (see above) is hereby encouraged.

prosecute a decision of the last resort. However, in practice, this approach is not always taken. As Andrews observes:

> '... some authorities will prosecute purely on the basis of a perceived expectation of conviction which, amongst other advantages to the local authority, gives a chance of recovery of all or part of the investigation costs ... It is submitted that many prosecutions are pursued which do not satisfy the seriousness of the criteria envisaged by LACOTS ...'[1]

5.64   However, under Agency powers, local authority enforcement will be monitored. A more detailed look at these powers and their limitation can be found at **6.71** below.

5.65   Certainly, the consultation document on local authority enforcement dated May 2000, appears to propose that a factor to be considered in the monitoring of enforcement is consistency in terms of enforcement action and in terms of implementing enforcement policies. However, what is equally apparent from the proposals is the emphasis placed on 'formal enforcement action' at the expense of informal measures in the monitoring process. In such circumstances, a decision to prosecute may be taken more readily.

Caution

5.66   As an alternative to prosecution, if a defendant admits the offence, a local authority can issue a formal caution. The use of a caution is outlined in Home Office Circular 18/1994. A caution is not a conviction, but it may be referred to in court for the purposes of sentencing. The purpose of a formal caution is to deal quickly and simply with less serious offences, to divert less serious offences away from the courts and to reduce the chances of repeat offences.

5.67   In its Guidance, LACOTS states that there must be evidence of the defendant's guilt which would be sufficient to give a realistic prospect of conviction. Therefore, a caution should not be used in cases which local authorities consider to be weak. The defendant must admit the offence and must understand the consequences of a caution.

ANCILLARY POWERS OF LOCAL AUTHORITIES

Improvement notices

5.68   Where an authorised officer has reasonable grounds for believing that the proprietor of a food business is failing to comply with Regulations (concerning the processing or treatment of food in its preparation or requiring the observance of hygienic practices), he may serve an improvement notice (s 10 of the Food Safety Act 1990). However, before serving an improvement notice, the business must be given written notice that the officer is considering serving an

---

1   Claire Andrews, *The Enforcement of Regulatory Offences* (1998), p 27.

improvement notice and why that action is considered necessary. The business must be given the opportunity to make representations which must be considered by the authority (Deregulation (Improvement of Enforcement Procedures) (Food Safety Act 1990) Order 1996 (SI 1996/1683)). Code of Practice No 5 (Use of Improvement Notices) has not yet been revised to take into account the 1996 Order.

5.69   Factors to consider when issuing an improvement notice are set out in the Code of Practice No 5, and include:

–   the risk to public health arising from the contravention (the enforcement action should be proportionate to such risk);
–   a record of non-compliance;
–   a continuing contravention (eg unhygienic conditions); and
–   an imminent risk to public health.

In addition, LACOTS' Guidance suggests that improvement notices might be appropriate when:

–   there have been significant contraventions;
–   there is a lack of confidence in the proprietor to respond to informal action;
–   there is a history of non-compliance with informal action;
–   standards are generally poor;
–   the consequences are potentially serious to public health; and
–   action needs to be taken as quickly as possible.

LACOTS suggests that improvement notices are not appropriate for minor technical contraventions.

5.70   An improvement notice must state that there is a failure to comply with Regulations (including the officer's grounds for believing there to be such a failure), must particularise the failures and the action considered necessary by the officer to comply, and must state the time for compliance which must not be less than 14 days. There is a prescribed form for the notice in the Food Safety (Improvement and Prohibition – Prescribed Forms) Regulations 1991 (SI 1991/100) and LACOTS and the Institute of Environmental Health have issued guidance on the drafting of improvement notices. If a notice is deficient and does not contain all the necessary details, it cannot be corrected and proceedings brought for breaches of the terms of a notice will be dismissed.[1]

5.71   The failure to comply with an improvement notice is an offence. However, if an officer negligently requires unnecessary works to be completed on pain of closure, the council may be at risk of being sued and having to pay

---

1   *Bexley London Borough v Gardiner Merchant* [1993] COD 383.

compensation,[1] although the availability of such a civil remedy appears to have very limited application.[2]

5.72 An appeal against a local authority's decision to serve an improvement notice lies with the magistrates' court (s 37 of the 1990 Act). Appeal against the decision of the magistrates' court lies to the Crown Court (s 38(a)). On appeal, the court can cancel the notice. If it chooses to affirm the notice, it can do so either on the original terms or on different terms that the court considers appropriate (s 39). However, the court cannot amend the notice to make it less stringent than the law requires.[3]

Prohibition Orders

5.73 Where a person has been convicted of an offence, the same court that has convicted the person may also impose a Prohibition Order on the use of a particular treatment or process or the use of any premises or equipment for that business or any food business (in the case of unsuitable premises) if the court considers the 'health risk condition' to have been fulfilled (s 11). If such an Order is made, a copy of it must be affixed to a conspicuous place on the premises. Once an authority is satisfied that the health risk condition is no longer fulfilled, it must, within 3 days of reaching the decision, issue a certificate that the Prohibition Order no longer has effect. Alternatively, a prohibited person can make an application to the authority for the lifting of the prohibition and this application must be determined within 14 days. If an authority refuses the application, it must give its reasons for doing so. There is a prescribed form in the Food Safety (Improvement and Prohibition – Prescribed Forms) Regulations 1991. An appeal against the authority's decision not to issue a certificate lies with the magistrates' court and then the Crown Court.

5.74 The 'health risk condition' is fulfilled where there is risk of injury to health caused by any process or treatment used, the construction or state of premises or equipment used for the purposes of any food business.

5.75 If a person is convicted of failing to observe Regulations requiring hygienic conditions in the preparation of food, the court that convicts him can also prohibit the proprietor or manager from participating in the management of any food business (generally or of a specified type) (s 11(4)). If an Order is imposed under s 11(4), a local authority has no power to lift the prohibition; only a court may direct that it no longer applies. Such a direction is sought on an application by the proprietor or manager and the court has regard to all the circumstances, including his conduct since the Order was made. A direction cannot be granted less than 6 months after the Order has been made nor within 3

---

1   *Welton v North Cornwall District Council* [1997] 1 WLR 570.
2   *Welton* was considered and distinguished in the more recent case of *Harris v Evans* [1998] 3 All ER 522 at 536, in which it was suggested that a remedy would not lie in negligence where an officer had served a statutory notice and that decision was open to challenge under the statutory regime.
3   *Salford City Council v Abbeyfield (Worsley) Society Ltd* [1993] COD 384.

months of a previous application to lift the prohibition. Any appeal against the magistrates' decision is made to the Crown Court (s 38).

5.76   Once a Prohibition Order has been made, a local authority must serve a copy of the order on the business. The contravention of an order is an offence.

Emergency prohibition notices and Orders

5.77   Section 12 of the 1990 Act contains similar provisions to s 11 on serving Prohibition Orders on a food business. This power allows local authorities to take immediate action when they consider it necessary and, unlike s 11, there is no requirement to prove the commission of an offence. A similar health risk condition is required to be fulfilled under this provision, except, in the case of the use of s 12 powers, it must be considered that there is an imminent risk of injury to health. The Code of Practice No 6 (Prohibition Procedures) gives the following examples of circumstances which might pose an imminent risk:

–   serious infestation by pests resulting in an actual or real risk of food contamination;
–   very poor structural conditions, poor equipment, accumulation of refuse or filth;
–   serious drainage defects; and
–   serious breaches of the Food Hygiene (General) Regulations 1970 (now to be read as referring to the Food Safety (General Food Hygiene) Regulations 1995 – see Chapter 3) involving an outbreak of food poisoning.

Additional guidance is given by LACOTS in the enforcement policy guidance document.

5.78   If a local authority considers there to be an imminent risk to health, it can serve an emergency prohibition notice (s 12(1)). A copy of the notice must be affixed to the premises as soon as practicable. The emergency prohibition notice will then expire after 3 days (including the day it is served) unless an application has been made to the magistrates' court for an Emergency Prohibition Order and will expire once that application is determined or abandoned.

5.79   Once the authority has applied for an Emergency Prohibition Order, it must give notice of the application to the business at least 1 day before the hearing date. If the court grants the Order, it must be served on the proprietor of the business and affixed to the premises as soon as practicable.

5.80   Both emergency prohibition notices and Orders cease to have effect once the local authority has served a certificate so stating. As with a prohibition notice, such a certificate must be served within 3 days of the council considering that the imminent risk no longer exists or within 14 days of an application made by the business. Again, if a certificate is not granted, reasons must be given.

5.81   Section 12(10) seeks to protect businesses from unnecessary use of these powers. It states that a proprietor will be entitled to compensation for any loss suffered if a notice is served, unless a successful application to the magistrates' court is made by the local authority. Therefore, Code of Practice No 6 states that any offer by a proprietor to close the premises without the need for formal action should not be prompted. Such a voluntary closure results in the loss of any rights to compensation, if it subsequently turns out not to have been required. The appeal provisions are similar to those for improvement notices and Prohibition Orders.

Inspection and seizure

5.82   Section 9 of the 1990 Act gives an authorised officer the power to inspect at all reasonable times and at any stage between production and distribution any food intended for human consumption (which has been sold, offered or exposed for sale or which is in the possession of a person for the purposes of sale or preparation for sale).

5.83   If, following an inspection, the officer considers that there has been a failure by the business to comply with food safety requirements or if the officer comes to believe (not by means of an inspection) that food is likely to cause food poisoning or disease to humans, that officer can exercise the remaining powers under s 9 and take the appropriate steps to seize the food.

5.84   By virtue of s 9(3)(a) of the 1990 Act, an environmental health officer may give notice to a person that until that notice is withdrawn, the food must not be used for human consumption or must not be removed (except to a place specified in the notice). It is an offence knowingly to contravene the provisions of a notice. If an environmental health officer gives such a notice, as soon as is reasonably practicable, and in any event within 21 days of its issue, he must determine whether the food complies with the safety requirements. If it does comply, the notice must be withdrawn immediately. If it does not comply, the food must be seized and dealt with by a magistrate. Alternatively, the officer may seize the food immediately in order to have it dealt with by a magistrate (s 9(3)(b)).

5.85   Once the food has been seized, a person who may have committed an offence under s 7 or s 8 of the 1990 Act has a right to be heard by a magistrate and can call evidence if he so wishes (s 9(5)). It may be a denial of natural justice to prevent an expert, who gives evidence on the question of whether the food fails to comply, to be cross-examined by the defence.[1]

5.86   If the magistrate considers that the food does fail to comply with the safety requirements, it must condemn the food and order its destruction or disposal so that it may not be used for human consumption. The owner of the food must pay the expenses incurred in this disposal.

5.87   If it turns out that the food is compliant, either before or after the determination by the magistrate, the local authority must pay the company compensation for any depreciation in value of the food as a result of the issuing of a notice or the seizure of the food (s 9(7) of the 1990 Act).

---

1   *Errington v Wilson* [1995] SC 550.

5.88   Guidance on the exercise of the powers contained in this section is contained in Code of Practice No 4 (Inspection, Detention and Seizure of Suspected Food). Regard should also be had to the guidance contained in Code of Practice No 16 (Food Hazard Warning Systems) when a local authority is considering issuing a public hazard warning, in order to alert the public and other food authorities of a serious problem. This Code sets out the detailed procedures to be followed in this event.

5.89   A failure by a local authority to follow the statutory regime may result in its actions being held to be unlawful. In *R v Liverpool City Council ex parte Baby Products Association and Another*,[1] a case concerning products which were allegedly unsafe within the meaning of the Consumer Protection Act 1987 and the General Product Safety Regulations 1994, the local authority issued a press release declaring certain baby walkers to be unsafe. The effect of such an action was to circumvent the statutory regime in place for dealing with such situations and effectively to cause companies to recall their products and cease their supply. The High Court considered that it was not open to local authorities to circumvent statutory procedures and, thereby, deprive companies of the safeguards to which they were entitled, no matter how cumbersome or slow the statutory procedures were in practice. This decision may be the subject of appeal but, if it stands, may have implications for non-statutory warnings in food law.

Powers of entry

5.90   Section 32(1) of the Food Safety Act 1990 provides general inspection powers to allow authorised officers to enter premises within the local authority, at all reasonable hours, for the purpose of ascertaining whether a contravention of the 1990 Act or its Regulations has occurred. In addition, authorised officers have the power to enter business premises in any area in order to obtain evidence relating to a contravention they believe to have been committed within their own area, and food authorities have a general power to enter premises for the purpose of performing any of their functions under the 1990 Act. However, if the premises are a private dwelling, 24 hours' notice must be given. In order to exercise these powers, the officer must be authorised by a 'duly authenticated document', showing the authority.

5.91   In certain circumstances, an officer can apply to a magistrate for a warrant, for example when entry is refused or it is anticipated that it will be refused or when the premises are unoccupied or there is an emergency. Once a warrant has been granted, entry can be executed using reasonable force.

5.92   An officer who enters the premises can inspect any records, including computer records, relating to the food business as a routine practice and not simply as part of an investigation into a suspected contravention. If he considers that records might be required as evidence in proceedings under the Food Safety Act 1990 or its Regulations, he may seize them. However, any material collected

---

1   (1999) *The Times*, 1 December.

must remain confidential and must not be disclosed other than in the performance of his duties and a breach of confidentiality may lead to the prosecution of the officer.

5.93 The extent of the powers given to officers was examined by the Divisional Court in *Walkers Snack Foods Ltd v Coventry City Council*.[1] In this case, the company Walkers was charged with two offences of obstruction under s 33 of the Food Safety Act 1990 and a s 14 offence (see **3.25**). The environmental health officers visited the company's factory, which was outside their authority, after they had received a complaint of a piece of plastic contained in a bag of crisps. An employee of the company had refused to allow the officers free access to the production line and records after having taken advice from a trading law consultant.

5.94 It was argued by Walkers that officers were not entitled to investigate a due diligence defence as such a position would be to extend the scope of s 32(1)(b) of the 1990 Act, which enables officers to obtain evidence of a contravention. However, the Divisional Court did not accept that the powers of a visiting authority were so limited as to prevent it from investigating the due diligence procedures and, therefore, held that a company is required to disclose these documents during an investigation. For a discussion of this case in the context of the Agency's powers of entry, see Chapter 6.

5.95 Codes of Practice No 8 (Food Standards Inspections) and No 9 (Food Hygiene Inspections) provide guidance on the exercise of these powers.

5.96 It should be noted that the Police and Criminal Evidence Act 1984 (PACE) and the Codes of Practice made thereunder do apply to investigating officers generally and not simply to police officers (PACE, s 67(9)). As such, investigating officers should issue a caution when there are grounds to suspect that an offence has been committed (although failure to do so may not render the evidence inadmissible).[2] The need to issue a caution has been considered more recently in *Walkers Snack Foods Ltd* (above). In that case, there was no need to caution an employee of the company because the court considered that questions put to her by the enforcement officer did not constitute an interview, but were simply an exercise of the officer's powers under the Act. As such, Code C did not apply to them.

5.97 In *Dudley Metropolitan Borough Council v Debenhams plc*,[3] the Divisional Court held that a routine inspection by a trading standards officer was a search and, therefore, that Code B of the Police and Criminal Evidence Act 1984 applied to it. As such, it was necessary for officers to give notice on arrival at the premises. However, since the 1995 amendment to Code B, that Code is specifically excluded from applying to officers who are exercising a statutory power of entry or of inspection of goods where their powers are not dependent

---

1   [1998] 3 All ER 163.
2   *Pennycuik v Lowe* (1991) *The Times*, 13 December.
3   (1994) 159 JP 18.

on them suspecting that an offence has been committed. The decision in the *Dudley Metropolitan Borough Council v Debenhams* case, ie that a notice should be given, would therefore appear no longer to be the case.

Sampling

5.98   Section 29 of the 1990 Act gives officers the power to purchase a sample of food or food ingredient or to take a sample of food or food ingredients which appear to be intended for human consumption or food source or contact material. Where food is on premises, officers are authorised to enter under s 32. Officers may also take a sample of any article or substance which is found on food premises and which may be required as evidence in proceedings.

5.99   A substance handed in by a consumer to a local authority is not a sample and, therefore, does not have to be treated as one.[1]

5.100   Test purchases made without the officer revealing his identity are not likely to be held to be unfair and, therefore, the evidence obtained as a result of such a purchase is unlikely to be excluded under s 78 of the Police and Criminal Evidence Act 1984.

5.101   When taking a sample, regard must be had to the Food Safety (Sampling and Qualifications) Regulations 1990 (SI 1990/2463) (which require the procured sample to be divided into three parts – one part being given to the proprietor) and to Code of Practice No 7 (Sampling for Analysis or Examination). Once the sample has been taken, it will usually be submitted to a public analyst.

Obstruction of officers performing their duties

5.102   Under s 33 of the Food Safety Act 1990, it is an offence to:

– intentionally obstruct an officer when he is executing his duties under the 1990 Act;
– fail to give an officer assistance or information, without reasonable cause, which the officer reasonably requires; and
– knowingly or recklessly to give false or misleading information.

5.103   Section 33(3) of the 1990 Act protects individuals from incriminating themselves. However, in *Walkers Snack Foods Ltd*,[2] it was held that s 33(3) relates to individuals, but it did not confer any protection on a company that was answering questions through individuals. This decision may be open to challenge under the Human Rights Act 1998. Article 6 of the European Convention on Human Rights, which provides for the right to a fair trial, has been held by the ECHR to protect the right against self-incrimination.[3] Whether Art 6 gives rights to companies is something that does not appear to have been decided by the

---

1   *Arun District Council v Argyle Stores Ltd* (1986) 150 JP 552.
2   [1998] 3 All ER 163.
3   *Saunders v UK* (1997) 23 EHRR 313.

courts. However, there is a line of authority, which appears to begin with *Air Canada v UK*,[1] in which the right under Art 6 is considered in relation to a company.[2]

5.104 There may be good arguments to suggest that a company should not benefit from protection under Art 6. First, they are obviously not 'human'. Secondly, and perhaps more significantly, Art 1 of the First Protocol states specifically that protection of property rights apply to natural and unnatural persons. Where such a distinction is made, the absence of such a reference in the remainder of the Convention might suggest it should be limited in its application. However, it is probably unlikely – given the line of authorities and the current climate – that a court would find that Art 6 could not be relied upon by a company and the decision in *Walkers Snack Foods Ltd* may be open to challenge on this basis.

5.105 It is no defence to an offence of failing to give assistance or information to rely upon advice given by a consultant,[3] nor for a member of staff to be acting under the supervision of its superior.[4]

CONSEQUENCES OF A FAILURE PROPERLY TO EXERCISE A FUNCTION BY THE LOCAL AUTHORITY

5.106 Local authorities must act within the powers expressly or impliedly given to them by the enabling statute (in the case of the 1990 Act, by ss 5 and 6) or which is 'calculated to facilitate, or is conductive or incidental to, the discharge of any of their functions' (s 111 of the Local Government Act 1972). Furthermore, the particular officer performing the function must also be properly authorised (see above). The unauthorised performance of any function will be *ultra vires* and can be challenged by judicial review.

5.107 Where a decision is challenged by way of judicial review, the High Court may grant one of the prerogative Orders of *Certiorari* (quashing the decision), Prohibition (prohibiting the act) or *Mandamus* (compelling performance of a duty), or may grant a private law remedy of an injunction or a declaration.

5.108 However, if it is alleged that the local authority did not have the authority to act in the way that it did, an alternative challenge can be exercised through the statutory audit under Part III of the Local Government Finance Act 1982. If it appears that expenditure is being incurred by a local authority on the performance of an *ultra vires* decision, which has not been sanctioned by the

---

1   (1995) 20 EHRR 150.
2   There are a number of similar later authorities, for example *R v Broadcasting Standards Commission, ex parte BBC*, 6 April 2000 (unreported), Court of Appeal.
3   [1998] 3 All ER 163.
4   *Mulvenna v Snape* (1995) 159 JP 717.

Secretary of State, the auditor can seek a declaration that the decision is unlawful and can require repayment of the expenditure.[1]

5.109   A failure to apply a policy resulting in a decision to prosecute (or a failure to prosecute) is open to challenge by way of judicial review.[2] However, the test for a successful challenge may be strict and similar to the test for the challenge of a decision of a Crown Prosecutor (ie that the decision was made regardless of or clearly contrary to the prosecution policy or without enquiry or dishonestly).[3]

5.110   The fact that a decision may be *ultra vires*, does not, of itself, provide a defence to a prosecution, unless the defendant actually successfully challenges the decision in a separate judicial review application. However, it is sometimes open to defendants to successfully defend a prosecution in the magistrates' court by arguing that a particular decision is an abuse of process.

5.111   It may be an abuse of process to commence proceedings before the decision to prosecute has been taken.[4] If a prosecution is commenced unlawfully, it may be quashed if the individual, without the authority to commence proceedings, does not have the power to bring them in his individual capacity. In addition, the adherence to an unlawful enforcement policy might be open to challenge. For example, in *R v Daventry District Council, ex parte Olins*,[5] a policy not to reveal the identity of complainants was successfully challenged, although the actual basis for the funding of an abuse of process was delay on the part of the prosecutor in providing the complainant's details.

5.112   If a prosecution is contrary to the enforcement guidance given to local authorities, even where judicial review or an abuse of process submission is not open to a defendant, a local authority may well face criticism by the court and may be penalised in costs.[6]

5.113   Finally, a most serious sanction for a local authority that continually fails in its duties is the power of central government to take over proceedings or to require a different food authority to take over the functions of the defaulting authority under s 42 of the 1990 Act (see Chapter 3).

5.114   These sanctions appear to have been strengthened by the Agency. Not only does the Agency have the function of monitoring local authorities, but it also has the power to exercise these functions on behalf of the government, although the actual extent of the Agency's powers to take over enforcement action may not be as extensive as has been trumpeted (see Chapter 6).

---

1   For a more detailed account of the doctrine of *ultra vires*, see SH Bailey, *Cross on Principles of Local Government Law* 2nd edn (Sweet & Maxwell, 1997).
2   *R v Director of Public Prosecutions, ex parte Chaudhary* [1995] 1 Cr App R 136.
3   See Claire Andrews, *The Enforcement of Regulatory Offences* (1998) at 2.11(vi), p 23.
4   *R v Brentford Justices, ex parte Wong* [1981] QB 445.
5   (1990) 154 JP 478.
6   *Smedleys Ltd v Breed* [1974] AC 839.

WEAKNESSES IDENTIFIED

5.115   In his report,[1] Professor James identifies the third weakness in the present system[2] as being that the enforcement of food law is uneven throughout the UK. He states that Regulations under the 1990 Act are enforced to varying standards from authority to authority, despite the existence of HAP, which can cause problems for nationwide food businesses.

5.116   In addition, the enforcement of food legislation is only one aspect of a local authority's responsibilities and, therefore, inevitably, it competes for funding with all of the other responsibilities. Different authorities have different priorities and budgetary constraints. A food prosecution can be expensive and financially risky for a local authority. Investigation costs can be considerable, particularly if the case is serious, for example involving a food poisoning outbreak, with supplies of food from the business being made throughout the country, and legal fees are not insubstantial. Although the court has the power to order a convicted defendant to pay the prosecution costs, there is no guarantee that the court will allow the whole amount to be recovered. Furthermore, there is always the possibility that the prosecution will not succeed and, even if the local authority does not have to pay the defendant's costs (which will normally be awarded from central funds under s 16 of the Prosecution of Offences Act 1985, although there is power under reg 3 of the Costs in Criminal Cases (General) Regulations 1986 to award costs against the local authority personally), they will have incurred considerable costs themselves, which they cannot recover.

5.117   The government White Paper *The Food Standards Agency – A Force for Change* (see **1.27**) also identified the difficulty in some areas of over-zealous enforcement. Despite numerous sources of guidance on when enforcement action is necessary, some local authorities appear to be too ready to go to court and the White Paper stated the need for clearly focused coherent guidance. The problem may not be that guidance is lacking, but that local authorities have been relatively free to adopt or reject that advice. Of course, LACOTS's Guidance and HAP are not mandatory and cannot be enforced. The Codes of Practice can be forced onto local authorities only by a direction from central government and local authorities presently cannot be compelled to sign up to the Enforcement Concordat.

5.118   In fact, there are those who consider the principle of local authority enforcement to be inherently unworkable. The authors of *Butterworths' Law of Food and Drugs* comment:

> 'Despite the imaginative and ingenious arrangements made by the government to overcome the fundamental weakness of local government in matters of law enforcement, it is submitted that local authority government is unsuited to the task.

---

1   See **1.25**.
2   For a discussion of the first two weaknesses identified, see **4.19–4.30**.

Its vulnerability to political interference and prejudice and its financial instability remain.'[1]

5.119   It remains to be seen what real impact the Agency will have on local authority enforcement. However, it certainly indicated a commitment to fulfil its role in this regard when, within 3 days of its establishment, it issued consultation in relation to the standards of enforcement it will expect and the procedures by which it intends to monitor those standards.

---

1   At Division A.

Chapter 6

The New Food Standards Agency

ORGANISATION OF THE AGENCY

Structure of the Agency

6.1 The original proposal as to how the Agency would be structured was that it should be modelled on the Health & Safety Executive/Commission. It was thought that there were striking similarities between the need for regulation of health and safety at work, which became apparent in the 1970s, and the growth in public concern over food issues in the 1990s.

6.2 Those aspects of the Health & Safety Executive/Commission which Professor James considered to be analogous and helpful as a proposed model for the Agency are detailed in Appendix V of his report. Essentially, the Commission has the role of policy adviser to Ministers, while the Executive is responsible for enforcement. Professor James highlighted the cooperation and division of responsibility that exist between local authorities and the Executive, where, broadly speaking, the local authorities enforce the provisions of the Health and Safety at Work Act 1974 in relation to low-risk premises, with the Executive taking responsibility for high-risk premises. It was not suggested that this route, or an analogous one, should be taken by the Agency – indeed, it is difficult to think of any meaningful distinction which could be drawn to divide responsibility for enforcement between local authorities and the Agency.

6.3 The Health & Safety Commission has the power to issue mandatory guidance on enforcement issues to local authorities, although it has no power over the funding of local authority enforcement work. It is subject to Ministerial control on a number of levels – notably in that the Secretary of State for the Environment has the power of appointment and dismissal over the commissioners, funding comes from a grant-in-aid from the Department of the Environment and the Secretary of State has powers of direction over the Commission and has to approve its annual plan of work. As will be seen, similar powers exist in relation to the Agency and have been viewed by some as a potential stumbling block to establishing the Agency as a credible and independent body. Professor James' view was that there was a case for strengthening the operational autonomy and security of that part of the Agency which was to perform a role equivalent to that of the Commission.

6.4 The provisions of the 1999 Act that deal with the administrative set-up of the Agency are ss 2–5 and Sch 1 and Sch 2.

6.5 The Agency consists of a chairman, a deputy chairman, and between 8 and 12 members. The members are appointed as follows: one by the National Assembly for Wales, two by the Scottish Ministers and one by the Department of

Health and Social Services for Northern Ireland. The remainder are appointed by the Secretary of State for Health.

6.6   The chairman and deputy chairman are appointed jointly by the Secretary of State for Health and his counterparts in the 'appropriate authorities' (defined in s 36) for Scotland, Wales and Northern Ireland. The 'appropriate authorities' are: in Scotland, the Scottish Ministers (a collective term for the members of the Scottish Executive; in practice it is expected this will be the Minister with responsibility for health); in Wales, the National Assembly for Wales; and, in Northern Ireland, the Department of Health and Social Services. These authorities are required to consult each other before making any appointments (s 2(2)).

6.7   The following appointments have been made:

- chairman: Sir John Krebs; and
- deputy chairman: Suzi Leather.

6.8   It has been a matter of some controversy as to who is represented on the Agency. Section 2(3)(a) of the 1999 Act states that the authorities making the appointment shall have regard to the desirability of securing a variety of skills and experience amongst the members. This is to include experience in matters relating to food safety or other consumer interests in relation to food. The model of the Irish Food Agency, where only consumer interests are represented, has not been followed.

6.9   It is a matter of some importance that the Agency has access to the skills of those who have experience not only of representing the interests of consumers, but also of retailers and manufacturers in the area. Amendments were proposed in Standing Committee to specify that there should be members appointed specifically with practical experience of matters such as primary food pro-duction, food processing, storage and distribution and food retailing. The government's position was that members would not be appointed to represent any particular interest and that the recruitment of members would take into account the desirability of having members with experience in all of the relevant areas.

6.10   The Act provides for the setting up of advisory committees to assist the Agency. There is to be an advisory committee each for Wales, Scotland and Northern Ireland to give advice or information to the Agency about matters in those areas. The Agency is required by s 23(2)(c) to take such advice and information into account in exercising its functions. Provision also exists for the setting up of an advisory committee for England, or for any region of it, for the same purpose. The Agency is also permitted to set up other advisory committees – presumably to deal with issues in specific geographical areas. Schedule 2 deals with the administrative provisions in relation to these committees.

6.11   Each committee is to have a chairman who is also a member of the Agency and such other persons as the appropriate authority thinks fit (after consulting with the Agency). Provision is made, in para 7 of Sch 2, for the absorption of existing non-statutory advisory committees into this procedure. The Explanatory Notes to the Act suggest that there is currently no intention of establishing committees for the English regions. The Secretary of State has the power to direct that an advisory committee for such a purpose shall be set up. The Agency has power to establish 'other advisory committees' according to s 5(3).

6.12   The current list of members is as follows:

–   Sir John Arbuthnot (Board Member for Scotland and Chair of the Scottish Advisory Committee);
–   Michael Gibson (Board Member for Scotland);
–   Ann Hemingway (Board Member for Wales and Chair of the Welsh Advisory Committee);
–   Michael Walker (Board Member for Northern Ireland and Chair of the Northern Ireland Advisory Committee);
–   Richard Ayre;
–   Karol Bailey;
–   Jeya Henry;
–   Valerie Howarth;
–   Robert Rees;
–   Bhupinder Sandhu;
–   Vernon Sankey; and
–   Gurbux Singh.

6.13   It was suggested by the opposition in Standing Committee that the devolved regions were over-represented, in terms of population, on the Committee, and that there should be 15 rather than 12 members to take account of this. To a certain extent, one can dismiss such concerns as being more relevant to the debate over devolution, however the risk of action being taken in certain regions which would make food safety enforcement non-uniform (such as the Welsh Assembly's proposal to lift the ban on beef on the bone before steps were taken on a UK-wide basis) is a concern that the government seems to have borne in mind in seeking to ensure that the regions have direct representation on the Board.

6.14   The authorities making the appointments are also required, by s 2(3)(b), to consider whether any prospective member has any financial or other interests that might compromise his or her position as a member. Paragraph 9 of Sch 1 requires the Agency to establish a register of private interests.[1] However, the government made it clear that the existence of such a financial interest will not necessarily be a bar to membership of the Agency. When questioned by the Food Standards Committee, the Minister of State at MAFF said, 'Nobody will be excluded from applying and their interest and their expertise could be relevant anyway … nobody is ruled out because of a beneficial interest which may be a

---

1   This can be viewed at www.foodstandards.gov.uk/register.htm.

pension, shareholdings …'.[1] Schedule 1 also contains detailed information on such matters as tenure of office of members of the Agency, remuneration, and pensions.

6.15 The Agency also has a chief executive, who will essentially run the Agency. Again the appointment is to be made by the appropriate authorities already mentioned. Directors for Wales, Scotland and Northern Ireland are also to be appointed. These directors are to be responsible to the chief executive for the activities of the Agency in their regions of the UK. The first appointees are to be made by the 'appropriate authority', with subsequent appointments to be made by the Agency, subject to the approval of that authority.

6.16 The James Report, in Part II, para 11, made it clear that the staff of the Agency should not be on a normal civil service career path, and it should be clear that their responsibilities are to the Agency and not to Ministers. Paragraph 8 of Sch 1 to the Act provides that the Agency shall appoint its own staff on such terms and conditions as it may determine. Therefore, it appears that the responsibility for ensuring that its staff know where their primary responsibilities lie will rest with the Agency. The majority of the staff are expected to be drawn from the JFSSG (a combination of MAFF and DoH staff), which, according to the government, have effectively been doing the work of the Agency prior to its establishment. Whilst this will no doubt improve the prospects of a smooth transition, it may be that it does not assist in developing a clear 'change of culture' in the manner that Professor James envisaged.

6.17 Proposals were made by the Select Committee for local authority enforcement personnel to be seconded to the Agency. Speaking in the Commons Second Reading of the Bill, the chairman of the Select Committee stated:

> 'On enforcement and monitoring, we made a recommendation on seconding people from local government who are responsible for day-to-day enforcement. I am pleased that the government has accepted it. Those people would not represent a new army of food thought police, as has been suggested; they are people who are already working in our communities.'[2]

6.18 It might be thought that such a level of cooperation will not produce the fresh start that the government and those involved in the food industry might have hoped for. One of the Agency's primary roles, at least in the eyes of those who are affected directly by it, will be the regulation and monitoring of local authority enforcement. If those who are setting the standards and marking performance are also involved at a local authority level, it is easy to see that there may be questions asked as to where an employee's loyalties lie. Equally, if the Agency were to find itself having to take over enforcement duties from a failing local authority under s 12 of and Sch 3 to the 1999 Act, it would undoubtedly find it useful to have personnel on board with hands-on enforcement experience.

---

1   *Minutes of Evidence to the Food Standards Committee,* p 140.
2   *Hansard* vol 333, no 107, col 822.

6.19   The appointment of members to the Agency, and the other staffing issues dealt with above, will clearly be closely scrutinised. It is immediately apparent, for example, that the Secretary of State for Health has a great deal of power in terms of appointing members of the Agency. This is in marked contrast to the recommendation by Professor James in para 12 of Part II of his Report that appointments should be made by the Prime Minister, or the Council of Ministers, after consultation with consumer and public interest groups, representatives of the food industry, the leader of the opposition and the chair of the relevant select committee. This was doubtless viewed as somewhat over-complicated, but one can easily anticipate that there will be allegations that the Agency is not genuinely independent when it is made up to a large extent of members chosen by the government alone.

Funding

6.20   Unsurprisingly the issue of funding for the Agency has been a matter of much controversy. The original proposal, as set out in the White Paper, was that the costs associated with the Agency would be raised through an annual levy on food retailers and caterers. A flat-rate charge was initially suggested, regardless of whether the food premises in question was a major supermarket or a small sandwich shop. Concerns were raised about the fairness of such a proposal and, indeed, the Food Standards Committee stated that it believed that the flat-rate principle was contrary to natural justice. Although some of the bodies consulted felt that it was appropriate for the food industry itself to bear the costs of implementing a national food safety policy, there was also the powerful argument that such costs inevitably would be passed on to the consumer, in effect becoming a 'tax on food' which would hit the poorest hardest.

6.21   Such was the controversy that the Agency is now to be funded from general taxation. Explicit provision is made for payments by the National Assembly for Wales to the Agency and it is envisaged that payment will also be made by the Scottish Parliament and the Northern Ireland Assembly. Given the government's earlier insistence that the Agency should be paid for by the food industry itself, it is remarkable that the proposal for the levy was abandoned in this fashion. The shortage of legislative time in which to pass the Act may have been a governing factor. The Bill itself was passed with surprising speed and it is highly likely that this could not have happened if funding had remained such an issue.

6.22   Section 39 spells out that the Agency is to be funded by Parliament, although the MHS, which is now part of the Agency, will continue to levy its own charges. It also makes provision for sums to be paid by the devolved authorities. Detailed provisions in relation to accounts and auditing of the Agency are set out in Sch 4.

Objectives and practices

[handwritten annotations: "Making me consumer can choice!", "aware so they are made an informed", "Labelling inc."]

6.23   The 'main objective' of the Agency is defined in s 1(2) as: 'To protect public health from risks which may arise in connection with the consumption of food (including risks caused by the way in which it is produced or supplied) and otherwise to protect the interests of consumers in relation to food.' *[handwritten: "Labelling again"]*

6.24   The Explanatory Notes to s 1(2) state emphatically that this is not a clause that confers any wider powers on the Agency other than those which it is given by the relevant sections of the Act, but that it 'sets the context in which the Agency's powers must be used'. Thus, an aggrieved party may be able to rely on this section if he alleges that the exercise of any of the Agency's powers had a different objective – although one suspects that the 'main objective' is apt to be given an interpretation as wide as the 'overriding objective' in the Civil Procedure Rules[1] and equally will be capable of meaning all things to all men. Certainly the argument could be employed if an aggrieved party felt that a power had been exercised for purely political reasons.

6.25   The expression 'interests of consumers in relation to food' is defined in s 36(3) as including 'interests in relation to the labelling, marking, presenting, or advertising of food, and the descriptions which may be applied to food'. Thus, the Agency is not simply involved with the quality and safety of food itself, but also the consumer protection issues relating to the marketing of food. The issue of nutrition will, it seems, also be within the Agency's remit, despite the absence of any direct reference.[2]

6.26   The Agency is required by s 22 of the 1999 Act to prepare and publish a statement of the general objectives it intends to pursue and general practices it intends to adopt in carrying out its functions. The first such statement must be produced within 3 months of the date of the first meeting of the Agency. These objectives are to include:

–   securing that its activities are the subject of consultation with, or with representatives of, those affected and, where appropriate, with members of the public;
–   promoting links with government departments, local authorities and other public authorities, and the devolved Parliaments in relation to food safety or other consumer interests in relation to food, with a view to ensuring that the Agency is consulted by such authorities from time to time in relation to these matters; and
–   securing and making available records of its decisions, and the information on which they are based in order to achieve transparency.

6.27   The Agency is to consult with the appropriate authorities on the content of such a statement and it must be approved by them before it is published. It is clear, therefore, that central government will have a significant role in setting the

---

1   1/CPR/1.1.
2   For a discussion of this issue, see **6.35**.

agenda for the Agency. The Explanatory Notes to s 22(2) state explicitly that the Secretary of State and the other appropriate authorities may amend the draft statement prepared by the Agency, but must consult the Agency before doing so. The Agency is required, by s 23(1), to 'pay due regard' to this statement of objectives and practices. The Select Committee on Agriculture[1] commented:

> 'One of the first tasks for the Food Standards Agency will be to draw up and publish the risk assessment criteria under which it will operate. We recommend that it consults widely on these criteria before they are adopted. A clear definition of the respective responsibilities of the government, the food industry and the individual consumer is also required.'[2]

6.28   The first of these statements is yet to be produced.

FUNCTIONS OF THE AGENCY

Development of food policy and provision of advice to public authorities

6.29   This function is set out in s 6 of the 1999 Act. Section 6(1)(a) gives the Agency the role of developing policy or assisting in such development in relation to 'matters connected with food safety or other interests of consumers in relation to food'. Section 6(1)(b) states that it shall also provide advice, information or assistance in respect of such matters to any public authority.

6.30   Professor James' Report recognised that there was a public desire for the de-politicisation of food legislation. It was also felt that a major weakness in the current system of food law was that there was a lack of coordination between the different bodies involved in food policy. Therefore, the idea that the Agency could become something of a law commission on food policy was an attractive one. The government's intention is that the Agency will be the primary source of policy advice in relation to food safety and associated areas to the government as a whole, and to the devolved authorities:

> 'The Food Standards Agency is being established as the principal authority in Government on food safety and standards matters. It will be the chief source of policy advice to Ministers and other public authorities. Its functions will include drafting and making recommendations on legislation, negotiating in the European Union and internationally on behalf of Ministers, and providing the necessary information and assistance to support decision making.'[3]

6.31   The Agency is also required, by s 6(3) to comply with any request made, under s 6(2), by a public authority (limited to Ministers, government departments, the Welsh Assembly, the Scottish Ministers and Northern Ireland

---

1   Quoted by James Paice, MP for SE Cambs in Commons Second Reading.
2   Vol 333, no 107, col 854.
3   Nick Brown, Minister for Agriculture, Fisheries and Food, Commons Second Reading, *Hansard* vol 333, no 107, col 788.

Departments) to provide such advice, information and assistance as they may require in relation to food matters. The Agency has a duty to comply with such requests so far as is reasonably practicable. It is envisaged that the Agency will be proactive as well as reactive in this regard:

> 'The Bill presupposes that the Agency will offer advice to public authorities without being requested to do so, on the assumption that the Agency will be proactive. As the main provider of advice and policy to the government on food standards, it will be expected to search the horizon, scan where problems may arise and be proactive in warning and advising Ministers.'[1]

6.32   It will be interesting to see how the Agency copes with the different demands placed on it by Whitehall and by the devolved governments. One can easily envisage a situation where the devolved authority seeks advice on an area which central government might prefer to keep quiet about (the Welsh Assembly's plans to legalise the sale of beef on the bone being a useful example). Whether such advice is acted on and, more importantly, published, will be an important touchstone of the Agency's independence.

6.33   It is also envisaged that the Agency will represent the UK at working level in relevant EU and other international fora. Whilst policy decisions will still rest with Ministers, it seems that Agency staff will act on day-to-day matters in relation to the EU in the manner in which the staff of the JFSSG have operated. The need for the Agency to establish good relations with Directorate General XXIV is stressed in the White Paper.[2] The Agency is also to represent the UK on the Codex Alimentarius Commission.[3]

Provision of advice, information and assistance to other persons

6.34   In addition to advising government departments and other public authorities, the Agency is required by s 7(1)(a) to provide advice and information to the general public in respect of matters connected with food safety or other food-related issues of interest to consumers. According to s 7(1)(b) the Agency is required to provide advice, information or assistance on such matters to 'any person who is not a public authority'. The Explanatory Notes to the Act cite the following as examples of how the Agency might perform its functions:

- run information campaigns on issues of current interest or importance;
- publish scientific data arising from research or surveillance and advise on its interpretation;
- publish information on enforcement activities, such as the BSE/meat enforcement publications;
- produce leaflets on food hygiene, labelling, etc;
- issue advice for people with food allergies;

---

1   Jeff Rooker, Standing Committee B, 6/7/99, col 119/120.
2   At paras 3.12–3.13.
3   White Paper, paras 3.12–3.16.

- pass on information about developments in food science to the public as a whole and to particular groups (eg food producers);
- produce guidance on food safety matters for the food industry; and
- issue food hazard warnings, alerting the public to particular problems.

6.35 No specific mention is made of advice as to nutrition in the examples given and this is perhaps surprising given that one of the primary recommendations of the James Report was that the Agency should have responsibility for matters of nutrition. There was considerable debate about the apparent failure to focus on the issue of nutrition in the text of the 1999 Act. The White Paper states that the Agency is to:

> 'Contract with the Health Education Authority and other health education bodies or agents, including the relevant body in Wales, to undertake health promotion and education activities relevant to nutrition, diet and food safety'.

6.36 However, nutrition does not merit an individual mention in the body of the 1999 Act. In answer to questions on this point, the Minister for Agriculture, Fisheries and Food referred to the proposed division of responsibility for matters of nutrition set out in the White Paper (see below) and stated:

> 'The fact is that the White Paper is a statement of government policy. It is not an idea thrown out for discussion, it is a statement of government policy. The way that the Bill has been drafted enables that policy to be conducted by the Agency'.[1]

6.37 The Minister of State at MAFF (Jeff Rooker) confirmed this approach in the Second Reading in the Commons:

> 'In "The Food Standards Agency: A Force for Change", published in January 1998, about three dozen aspects of nutrition were set out. Some of them were designated as the exclusive remit of the Department of Health, some of the Food Standards Agency, and some of both. That remains the position. It is set out in substantial detail in three columns of the White Paper. That is exactly the way things will operate; there has been no change since the publication of the White Paper.'[2]

6.38 This position was confirmed and expanded upon in Standing Committee:

> 'We have already said that the Agency will deal with nutrition, and we have discussed the relevant aspects of that. I have three examples, as set out in the White Paper, which we have not moved from in the past 18 months. First it will undertake surveys of the nutritional value of individual foods such as milk, bread and ready-prepared foods to determine nutritional and micronutritional content. That is already done by the joint food safety and standards group. Secondly, it will develop analytical techniques to assess the nutritional content of food. Thirdly, it will provide policy guidance and regulation on matters relating to nutritional labelling of foods.'[3]

6.39 Thus, the position appears to be that certain aspects of responsibility for nutrition are within the Agency's remit, with the definition of the Agency's role

---

1   *Minutes of Evidence to the Food Standards Committee*, p 121.
2   Vol 333, no 107, col 815.
3   Jeff Rooker, Standing Committee B, 6/7/99, col 124.

being sufficiently wide to cover such matters, and that MAFF is to have no residual responsibility in this area. The division proposed in the White Paper was that the Agency should have sole responsibility for:

–   the monitoring and surveillance of the nutrient content of food and the nutrient content of the diet;
–   providing authoritative factual information about the nutrient content of individual foods and advice on the diet as a whole;
–   securing expert scientific advice on the relationship between diet, nutritional status and health to support the definition of a healthy diet and to inform policy from the Committee on Medical Aspects of Food and Nutrition Policy (COMA);
–   where appropriate, proposing legislation relating to nutritional aspects of food, including labelling and claims, dietary supplements sold as food, fortified foods and functional foods;
–   providing practical guidance in relation to nutritional aspects of the food chain, including production and catering;
–   commissioning food and diet research appropriate to the functions of the Agency;
–   representing the UK in international negotiations on issues relating to the nutritional aspects of food; and
–   formulating policy and providing advice to Ministers on these issues.

6.40   The following matters listed were proposed to be within the joint remit of the Agency and the DoH:

–   providing the joint secretariat to COMA (COMA is to advise UK health departments and the Agency);
–   surveillance of the nutritional status of the public;
–   defining the health education message on nutritional issues, taking account of both food and wider health issues; and
–   policy formulation and advice on these issues, for example in relation to the 'Our Healthier Nation' campaign, and public health aspects of food fortification.

6.41   Health departments are to retain responsibility for:

–   wider public health issues, including conditions (eg cardiovascular disease, cancer, osteoporosis and obesity) where nutritional status is one of a number of risk factors;
–   consideration of vulnerable groups and inequality issues;
–   health education on wider behavioural issues than just nutrition (eg smoking, drinking and physical activity);
–   dietary supplements controlled by the Medicines Act 1968 (through the Medicines Control Agency);
–   health surveillance of the population; and
–   international negotiation on health matters.

6.42 Opposition members of Parliament described s 7 as '... a lawyer's paradise',[1] suggesting that pressure groups might seek to use this section to force the Agency to publish guidance and provide advice on their particular concerns and, if the Agency refused to do so, seek to compel them by judicial review. The government's response to this was as follows:

> 'To some extent, the Agency would be required to give information that it was reasonable to give to people who requested it, but there is no presumption in the Bill that the agency would have to answer every jot and tittle that was put to it.'[2]

6.43 The inclusion of the phrase 'the Agency considers' is intended to make plain that the matters upon which the Agency is required to inform and advise the public under the terms of this section are to be within its own discretion:

> 'Removing the words "the Agency considers" ... would water down the Agency's independence. That is the bottom line when it comes to [s] 7(1)(a), and it would be open to people to challenge the Agency in the courts. Frankly, the decision should be made by the Agency ... I do not want judges to decide what people can eat or what should be in the food chain.'[3]

Acquisition and review of information

6.44 The Agency has the function (s 8(1)) of obtaining, compiling and keeping under review information about matters connected with food safety and other interests of consumers in relation to food. This is to include (s 8(2)) such matters as monitoring developments in science and technology and carrying out commissioning or coordinating research on matters relating to food. The somewhat self-evident purpose of this function is stated (in s 8(3)) to be that it will ensure that the Agency has sufficient information to enable it to take informed decisions and to carry out its other functions effectively. The somewhat self-serving nature of this section may be explained by the fact that is intended to satisfy in part the second of the 'guiding principles' set out in the White Paper:

> 'The Agency's assessments of food standards and safety will be unbiased and based on the best available scientific advice, provided by experts invited in their own right to give independent advice.'

6.45 Any research and development projects within the remit of the Agency which have been funded by either MAFF or other departments such as the DoH, are to be transferred to the Agency. The extent to which the Agency is able to commission and fund its own research will doubtless be a matter of controversy in the future. The Agency's budget for research is expected to be in the region of £25 million.[4] At the time of the Standing Committee, there were 400 research projects under way, responsibility for which will be transferred to the Agency.

---

1   David Maclean, Standing Committee B, 6/7/99, col 140.
2   Jeff Rooker, Standing Committee B, 6/7/99, col 142.
3   Jeff Rooker, Standing Committee B, 6/7/99 col 143/4.
4   See comments in Standing Committee B, 6/7/99, col 149/150.

General functions in relation to animal feedingstuffs

6.46   This is an area given heightened significance in the light of what is now known of the probable origins of BSE in cattle. Section 9 of the 1999 Act confers the same functions on the authority in relation to 'matters connected with the safety of animal feedingstuffs and other interests of users of animal feedingstuffs' as are conferred by ss 6, 7 and 8 in relation to 'matters connected with food safety and other interests of consumers in relation to food'. Thus, the Agency is empowered and required, so far as is reasonable, to provide advice and assistance to public authorities and members of the public on issues relating to animal feedingstuffs, defined as 'feedingstuff for any description of animals, including any nutritional supplement or other substance which is not administered through oral feeding' (s 36(1)).

6.47   Prior to the foundation of the Agency, feedingstuffs were regulated by means of Regulations under the 1990 Act, the Agriculture Act 1970, and the European Communities Act 1972, and by Orders made under the Animal Health Act 1981. The Agency is to acquire some of the functions of the Minister of Agriculture, Fisheries and Food in this regard, in that it will have responsibility for Regulations under the 1990 Act (Sch 3, para 7 of the 1999 Act) and MAFF shall cease to have that responsibility (s 26(1)(a)). However, MAFF retains the primary policy-making role in relation to the other Acts, albeit that the Agency will be able to advise as to any statutory or policy changes which it considers desirable. The government's view was that MAFF's veterinary expertise is important in this area, where Orders under the Animal Health Act in relation to feed are used to control feed-borne diseases of animals (Explanatory Notes, para 33). There is to be cooperation between MAFF and the Agency in this area to ensure that there is consultation and that any duplication of work is avoided so far as possible.

6.48   The issue of labelling of animal feed was debated in Standing Committee B, with the Minister giving the assurance that this aspect is covered by the combination of ss 6, 7 and 9 (col 159). It seems that the government envisages that the Agency will oversee a tightening of the requirements in relation to such labelling, although the Agency is given no more power in this regard than was previously available to MAFF, and it remains to be seen how the Agency will choose to exercise this power. Indeed, the Agency may find itself in conflict with MAFF on issues such as this, given that MAFF retains its role as 'a sponsor of the agricultural industry' (so described by Jeff Rooker in Standing Committee B).

POWERS OF THE AGENCY

Observations with a view to acquiring information

6.49   The Agency is empowered by s 10 to carry out observations in order to acquire the information needed to carry out its functions under ss 8 and 9 in relation to any aspect of the production or supply of food or food sources and any aspect of the production, supply or use of animal feedingstuffs (s 10(1)). Section 10(2) gives examples of the types of premises that may be observed including food premises, food businesses, agricultural premises and businesses (defined in s 1 of the Farm Land and Rural Development Act 1988), premises involved in fish farming and those involved with animal feedingstuffs. Examples given in the Explanatory Notes to s 10 as to the type of observations which may be made are surveillance programmes to investigate the presence of pathogens that could carry risks for human health levels, or of a particular contaminant, such as lead, in particular foodstuffs, or surveys of hygiene practices in food businesses.

6.50   Opposition MPs termed this a 'nosey parker' clause, but the government contended that it is in reality simply a replacement for s 25 of the 1990 Act, albeit that it allows for surveillance to take place earlier in the food chain than the previous legislation allowed. An important distinction, however, is that s 25 required the Minister to make an Order in relation to surveillance of a particular producer or a specific sector of the industry, whereas the Agency has the power of entry itself.

6.51   Furthermore, such information as was obtained as a result of the making of such an order was not to be disclosed without the consent of the person concerned, unless the Minister ordered otherwise, or if the information was to be used in the prosecution of any offence thereby disclosed, and an offence was committed if such disclosure took place (s 25(3)). The Agency has power to publish any information which it receives, subject to the safeguards in s 19.[1]

6.52   It does not appear that this power is itself to be used for enforcement purposes:

> 'The clause gives us the power of observation, or, more accurately, surveillance as it would normally be termed, at any point in the food chain in order to obtain information, although not for the purpose of enforcement. If something is discovered, it can be drawn to the attention of the enforcement authorities, but samples taken for enforcement purposes cannot be used for enforcement.'[2]

> '... enforcement in the context of food safety legislation has a specific meaning, which can lead to criminal prosecution. These powers will not lead to criminal prosecution; they are about inserting an intermediate stage between the process of collecting information by agreement, which happens in the vast majority of cases, and securing the power of entry to take samples, thereby ensuring that the information is complete. While enforcement powers can result in criminal prosecution if failures are found, these powers are about getting a better understanding of problems and using the information to work with the industry to solve them.'[3]

6.53   The Explanatory Notes to s 10 also make it clear that this is essentially an information-gathering power rather than an investigative one, stressing that 'any

---

1   See also s 11(7) in relation to unauthorised disclosure by individuals.
2   Jeff Rooker, Standing Committee B, 6/7/99, col 165.
3   Tessa Jowell, Standing Committee B, 7/7/99, col 195.

information obtained could not in general be used for the purposes of food law enforcement'. However, they go on to comment:

> 'Where apparent problems are identified in the course of a surveillance exercise, the information gathered would normally be passed to the relevant enforcement authorities who would then take a decision on the need for further investigation.'

6.54   See also the Explanatory Notes to s 19(9) (and the detailed discussion of the power to publish):

> 'the Agency could pass on confidential information to enforcement authorities to assist them in carrying out their enforcement functions'.

6.55   Therefore, food businesses should bear this in mind when they receive a request under s 10. Of course, the majority of the information the Agency seeks is likely to be relatively non-contentious, and it is in the interests of businesses to cooperate. However, it is also easy to conceive of situations whereby the Agency may obtain and seek to publish information which a business would rather was not in the public domain. A business which is reluctant to cooperate may seek to draw some support from the words of the Minister in Standing Committee:

> '... [s]10 is not intended to target individual companies. The purpose of the surveillance is to take representative samples of the part of the food chain that contains the product under investigation. The surveillance is not targeted against companies; it is intended to be general and representative, as is the information produced.'[1]

6.56   However, s 11, which deals broadly with the authorisation of individuals to exercise the powers of observation specified in s 10, also creates various offences in relation to obstruction of such a person.

Powers of entry for persons carrying out observations

6.57   Section 11(4) allows an authorised person, who may be a member of the Agency's staff or not, to enter any premises, take samples of any articles or substances (including any food source) found there, inspect and copy any records, and require any person carrying on a business to provide him with any such facilities, records or information or other assistance as he may reasonably request. Authorisation is to be made in writing and is to be issued only in pursuance of a decision taken by the Agency itself, or by a committee, sub-committee or Member of the Agency acting on its behalf (s 11(2) and(3)).

6.58   The authorised person is required, if asked, to produce his authorisation and to provide a document identifying any sample taken or document copied (s 11(5)). It was suggested in Standing Committee that this section be amended to ensure that the authorisation would make clear the purpose for which the powers were being exercised[2] but it seems that such an amendment was not forthcoming. It is submitted that the spirit of the legislation indicates that the purpose should

---

1   Jeff Rooker, Standing Committee B, 6/7/99, col 167.
2   Tessa Jowell, Standing Committee B, 7/7/99, col 198.

be identified and this is further supported by the comments made in Standing Committee: 'When authorisation is provided to secure the power of entry, the purpose of that visit will be set out clearly in such authorisation'.[1]

6.59 It seems that persons exercising powers conferred by authorisation under this section will not be able to employ their power to enter premises without having first informed the business in question in advance. An amendment was suggested to require prior appointments for visits, but this was rejected, the Minister commenting:

'In practice that would normally occur and even where there is no cooperation, the business would be forewarned of the intention to visit. However, because we must be able to respond to emergencies, it is not right to stipulate time and date in every case; that would obviously weaken the agency's ability to monitor food safety effectively. ... We accept that the Agency or the representatives of the Agency should enter premises only at a reasonable time.'[2]

6.60 It is laudable to give such persons wide powers if the objective is merely to gather information and to advance public knowledge in a particular area of food safety and standards. The concerns raised above in relation to the Agency's enforcement functions are relevant if material comes to light during an 'observation' which later would prove helpful in any prosecution of the person or company involved. Section 11(7) provides that it is an offence to disclose such information obtained with regard to any trade secret, but it does not make clear (nor do the Explanatory Notes and the debates[3]) whether that information could be employed in any subsequent enforcement action, for example in relation to the rebutting of a due diligence defence.

6.61 Although the use of such material in a regulatory prosecution may well come down to a question of admissibility at trial (and it seems that a prosecution could not result directly from an incident identified during an investigation, as samples taken are not to be used in enforcement proceedings[4]), one can none the less draw parallels with the Department of Trade and Industry's powers of investigation which compel a suspect to answer questions and provide assistance, with the sanction of proceedings for contempt. Given that the use of information obtained in this manner in the subsequent prosecution of an individual was found to be an infringement of Art 6(1) (the right to a fair trial) of the Convention,[5] it may be that similar arguments could be employed in this regard.[6] The Human Rights Act 1998, which comes into force in October 2000, renders it possible to raise breaches of Convention rights (this is likely to be limited in practice to Art 6 – the right to a fair trial), either as a defence (s 7 of the Human Rights Act 1998) or in relation to questions of admissibility of evidence.

---

1   Tessa Jowell, Standing Committee B, 7/7/99, col 200.
2   Tessa Jowell, Standing Committee B, 8/7/99, col 197.
3   See above.
4   See above.
5   *Saunders v UK* (1997) 23 EHRR 313.
6   However, see also *R v Hertfordshire County Council, ex parte Green Environmental Industries and Another* 17 February 2000, unreported, House of Lords.

Surprisingly, whether the Convention gives enforceable rights to corporations does not appear to have been decided, but is likely that a company can rely upon those rights (see Chapter 5).

6.62   Section 11(8) creates the offences of intentionally obstructing an authorised person (s 11(8)(a)); failing without reasonable excuse to comply with any requirement to assist the authorised person under s 11(4)(e) (s 11(8)(b)); and furnishing information in purported compliance with a request from the authorised person which the supplier knows to be false or materially misleading or is reckless as to whether it is false or materially misleading (s 11(8)(b)). Offences are punishable on summary conviction with a fine of up to level 5 on the standard scale.

6.63   The use of the expression 'intentionally obstructs' mirrors the provision in s 33(1) of the 1990 Act, which replaced the former offence of 'wilfully obstructing' created by s 91 of the Food Act 1984. 'Wilfully obstructing' has been held, in the context of obstruction of the highway under s 121 of the Highways Act 1959, not to imply any element of *mens rea*, in the sense that a person will be guilty of the offence if he intentionally and by his own free will causes the obstruction – there is no need to prove additionally that he knew what he was doing constituted an unlawful act.[1] By analogy, it is submitted that the use of 'intentionally' further clarifies that there need not be any knowledge of the specific nature of the wrongdoing for this offence to be proved.

6.64   As to what might constitute 'obstruction', to a significant extent this will be a matter of common sense, although it necessarily implies that the accused took some step to prevent the authorised person from carrying out his functions. A mere failure to assist or to answer questions would fall more logically within s 11(8)(b). This view receives some support from *Green v DPP*,[2] a case in which the appellant advised his brother, in no uncertain terms, to say nothing to police officers who sought to question him in the street. The Divisional Court concluded that such conduct did not amount to obstructing the police in the execution of their duty.

6.65   The Minister gave assurances that certain matters (refusal to allow entry because a member of staff was not available to escort the authorised person or because a dangerous experiment was being conducted) would not constitute obstruction.[3] On the face of it, such matters could be viewed as 'intentional obstruction', in that the authorised person would be prevented at that time from carrying out his functions. One could argue that s 11(8)(a) should be read as 'intentionally obstructs *without lawful excuse*', although the contrary argument would be that such words are incorporated within s 11(8)(b) and, had the intention been to include this *caveat* in s 11(8)(a), it would have been made explicit.

---

1   *Arrowsmith v Jenkins* [1963] 2 QB 561.
2   [1991] Crim LR 784.
3   See **6.85**.

6.66   The offence in s 11(8)(b) of failing without lawful excuse to comply with any requirement imposed under s 11(4)(c) extends only to the situation where such a requirement is 'reasonable'. Thus, a person who refuses to comply with a request on the basis that it would put an onerous burden upon him will be able to argue in his defence that the requirement was not reasonable and, if successful, will be entitled to be acquitted.

6.67   The offences created are, as is stated above, similar to those in s 33 of the 1990 Act, with the significant difference that the latter specifically preserves the individual's privilege against self-incrimination (s 33(3)), whereas there is no such provision in s 11 (nor is there, in relation to s 16, which creates offences relating to the powers in ss 13 and 14). The exclusion of such a provision may be taken as a confirmation of the government's assertions that any information gathered in such a fashion cannot be employed for enforcement purposes, whether directly or indirectly.

6.68   In any event, the protection afforded to corporations by s 33(3) arguably has been eroded substantially, by the decision of the Divisional Court in *Walkers Snack Foods Limited v Coventry City Council*,[1] which concluded that the right in s 33(3) applied only to the individual being questioned, and did not confer any right to refuse to answer incriminatory questions about an individual's employer. As, of course, a corporation can only speak through its employees, it may be that this decision would be open to challenge in the light of the provisions of the Human Rights Act 1998 (see **5.102–5.105**).

6.69   The Explanatory Notes to s 11 seem to confirm that the Agency would be empowered to publish information acquired as a result of such observations. When dealing with s 11(7), the Explanatory Notes state that 'this provision does not in any way restrict the provision of any information to the Agency, or affect the Agency's own powers to publish information'. This strongly suggests that such information will be available to any local enforcement body if it seeks it in relation to a prosecution, although, of course, questions of admissibility would arise. It would be unfortunate if this provision were to be seen to have that effect, as it may encourage businesses to be less cooperative than they might otherwise be with such investigations.

6.70   There seems little doubt that the provisions of Code C of the Police and Criminal Evidence Act 1984 (relating to searches) will not apply to those exercising powers under this section, in that they are not persons 'charged with the duty of investigating offences' within s 67(9) of that Act.

Monitoring of enforcement action

6.71   It is a long-standing criticism of enforcement action in the food industry that the method of enforcement, ie by local authorities, results in a piecemeal and inconsistent pattern of enforcement throughout the UK. The introduction of

---

1   [1998] 3 All ER 163.

LACOTS and HAP went some way towards providing those at the sharp end of enforcement action with something approaching a national standard of what is expected of them. None the less, it is still common to find prosecutions occurring in relation to matters which have been viewed as satisfactory by the officers of a particular company's home authority. Therefore, any move towards standardising enforcement throughout the country is welcome, although the government has made clear that it is not seeking to set up a national enforcement body: '[ss] 12, 13, 14 and 15 are not about getting control or bringing in a national enforcement operation, but making sure that we monitor and raise standards of enforcement'.[1]

6.72 Section 12 gives the Agency the function of 'monitoring the performance of enforcement authorities in enforcing relevant legislation', including the setting of standards of performance for enforcement authorities generally or for any specific authority. Section 12(3) requires the Agency to include in its annual report (see s 4) details of its activities in relation to enforcement where it is the enforcement authority. At present, that is simply the enforcement of the meat hygiene regulations (previously enforced by the MHS, which becomes part of the Agency) and the dairy hygiene regulations, although the Agency has the power to take over local authority enforcement responsibilities as well (see Sch 3).

6.73 Under s 12(4), the Agency may make a report to any enforcement authority on its performance and such a report may include guidance as to what the Agency considers could be done to improve the performance. Under s 12(5), the Agency may direct that the authority publish all or some of the contents of such a report and notify the Agency of what steps have been taken or are to be taken in response to the report. The transparency that this provision could bring to local authority enforcement will doubtless be welcomed by many national businesses who find inconsistency of enforcement to be a problem. However, s 12 contains no power beyond, effectively, the ability to publicly embarrass the local authority in question. The decision as to whether to prosecute, for example, remains firmly in the hands of the local authority. It is to be presumed that the 'ultimate sanction' of withdrawal of responsibility for enforcement from the local authority will not be deployed to enforce compliance with guidance given by the Agency under s 12(4) except in the most extreme circumstances: '[It] is a powerful sanction to remove the enforcement power, so that point would be a long way down the line of failure.'[2]

6.74 The Agency has produced a draft standard for food enforcement which sets out the areas of local authority food law enforcement work and the expectations on the design and delivery of services across those areas. It covers:

– management arrangements, staff and equipment resources;
– enforcement policy;

---

1   Jeff Rooker, Standing Committee B, 8/7/99, col 227.
2   Jeff Rooker, Standing Committee B, 8/7/99, col 207.

- inspection and sampling programmes;
- arrangements for cooperating with other relevant agencies including 'home authority' arrangements;[1]
- arrangements for the investigation and control of outbreaks and liaison with the Agency on the handling of national food standards; and
- services to the general public and local food businesses.

6.75 It will be interesting to see how the Agency interacts with LACOTS. The Food Standards Committee Report indicated that local authorities and, in particular, LACOTS gave a somewhat reserved reaction to these powers of the Agency. One can see how it might be thought that LACOTS has little role, given the potential exercise of the Agency's powers. Whether the expression 'standards of performance' will relate to factors such as the volume of enforcement action taken by any particular authority or will relate instead to the manner in which enforcement powers are exercised by local authorities is a matter for conjecture at this stage. However, the Minister made it clear in Standing Committee that the standards would not be merely a bean-counting exercise, in terms of the number of visits an authority is able to make to food premises, for example.[2]

6.76 The Agency has now published a consultation document on food law enforcement, which includes provisions on monitoring. A draft monitoring form has been produced and is expected to be in use by January 2001. The scheme is intended to provide information on:

- local authority implementation of the food law enforcement standard requirements – this is a separate document which sets out what is expected of local authorities in terms of enforcement (see above), including the requirement for a service plan;
- local authority inspection activities and whether they are inspecting food premises at an appropriate frequency;
- formal enforcement actions taken;
- inspection outcome measures;
- food complaints made to local authorities;
- local authority sampling and the extent of enforcement activity resulting from it; and
- food control activities at ports in relation to imported foods.

6.77 Subject to the outcome of consultation on the food law enforcement standard, the Agency proposes that the document shall be issued to local authorities in September 2000 in order that it is reflected in enforcement plans for 2001/2002.

---

1 See HAP at **5.19–5.29**.
2 Standing Committee B, 8/7/99, col 206.

Powers conferred in relation to the monitoring of enforcement

6.78   Section 13 gives the Agency the power to request from any enforcement authority, or from any member, officer or employee of that authority, any information which it has reasonable cause to believe that person can give and to make available any records which it reasonably believes that person holds. The Agency may also exercise this power over any person who is subject to a duty under 'relevant legislation'. 'Relevant legislation' is defined in s 15(1) as the following statutes and regulations or orders made thereunder:

- the Food Safety Act 1990;
- the Food Safety (Northern Ireland) Order 1991; and
- Part IV of the Agriculture Act 1970, insofar as it relates to matters concerned with animal feedingstuffs.

6.79   Section 14 gives power to the Agency to authorise any individual to exercise a power of entry for the purpose of carrying out the Agency's function under s 12, in much the same way as s 11 confers powers in relation to the function conferred by s 10. Thus, an authorised person may, by s 14(4), enter certain premises[1] and take samples of any articles or substances found there, inspect and copy any records and require any person present to provide any facilities, records, information or other assistance as the authorised person may reasonably request.

6.80   Authorisation is to be made in writing and is to be issued only in pursuance of a decision taken by the Agency itself, or by a committee, sub-committee or member of the Agency acting on its behalf (s 14(2) and (3)). The authorised person is required, if asked, to produce his authorisation and to provide a document identifying any sample taken or document copied (s 14(5)). As with s 11(7), s 14(7) makes it an offence for any authorised person to disclose any information obtained through exercise of this power with regard to any trade secret, unless such disclosure is made in the exercise of his duty.

6.81   It was made clear that although s 19 gives the Agency the power to publish information which it obtains through exercise of this power (as it does in relation to all of its functions), issues of confidentiality will be taken into account:

> 'We recognise that local authority officers and councillors would be concerned about the agency publishing confidential internal records. Again, however, it would take that step only after jumping over the hurdles in [s 19] in the public interest. It would be the norm for the Agency to publish advice to Ministers as a default, but it would have to be in the public interest for it to publish advice from anyone else. It would, therefore, have to respect the confidentiality of personal data. ... The agency

---

1   Defined in s 14(5) as those occupied by the enforcement authority or any laboratory at which work related to enforcement by the authority has taken place (eg public analysts' laboratories), and any premises at which enforcement powers are, or have been, exercisable (the Explanatory Notes to s 14(5) give the examples of food shops, food manufacturers and slaughterhouses).

will certainly not go round being unreasonable because it will be constrained by normal administrative law in what it can do.'[1]

6.82 Section 16 creates offences in relation to the obstruction of persons exercising powers conferred by ss 13 and 14. Thus, it is an offence intentionally to obstruct a person exercising powers under s 14(4)(a), (b) or (c) (s 16(1)); to fail without reasonable excuse to comply with any requirement imposed under s 13(1) or 14(4)(d) (s 16(2)); or to furnish information which a person knows to be false or materially misleading or to recklessly furnish such information (s 16(3)). These offences are all summary only and carry a maximum fine of level 5 on the standard scale.

6.83 These provisions make it clear that a great deal of importance is being put on the gathering of information on enforcement. No doubt many of those responsible for enforcement will feel that there was no need to back up the statutory powers for observation and entry in this regard with criminal sanctions, and it is submitted that it is unlikely that a local authority would seek to keep relevant information from the Agency. There is, of course, no question of an authority facing a criminal prosecution over any failings in its enforcement record as a result of information obtained in this fashion, and, therefore, the issues of self-incrimination raised in relation to s 11 do not arise.

6.84 It is submitted that a local authority would not be able to claim privilege over any information simply on the basis that its disclosure may expose failings which could lead to the Agency taking further action, such as removing the authority's enforcement powers.[2]

6.85 Discussion in Standing Committee focused on the issue of obstruction, with opposition MPs seeking clarification on whether certain conduct could constitute obstruction. Whilst the definition of 'intentional obstruction' is, of course, a matter for the courts,[3] the Minister confirmed that to refuse access to premises because no member of staff was available to accompany the authorised person, or because a dangerous experiment was in progress, would not constitute obstruction.[4]

Direct enforcement by the Agency

6.86 One of the most debated provisions of the 1999 Act, and the 'remedy of last resort' in relation to monitoring of enforcement, is the power to take over the role of enforcement from the enforcement authorities. It has been stressed, rightly, by the government that this is not a new power, although it has assumed some significance in debate. Part 1 of Sch 3 to the 1999 Act (which is given effect by s 18) confers certain functions under the 1990 Act on the Agency. The

1 Jeff Rooker, Standing Committee B, 8/7/99, col 213.
2 See *Halsbury's Laws of England*, vol 11(2), (4th edn Reissue), para 1160 – privilege against self-incrimination applies only where the answer might expose the person questioned to proceedings for a criminal offence, for forfeiture or for the recovery of a penalty.
3 See **6.63–6.65**.
4 Jeff Rooker, Standing Committee B, 8/7/99, cols 229–230.

Explanatory Notes to Sch 3, Part I state that this allows 'the Agency to act as an enforcement authority in similar circumstances to those in which the Minister of Agriculture, Fisheries and Food and the Secretaries of State for Health, Scotland and Wales can act'. However, the statutory position in relation to this power is rather more complex than that simple summary might suggest and benefits from some analysis.

6.87   It seems, fairly obviously, that this is to be viewed very much as an ultimate sanction, perhaps only as a last resort where an enforcement authority has failed to act on any report and/or directions given by the Agency to it under s 12.

> '[The Agency] may remove powers from a local authority in the case of an abject failure and hand them over to another local authority, or do the job itself. That is the ultimate sanction in ensuring that we raise standards and achieve a high degree of consistency in enforcement.'[1]

> '...this measure is the nuclear option. It would not be done in secret without any warning; it would be done as a result of a failure to meet enforcement standards, which have already been published and are in the public domain...'[2]

6.88   In consultation, the Local Government Association raised the relevant issue that the taking of such action would involve the removal of responsibility from a democratically elected body. It was suggested by the Food Standards Committee that the final decision to invoke this power should remain with the Secretary of State, having received advice from the Agency. In answer to questioning in the Commons Second Reading of the Bill on whether it should be the Minister who takes this decision, the Minister of State at MAFF stated:

> 'The Hon Member for North Shropshire (Mr Paterson) asked about the advice from the Select Committee on Agriculture and whether Ministers should be able to decide about removing the duty of enforcement from local authorities. That responsibility already resides with Ministers under the Food Safety Act 1990. That provision was part of the draft legislation, and remains in this Bill.'[3]

6.89   This was echoed in the House of Lords by Lord Carter:

> 'The Agency will be able to take over enforcement from a local authority in special cases; for example where it has greater breadth or depth of expertise. It will also be able to act as an enforcement authority for certain Regulations. However, in both cases that will be done at the direction of Ministers and will represent an exception to the general rule of local control over enforcement.'[4]

6.90   Lord Carter made the very relevant point that it is not for the Agency to decide unilaterally that it will take over enforcement powers, this is to be done at the direction of Ministers. The text of para 2(a) of Sch 3 to the 1999 Act makes this clear:

---

1   Jeff Rooker, Standing Committee B, 6/7/99, col 156/7.
2   Jeff Rooker, Standing Committee B, 15/7/99, col 369.
3   *Hansard*, vol 333, no 107, col 860.
4   Lords Second Reading, *Hansard*, vol 604, no 130, col 1823.

'2. The Agency –
  (a) may be directed to discharge duties of food authorities under section 6(3) [of
    the 1990 Act];'

6.91 From the debates which took place over these powers, one would have thought that a substantial new provision was being created, but as will be seen from s 6 of the 1990 Act, the circumstances in which such a power can be exercised are necessarily limited. Section 6(3) provides:

'The Ministers may direct, in relation to cases of a particular description or a particular case, that **any duty imposed on food authorities** by subsection (2) above shall be discharged by the Ministers or the Minister and not by those authorities.'[1]

6.92 Thus, the wording of s 6(3) does not immediately convey the impression that it is intended to permit Ministers to remove powers from any particular authority, rather that it permits the Minister to withdraw enforcement responsibilities in a particular area from food authorities generally, for example if a particular problem assumes national significance and it is better for enforcement in relation to that problem to be coordinated centrally. The passages quoted above certainly suggest that this provision is intended to be applicable to individual authorities which are identified as failing in their enforcement responsibilities, but it may be that there is room for argument that s 6(3) does not permit the removal of powers from individual authorities, but simply allows such powers, in a specific area, to be removed from all food authorities. The use of the phrase 'duties of food authorities' in para 2(b) might be said to lend weight to this argument, in that it does not make explicit that this power is to be exercisable in relation to *individual* authorities.

6.93 In this regard, it is interesting to note some of the Minister's comments in Standing Committee concerning this provision:

'First, the Bill contains no new powers. It transfers the operation of existing powers from one government department to another government department – the Food Standards Agency is a non-ministerial government department ... The powers referred to in Schedule 3 already exist in legislation.'

6.94 When questioned as to why the Secretary of State could not himself direct the local authorities, without the Agency being involved, the Minister replied:

'Believe it or not, the Secretary of State has no authority to do that. That is why we are setting up the Agency – its operation, which will set enforcement standards for local authorities and monitor them, will not be under day-to-day control ... The powers will not be given to the Agency, they will reside with the Minister who can direct the Agency to operate those powers.'[2]

6.95 This apparent confusion is resolved by para 6 of Sch 3, which states that the Agency ' may be empowered by an Order under section 42 [of the 1990 Act] to discharge any duty of a food authority'.

---

1   Emphasis added.
2   Jeff Rooker, Standing Committee B, 15/7/99, col 371.

6.96   Section 42 of the 1990 Act deals with 'default powers' retained by the Minister, which, according to s 42(1), allow the Minister, where he is satisfied that a food authority has failed to discharge any duty imposed by the 1990 Act and such failure affects the general interests of food consumers, to empower another food authority to discharge that duty in place of the authority in default.

6.97   Precisely how the Agency would undertake enforcement activity itself is not clear. It was suggested by the Minister of State at MAFF in answering questions posed by the Food Standards Committee that the Agency would be able to ask another local authority effectively to sub-contract enforcement work for an authority that was 'not up to the job'. Such an approach is envisaged by s 42 of the 1990 Act and obviously presents funding issues in that extra funds would have to be provided for the authority which was undertaking the extra work. Section 42(4) of the 1990 Act makes provision for the redistribution of resources in such circumstances, allowing 'the substitute authority or the Minister' to recover from the authority in default any expenses reasonably incurred in carrying out functions transfered in accordance with s 42(1).

6.98   It seems doubtful that the Agency itself would have the resources or know-how to take on all of the functions of an enforcement authority in this regard. Significantly, it would not have any local presence itself in the area that it had taken over, which suggests that the use of a successful neighbouring authority would be the only viable solution.

6.99   The true position in relation to this power, therefore, is that it is not the Agency's power at all. The Agency simply becomes another body upon which the Minister can confer enforcement responsibilities under his existing powers. Thus, this is not, in truth, an ultimate sanction to ensure compliance with the requirements of the Agency. If a local authority refuses to either comply with Agency directions or meet the standards set by the Agency, it is not open to the Agency itself to threaten to take away enforcement responsibility. The key question will remain whether (in accordance with the test in s 42(1) of the 1990 Act) the local authority has failed to discharge any duty in relation to the 1990 Act and such failure affects the general interests of food consumers.

6.100   No doubt the Minister would give a great deal of weight to the views of the Agency in this regard and if, for example, the Agency (in accordance with s 19 of the 1999 Act) were to publish a conclusion that a particular local authority was failing, the Minister would come under significant public pressure to exercise this power. However, the decision remains in the Minister's hands. The significance of the Agency in this area is chiefly that a Minister is much more likely to have information upon which he could base such a decision given the Agency's functions of monitoring and setting standards. It may be that the absence of any such information has contributed to the fact that this power (under the 1990 Act) has never yet been exercised.

6.101   The Agency, by para 2(b) of Sch 3, becomes a body which may be specified as an enforcement authority within s 6(4) of the 1990 Act. Essentially, this just adds the Agency to the list of enforcement bodies that the Minister can designate for the purposes of enforcing regulations in the food sphere, either generally or in relation to specific areas or cases. The Agency is, of course, already acting as an enforcement body, having taken over the enforcement responsibilities of the MHS from MAFF.

6.102   According to para 2(c) of Sch 3, the Agency may also take over the conduct of any proceedings which have been commenced by an enforcement authority, with the consent of that authority or at the direction of the Secretary of State. Presumably, such power is intended to be invoked in a case either of national significance or where the greater resources of the Agency make it more appropriate for it to assume the burden of prosecution.

6.103   What is clear in relation to direct enforcement is that (as of 1 April 2000) it is the Agency's responsibility to enforce the various provisions of the Meat Hygiene Regulations through the MHS (which has become part of the Agency) and the Dairy Hygiene Regulations. There is a sub-committee, the 'MHS Supervisory Board', chaired by the Deputy Chairman of the Agency, which is to conduct a strategic review of the MHS and to present recommendations on key issues to the Agency Board.

Publication by the Agency of advice and information

6.104   This power, in s 19, has been identified as an important factor in establishing the Agency as a credible body, independent of the government. Section 19(1) states that the Agency may publish any advice which it has given under ss 6, 7 and 9 (ie advice to any public authority, any member of the public or to anyone in relation to animal feedingstuffs), any information obtained through observations or monitoring under ss 10 and 12, and any other information in its possession, whatever its source.

6.105   The power is restricted only to the extent that there can be no publication if it is prohibited by an enactment, is incompatible with any Community obligation, or would constitute or be punishable as a contempt of court (s 19(3)). It is also to be exercised in accordance with the provisions of the Data Protection Act 1998. Apart from those restrictions, the power 'is exercisable free from any prohibition on publication which would apply apart from this section' (s 19(7)). Indeed, s 25 of the 1999 Act grants further power to the Secretary of State (and to the Scottish Ministers and the First Minister in Northern Ireland in respect of matters which are within their legislative competence) to make Orders relaxing any prohibition on disclosure in any other enactment which he considers may prevent the publication of information where the power to publish under s 19 would otherwise be exercisable (s 25(1) and (5)(b)).

6.106   In practice, publication is a matter of discretion and is fettered by s 19(4). The Agency is not required to publish everything (the government resisted proposed amendments imposing a duty to publish) and, before deciding to exercise the power, it must 'consider whether the public interest in the publication of the advice or information in question is outweighed by any considerations of confidentiality attaching to it' (s 11(4)). For example, the Explanatory Notes to s 19(4) cite the need to weigh the competing interests of promoting openness or making people aware of health risks as against issues such as personal privacy or commercial confidence.

6.107 Such considerations do not apply, however, where the advice or information relates to the performance of enforcement authorities, unless the advice or information relates to a person other than an enforcement authority or a member, officer or employee of an enforcement body acting as such (s 11(5)). So, for example, where information would touch on the affairs of a business being investigated by the enforcement authority, the Agency would have to carry out the balancing act required by s 11(4).

6.108 Clearly, the type of information that may be published includes policy advice to Ministers:

> '[The Agency's] decisions will be science based – that is not based on any economic interest of one sort or another – and placed in the public domain as policy advice to Ministers, especially the Secretary of State for Health. There will, of course, be consultation within government, as happens now, but the fact that the advice is transparent and science based means that there can also be public discussion. There may be overriding factors that the government wishes to take into account in modifying the advice or even rejecting it outright, but for the first time, Ministers will have to be able to explain their decisions. In the current climate, any Minister who introduced another factor would have to provide a pretty good explanation.'[1]

6.109 Publication of advice given to Ministers was one of the factors which received strong support from consumer groups in relation to the Act. If a Minister chooses not to follow the advice of the Agency, there will doubtless be pressure from the press and opposition parties to explain the reason why such advice was not followed, a factor which the government clearly recognises. One might think that this could lead to Ministers seeking to influence the Agency's decision as to whether to publish, albeit that such a suggestion was vigorously refuted in Standing Committee:

> '... it is for the Agency to decide what to publish; there will be no constraints from Ministers. The Agency will make and defend the case for what it publishes and what it does not; there will be no ministerial diktat or interference whatever. This is a culture shock for those who were previously Ministers.'[2]

6.110 Thus, a party seeking judicial review of a decision by the Agency (see **6.115** below) to publish or not to publish certain advice, research or information gleaned through its observations under ss 10 or 12 would do well to question whether any ministerial pressure was brought to bear on the Agency. For example, it might be argued that taking into account such pressure in reaching a

---

1   Minister for Agriculture, Fisheries and Food, Commons Second Reading, *Hansard*, vol 333, no 107, col 793/4.

2   Jeff Rooker, Standing Committee B, 6/7/99, col 129.

decision may constitute procedural impropriety (on the basis that an irrelevant factor was taken into account).

6.111 As has already been stated, the Agency has the *power* but not the *duty* to publish the information or advice in question. The government felt that a duty to publish may cause certain sources of information to be reluctant to come forward – although, of course, such sources will not be able to rely on any greater degree of confidentiality than is already provided by the provisions of s 19(4), unless the Agency itself agrees to it. It might well be inappropriate for the Agency to bind itself by agreeing with a source not to publish unless it has exercised its discretion in accordance with s 19.

6.112 Whilst matters of commercial confidence will no doubt play a part in any decision taken by the Agency to publish information, it is clear that the primary consideration is the public interest in disclosure: 'The Agency's default option will be to publish, rather than not to do so'.[1] The exercise of such a discretion is a matter which will almost certainly be subject to challenge by way of judicial review.

6.113 The Minister did provide some assistance regarding the situation where the Agency chooses not to publish certain information:

> 'The idea of the Agency having to publish its reasons for not publishing is seductive, but impractical. To publish one's reasons for not publishing is, in effect, to provide the information that one is not publishing.'[2]

6.114 Whether one agrees with this reasoning or not, it is a straightforward demonstration of Parliamentary intent in this regard. The question of publication of reasons for not publishing certain information (or for publishing it) is, of course, slightly different to the issue of whether there is, as a matter of administrative law, any duty to give reasons to the persons affected by any decision to publish or not to publish. This is potentially an important issue, as it is unlikely that the Agency will volunteer to disclose its reasoning as to any particular decision, and, in the absence of reasons for any such decision, an aggrieved party is unlikely to be able to present a convincing case on a substantive ground of review.[3]

6.115 Whilst a detailed examination of the administrative law aspect of the Agency is outside the scope of this book,[4] the following considerations are likely to be relevant to the issue of whether there is any duty on the Agency to give reasons for a decision to publish or not to publish:

– there is no right of appeal against any decision to publish;

---

1   Jeff Rooker, Standing Committee B, 8/7/99 col 242.
2   Jeff Rooker, Standing Committee B, 6/7/99, col 129.
3   See, for example, *R v Civil Service Appeal Board, ex parte Cunningham* [1991] 4 All ER 310 at p 322d, *per* McCowan LJ.
4   For such an examination, see De Smith, Woolf and Jowell, *Judicial Review of Administrative Action* 5th edn (Sweet & Maxwell, 1995), at 9-039 et seq.

– publication of confidential commercial information may have a significant financial effect, whether on a large corporation or a small business; and

– there is no statutory fetter to the giving of reasons (although the passage quoted at **6.113** above in Standing Committee may be taken as evidence of Parliamentary intention in this regard).

6.116 Whilst, undoubtedly, it would be onerous for the Agency to be required to give reasons in respect of all decisions taken under s 19, it is submitted that where, for example, information is supplied to the Agency and/or published against the will of the provider of the information, the principles of fairness or natural justice require that the provider is able to obtain reasons for such publication.

6.117 In relation to a decision not to publish, one can readily envisage a situation where a body or individual concerned with a particular issue, such as genetically modified foods, will demand the publication of all advice and research in the area, and seek review if it is not forthcoming. It is submitted that in such a situation the courts are more likely to take the view that there is no duty to give reasons, not least because in such a situation it would be difficult to identify significant injustice suffered by any individual or identifiable group by reason of the failure to publish.

Providing guidance on the control of food-borne disease

6.118 Section 20 of the 1999 Act enables the Agency to issue general guidance to local authorities or other public authorities on matters connected with the management of outbreaks or suspected outbreaks of food-borne disease, defined in s 20(5) as 'a disease of humans which is capable of being caused by the consumption of infected or otherwise contaminated food'. The examples given in the Explanatory Notes to s 20 are salmonella, E. coli 0157 (the organism responsible for both the Lanarkshire outbreak and the cause of the problems in the *Eastside Cheese* case) and campylobacter.

6.119 Any such guidance must identify the authority or authorities to which it is addressed and shall be published by the Agency in such manner as it thinks fit (s 20(2) and (3)). There is, it would seem, no discretion not to publish such guidance, although the manner in which this is to be done is a matter of discretion. It is not entirely clear whether this section is intended to permit the Agency to give general guidance of a pre-emptive nature in relation to such outbreaks or potential outbreaks or whether it is intended to permit the Agency to coordinate effectively the response to any such outbreak. The Explanatory Notes give the examples of guidance on tracing the food-related source of any outbreak or the speed with which action needs to be taken to limit the spread of food poisoning.

6.120 This is a matter of some interest given recent problems such as the E. coli outbreak in Lanarkshire. The enquiry into the outbreak criticised the speed with which the local authority reacted in dealing with the problems. It took quite some time before the source of the outbreak was located and, therefore, before those who were at risk could be protected. Although the report was highly critical of the actions of the local authority, it is difficult to see how a centralised body such as the Agency could have reacted with greater speed than the local authority in place.

6.121   The E. coli outbreak in Lanarkshire itself provides an interesting example of failures in local food safety enforcement. In addition to criticising the speed of reaction of the local authority, the Sheriff's inquiry commented that whilst experienced environmental health officers were involved in prosecution of food safety offences, it was left to the more junior officers to deal with matters of inspection. Shortly prior to the outbreak the butcher's shop in question in Lanarkshire had been inspected by the Environmental Health Authority, and had been passed as fit. This was despite evidence that cooked and uncooked meat were being served from the same counter. It will be interesting to see how the Agency's powers of monitoring are able to address failings such as this and whether a centralised body (albeit one with regional advisory committees set up in accordance with s 5[1]) is really able to make a difference in improving the speed and efficiency with which outbreaks of food-borne disease, which are invariably a local problem, are dealt with.

Supplementary powers

6.122   Section 21(1) of the 1999 Act gives the Agency the 'power to do anything which is calculated to facilitate, or is conducive or incidental to, the exercise of its functions'. This is an extremely general power. Section 21(2) gives the power to:

–   carry on educational or training activities;
–   to give financial or other support to activities carried on by others;
–   acquire or dispose of any property or rights; and
–   institute criminal proceedings in England and Wales and in Northern Ireland.

6.123   The Agency also has the power to make charges for facilities or services provided by it at the request of any person (s 21(3)).

6.124   The Explanatory Notes to s 21 state that this clause does not give the Agency any power to act outside the area of its functions. Even so, there are many matters which may help the Agency to perform its functions which one would not expect the Agency to have the power to deal with. For example, it would doubtless assist the Agency if it were to have its own revenue-creating powers. If the Agency decided to introduce a levy on food businesses (much in the way that it was originally intended that the Agency should be funded[2]), it would seem that, on paper, s 21 provides such a power.

---

1   See **6.9**.
2   See **6.20**.

6.125   Concerns were raised by members of the Food Standards Committee in relation to this power, although such concerns do not appear in the Committee's report. It may be that the answer to such concerns is that the exercise of this power, in common with the exercise of all of the other powers of the Agency, is subject to the constraints imposed by s 23(2), which is dealt with below.

6.126   The government's position is firmly that there is to be no levy:

> 'The clause dealing with the levy, and which would be the statutory foundation for such a charge has been removed from the Bill. There is no primary legislation, and therefore no levy – more permanent than that one cannot get.'[1]

6.127   In relation to the power to levy charges, it was made plain that such power was not to be used for the purposes of introducing a levy by stealth:

> 'The charges which may be levied by the Agency are for any facilities or services provided. That is not a backdoor way to charge food businesses. The power is there to allow the Agency to charge for services such as the photocopying of research reports. The Agency must have some discretion to charge. Any charges will be made in accordance with general and government guidance. These will be set only to cover the costs of providing a service.'[2]

EXERCISE OF THE POWERS BY THE AGENCY

6.128   Section 23 sets out the matters which the Agency must consider in relation to the exercise of any of its powers. In addition to paying 'due regard' to the 'statement of objectives and principles' required to be produced by s 22, the Agency must take the following factors into account (s 23(2)):

– the nature and magnitude of any risks to public health, or other risks, which are relevant to the decision (including any uncertainty as to the adequacy or reliability of the available information);
– the likely costs and benefits of the exercise or non-exercise of the power or its exercise in any manner which the Agency is considering; and
– any relevant advice or information given to it by an advisory committee (whether or not given at the Agency's request).

6.129   The Agency is not required to consider such factors where it would be unreasonable or impracticable to do so in view of the nature or purpose of the power or in the circumstances of any particular case (s 23(3)(a)). The somewhat banal example of such a situation given in the Explanatory Notes to s 23(3) relates to decisions on appointments. Examination of the Agency's decision-making by reference to this section will be the starting point for anybody seeking to obtain judicial review of the exercise by the Agency of any of its powers.

1   Minister for Agriculture, Fisheries and Food, Commons Second Reading, *Hansard*, vol 333, no 107, col 796.
2   Lord Carter, Lords Second Reading, *Hansard*, vol 604, no 130, col 1826.

6.130 The issue of the existence of a duty by the Agency to give reasons for the exercise of the power to publish is discussed at **6.115**. Detailed discussion of potential administrative law remedies against the Agency is beyond the scope of this book, however, as a matter of common sense, the Agency's decisions must *prima facie* be subject to review in much the same way as the decisions of MAFF and the DoH were prior to the formation of the Agency.

6.131 In addition to the factors spelt out in s 23, the Agency will be expected to follow the principles of the 'Better Regulation' Guide, produced by the Cabinet Office.

THE INTERACTION BETWEEN THE AGENCY AND CENTRAL GOVERNMENT

Direction by central government

6.132 Much importance has been placed, in terms of restoring public confidence in food, on the 'independence' of the Agency. The power to publish its advice and the laying out of principles to be followed in the exercise of its powers may be said to go some way towards achieving this objective, although how truly independent a 'non-ministerial government department' (the definition which the government has given the Agency) can (or should) be from central government is a moot point. Those who view the creation of the Agency cynically have drawn some support from s 24, which gives the Secretary of State powers to direct the Agency.

6.133 Section 24(1) permits the Secretary of State to give such directions to the Agency as he may consider appropriate, if he considers that there has been a serious failure:

– to comply with the requirements of s 23(1) or (2); or
– to perform any other duty which he considers should have been performed by it.

6.134 This power may also be exercised by the appropriate person within the devolved Parliaments within their particular sphere of competence (s 24(2)). The authorities must consult with the Agency before giving any such direction (s 24(6)). If the Agency fails to comply with any directions given in accordance with this section, the authority that gave the directions may give effect to them itself and, in so doing, may exercise any power of the Agency (s 24(7)). In such circumstances, the Secretary of State has the further power to remove all the members of the Agency from office and, until new appointments are made, to carry out the Agency's functions himself or appoint any other person or persons to do so (s 24(8)). In order to take this step, the Secretary of State must consult with and obtain the agreement of the other appropriate authorities.

6.135 The Food Standards Committee raised serious concerns about this power. The Minister for Public Health provided a memorandum to the Committee in relation to its concerns as to when these powers might be used. Two examples were given: 'gross misuse of public funds by the Agency and failure to exercise financial control' and 'serious disagreement with Health Ministers or the Chief Medical Officer on the magnitude and scale of risk to public health and the scientific basis for the Agency's advice'.

6.136 The Committee rightly identified the significant distinction between these two scenarios. Clearly, if the Agency is operating in a financially irresponsible fashion, few would argue that central government ought to be able to intervene. However, the fact that it is envisaged that the power will be exercisable where there is a dispute between the Agency and other governmental advisors is more significant. One can see how the presence of this power may discourage the Agency from taking and/or publishing a viewpoint which differs substantially from current government thinking, which would rather weaken the Agency's claim to independence.

6.137 The Committee's recommendation was that there should be further clarification as to the nature of any disagreement which would lead to these powers being invoked, and who should act as an arbiter in cases where there was obviously a fundamental difference of opinion as to the authority of any given piece of research which was ultimately responsible for such a disagreement. There was also a clear concern that this power would provide a means for political direction of the Agency.

6.138 In Standing Committee, it was stressed that this is not intended to be a device permitting Ministers to control the Agency indirectly:

> 'It cannot be used by Ministers simply to tell the Agency what to do on a routine basis. It would be wrong to dismiss the power as general or draconian. The directing authority would need to ensure that it was exercising the power fully in accordance with the terms in which it is couched, otherwise the authority would be subject to judicial review. It is likely that the wording of any direction will have to say clearly why that step was being taken. It is difficult to conceive of a direction being given without the directing authority giving some explanation, otherwise the direction would appear arbitrary.'[1]

6.139 Section 24(9) states that 'any directions given under this section shall be published in such manner as the authority giving them considers appropriate for the purpose of bringing the matters to which they relate to the attention of persons likely to be affected by them'. This section is somewhat loosely worded and, on the face of it, seems to confer on the authority seeking to direct the Agency a substantial degree of discretion in relation to publication.

6.140 In Standing Committee, the Minister for Public Health stated that she saw no reason why an express requirement to publish the reasons for issuing a direction could not be imposed on the authority seeking to direct the Agency and

---

1   Tessa Jowell, Standing Committee B, 13/7/99, col 284.

suggested a suitable amendment. The requirement that 'directions under subsection (1) must include a statement summarising the reasons for giving them' (which was not present in the draft Bill before Standing Committee) is included at s 24(3). Thus, if an interested party is minded to challenge any direction the Agency is given, it would appear that the reasons are to be published (although, presumably, if published by the authority giving the direction, subject to the provisions of s 24(9)). Of course, the Agency itself has the power to publish 'any ... information in its possession (whatever its source)' (s 19(1)(c)).

6.141 The power to direct also exists, somewhat less controversially, in relation to the giving of directions by the Secretary of State and his equivalents in the devolved Parliaments on the implementation of any obligations of the UK under the Community Treaties or any international agreement to which the UK is a party (s 24(4) and (5)).

Consultation and co-operation

6.142 Section 28 imposes a duty on a 'Minister of the Crown' (in practice, likely to be the Minister for Agriculture, Fisheries and Food and the Secretary of State for Health) and the devolved authorities on the one hand and the Agency on the other to make administrative arrangements for sharing relevant information on food-borne zoonoses. These are defined in s 28(5) as 'any disease of, or organism carried by, animals which constitutes a risk to the health of humans through the consumption of, or contact with, food'. This includes the familiar examples of salmonella, E. coli and campylobacter. Such arrangements may also include provisions for coordinating the activities of the Agency and the relevant authority in relation to such matters.

6.143 Section 29(1) requires the Minister of Agriculture, Fisheries and Food, and each Secretary of State with a responsibility for any matters connected with the regulation of veterinary products (defined in s 29(2) and including drugs and medicated feedingstuffs), to consult the Agency from time to time about the general policy they propose to pursue in carrying out their functions in relation to such matters. Section 29(3) permits the Minister or the Secretary of State involved to disclose any information to the Agency relating to matters connected with the regulation of veterinary products. This lifts a general restriction in the Medicines Act 1968 on disclosure of information relating to veterinary products. Once such information is in the hands of the Agency, it may be published or disclosed by the Agency in accordance with the Agency's powers of publication in s 19.

6.144 The Agency, according to s 34, must take account of the activities of the Food Safety Promotion Board in Ireland. This body was established by agreement between the UK and Irish governments on 8 March 1999 (see s 36(1)) and implemented by the North/South Cooperation (Implementation Bodies) (Northern Ireland) Order 1999. Its functions include the promotion of food safety, research into food safety, communication of food alerts and surveillance of food-borne diseases throughout Ireland. Clearly, this mirrors to a great extent the role of the Agency in the UK. Section 34 requires the two bodies to consult with each other with a view to ensuring that their activities are not duplicated unnecessarily.

Modification of the Act

6.145   Provision for modifying the 1999 Act by the making of an Order in Council are detailed in s 32. The Agency itself is required to be consulted before the making of any such Order. It seems that this power is included mainly for the purpose of dealing with the effects of devolution. It may be that certain matters are better dealt with by the appropriate authorities within the devolved Parliaments, and this section provides a measure of flexibility in that regard without the need for amendment of the Act. Section 33 contains further powers to modify the Act by Order in Council in the event that either the Scottish Parliament or the Northern Ireland Assembly passes an Act providing that any of the Agency's functions should no longer be exercisable in or as regards Scotland or Northern Ireland respectively. No provision is made in relation to the National Assembly for Wales, as that body does not have primary legislative powers.

Chapter 7
Food Agencies Internationally

7.1 In Appendix 3 to his Report, Professor James considered some of the bodies which exist in foreign countries for the regulation of matters of food standards. Whilst he thought that none of these models were directly appropriate to the UK context, it is none the less instructive to examine briefly how similar issues are dealt with in other jurisdictions. The nature and remit of such agencies varies with the jurisdictions, although it is unsurprising to find that the most highly developed system of centralised monitoring of food standards and safety exists in the USA.

7.2 It had been suggested that the US Food and Drug Administration (FDA) was an appropriate model for the UK Agency and certain MPs persisted in this view as the Bill was debated. Professor James' Report stated that it was inappropriate for a number of reasons. One of these is that the FDA does not have responsibility for meat (which, of course, the Agency does as part of its overall food safety responsibilities, in addition to the fact that the MHS is now a part of the Agency); another is that it operates in a different constitutional context and regulatory framework from the UK. He also suggested that, as the appointment of the Commissioner of the FDA is a political appointment, this would undermine its public protection mission.

THE US FOOD AND DRUG ADMINISTRATION

7.3 One of the most obvious differences between the FDA and the Agency is that the former is an enforcement body. Employees of the FDA carry out a number of the roles that are exercised by environmental health officers and trading standards officers in the UK. These include making inspections of sites, seizing goods, carrying out scientific tests, and, if appropriate, taking enforcement action by way of prosecution. The FDA has its own scientists who deal with scientific evidence in relation to any prosecutions (2,100 scientists out of a total staff of over 9,000, working in 40 laboratories, including 900 chemists and 300 microbiologists). Whilst the Agency may take over enforcement action in certain circumstances (see Chapter 6), enforcement is not one of its primary roles. One can see the advantages of maintaining a federal system of enforcement in the USA, and it remains to be seen to what extent the Agency is able to achieve consistency in enforcement throughout the UK. It is not simply the FDA which has responsibility for enforcement and inspection throughout the USA; State and local government agencies cooperate with the FDA in the development of uniform standards and regulations.

7.4 Such a system fits rather more logically within a federal structure than it does in the UK. Government initiatives in the area of regulation, such as the work of the Better Regulation Unit, have experienced limited success in implementing centralised standards, such as the Enforcement Concordat.

7.5   It is impossible to draw parallels between the FDA and the Agency as they are such different bodies. However, within the FDA, the Center for Food Safety and Applied Nutrition carries out functions broadly comparable to the sphere of influence envisaged for the Agency. The Center was reviewed, together with the whole of the FDA, by the Edwards Committee and major structural change was implemented in 1992. This divided the Center into a number of offices, established to focus on specific products and issues (under a 'Deputy Director for Programs') and, on the administrative and strategic side, further offices were set up under a 'Deputy Director for Systems and Support'.

7.6   By way of comparison, the organisational set up of the Agency is depicted in Appendix 3.

THE AUSTRALIA NEW ZEALAND FOOD AUTHORITY

7.7   This is a statutory authority whose stated aims are to:

–   protect public health and safety;
–   provide adequate information relating to food to enable consumers to make informed choices and to prevent fraud and deception;
–   promote fair trading in food;
–   promote trade and commerce in the food industry; and
–   promote consistency between domestic and international food standards where these are at variance.

7.8   The clear difference in approach here is that it does not involve issues relating to food production, although Professor James' Report states that there was consumer pressure for a broader 'paddock to plate' approach to be taken.

7.9   The Authority has recently published a draft Food Standards Code (released on 15 March 2000), which implements a wide variety of recommendations is anticipated to become law by late 2000 and which will completely replace existing food standards legislation in Australia and New Zealand by 2002. The Code sets out general provisions applicable in relation to all foods, including labelling and other information requirements, substances added to foods, contaminants and residues, foods requiring pre-market clearance (including genetically modified foods) and microbiological and processing requirements. There are further provisions setting standards for specific groups of foods, such as cereals, meat and fish and dairy products. It is an offence under Australian State and Territory legislation, and under the Food Act 1981 in New Zealand, for food to be sold that does not comply with a prescribed standard.

7.10   It must be doubtful whether the Agency would have the will or the time to devote to a reworking of UK food legislation to this extent, although it is anticipated that policy-making will be a primary role. The sheer magnitude of food legislation and the complexity of the institutions, both in the UK and Europe, which have an impact on food policy, militate against the possibility of any such codification happening in the UK, although there are many who would argue that some simplicity and consistency is long overdue. It may be that a universal code will be established by the proposed European Food Authority.[1]

THE CANADIAN FOOD INSPECTION AGENCY

7.11 This body was created in 1997 to 'consolidate the delivery of all federally mandated food inspection and quarantine services as well as plant protection and animal health programs' (in the words of its latest Annual Report). It has responsibility for administration and/or enforcement of a number of statutes and regulations which cover inspection services related to food safety, consumer protection, plant protection and animal health. However, it does not deal with development of policy or standards or with nutritional matters, which are the remit of Health Canada, a federal government department that is also responsible for assessing the work of the Canadian Food Inspection Agency.

7.12 Thus, the Canadian Food Inspection Agency is very much oriented towards enforcement and inspection, rather than policy development and the setting of standards, which are the Food Standards Agency's primary interests. The latest Report from the Food Inspection Agency highlights increased consumer interest in matters of food safety and nutrition, and stresses the need for accountability and openness in government handling of such issues.

7.13 It is striking how this mirrors experience in the UK and the demands which led to the introduction of the Food Standards Agency, although the Canadian solution is in some respects not as wide-ranging as that of the UK. However, the existence of a national body with responsibility for enforcement and inspection may yet prove attractive if the Agency fails to deliver improved standards in local authority enforcement. None the less, it must be said that the only experience UK consumers and food producers have of such a body is the MHS, which has certainly not been free from criticism.

THE FOOD SAFETY AUTHORITY OF IRELAND

7.14 Formally established on 1 January 1999, and intended to cover all issues of regulation of the food industry 'from farm to fork', the Authority describes itself as a 'statutory, independent and science-based body'. It has a Board of ten members, appointed by the Minister for Health and Children, which is advised by a Scientific Committee of 15 members, with the support of sub-committees set up to deal with specific areas.

---

1   See the discussion of the European White Paper in Chapter 2.

7.15   There are significant similarities between the Food Safety Authority and the Agency (perhaps unsurprisingly), including the power to publish reports on matters within its remit and the publication of an annual report. However, in relation to enforcement, the approach differs. The Authority is to operate the 'national food safety compliance programme' by means of service contracts with the agencies which currently have that responsibility, and those agencies will act as agents of the Authority. This is something of a compromise between local and central government enforcement. Presumably, the Authority will be able to terminate the 'service contract' of a local enforcement body if it does not match its standards. In that sense, it may be that the arrangement is not so different from the Agency, which has power to set standards and give guidance to local authorities and, if they do not measure up, the Minister may remove enforcement responsibilities from them.[1]

7.16   There is also to be an all-island body, the Food Safety Promotion Board, which has responsibility for certain areas throughout the Republic of Ireland and Northern Ireland (and with which the Agency is required to liaise (s 34 of the 1999 Act). These are:

- promotion of food safety;
- research into food safety;
- communication of food alerts;
- surveillance of food-borne diseases;
- promotion of scientific cooperation and linkages between laboratories; and
- development of cost-effective facilities for specialist laboratory testing.

7.17   This body was proposed as one of the 'implementation bodies' for the development of areas of common interest between the Republic of Ireland and Northern Ireland in the so-called Good Friday Agreement. Therefore, its future must be in some doubt given the uncertainty about the political situation in Northern Ireland at the time of writing.

Possibly use for conclusion?

EUROPEAN FOOD AUTHORITY

7.18   In its White Paper on Food Safety,[2] the European Commission sets out proposals for a European Food Authority. The White Paper echoes many of the concerns identified in the course of the establishment of the Agency, notably the pressing need to restore consumer confidence in food. The need to secure the best scientific advice and to publish such advice are also recognised as key to the improvement of the system. Proposals for a 'General Food Law' contained in the White Paper are discussed in Chapter 2.

7.19   Chapter 4 of the White Paper sets out the proposals for the European Food Authority. It is stated that a new body is desirable because structural

---

1   See the discussion of this power in Chapter 6.
2   COM(1999)719.

change is the most effective manner in which to achieve the changes required to protect public health and restore consumer confidence. The White Paper also refers to 'the generally accepted need to separate risk assessment and risk management.' (para 29). The proposal is that the Authority will be responsible (at least initially) only for 'risk assessment', which is defined in this context as having the objective of 'the provision of scientific advice'. Within this role, important aspects are extensive information gathering and analysis, and the formation of networks for monitoring and surveillance, in addition to research and development programmes.

7.20 It was considered important to keep the risk-management function separate, because that is a 'political' function, involving legislation and control and requiring judgments to be made not simply on the basis of science but also on 'a wider appreciation of the wishes and needs of society' (para 32). Inclusion of such functions within the European Food Authority would, it is said, cause three main problems:

- transfer of regulatory powers to an independent Authority could lead to diminution of democratic accountability;
- the 'control function' must be retained by the Commission in order to discharge its obligations under the Treaties; and
- an Authority with regulatory power could not be created under the current institutional arrangements of the EU and would require modification of the EC Treaty.

7.21 It is readily apparent, therefore, that the European Food Authority will have substantially less power than the UK Agency, or rather that its powers are to be limited to observation and advice without any enforcement role. Its stated tasks are as follows.

- Provision of scientific advice and information to the Commission on all matters having a direct or indirect impact on consumer health and safety arising from the consumption of food: this will encompass both risk and nutritional issues.
- Information gathering and analysis: the development and operation of food safety monitoring and information programmes will be a part of this, in addition to contact with agencies within Member States.
- Communication: the idea is that the Authority will become the first port of call for scientific information on food safety and nutrition. It will ensure that appropriate information on these subjects is published. It also appears that the intention is to give the Authority a role of direct communication with consumers.

7.22 Whilst some of the factors that influenced the EU's decision to keep enforcement away from the Authority are related simply to the competence of the European institutions and, therefore, are not applicable to the UK, the concern that risk management and risk assessment should be separated may have resonance for the UK Agency.[1] By way of example, the enforcement powers conferred by s 12 and Sch 3 of the 1999 Act permit the removal, from a democratically elected body, of enforcement powers, which is a matter that has caused some concern (see para 39 of the Food Standards Committee Report). As is explained in Chapter 6, however, these are not in reality powers of the Agency, rather they are powers retained by the Minister which already existed under the Food Safety Act 1990.

---

1   See, for example, concerns in relation to the MHS, discussed at **4.4**.

Appendix 1
Food Standards Act 1999

(1999 c. 28)

ARRANGEMENT OF SECTIONS

The Food Standards Agency

An Act to establish the Food Standards Agency and make provision as to its functions; to amend the law relating to food safety and other interests of consumers in relation to food; to enable provision to be made in relation to the notification of tests for food-borne diseases; to enable provision to be made in relation to animal feedingstuffs; and for connected purposes.

[11th November 1999]

EXPLANATORY NOTES

INTRODUCTION

1. These explanatory notes relate to the Food Standards Act 1999. They have been prepared jointly by the Ministry of Agriculture, Fisheries and Food, Department of Health, Scottish Executive, National Assembly for Wales and the Department of Health and Social Services in Northern Ireland in order to assist the reader in understanding the Act. They do not form part of the Act and have not been endorsed by Parliament.

2. The notes need to be read in conjunction with the Act. They are not, and are not meant to be, a comprehensive description of the Act. So where a section or part of a section does not seem to require any explanation or comment, none is given.

SUMMARY AND BACKGROUND

3. The Act gives effect to the proposals of the White Paper, 'The Food Standards Agency: A Force for Change' (Cm 3830). A draft Bill was published for consultation in the Command Paper 'The Food Standards Agency: Consultation on Draft Legislation' (Cm 4249) on 27 January 1999. The draft Bill was examined by the Food Standards Committee, whose report was published on 31 March 1999 (House of Commons Food Standards Committee Report of Session 1998–99 (HC 276) on the Food Standards Draft Bill).

4. The Act was introduced in the House of Commons on 10 June 1999 and received Royal Assent on 11 November 1999.

5. The main purpose of the Act is to establish the Food Standards Agency, provide it with functions and powers, and to transfer to it certain functions in relation to food safety and standards under other Acts. It sets out the Agency's main objective of protecting public health in relation to food and the functions that it will assume in pursuit of that aim, and gives the Agency the powers necessary to enable it to act in the consumer's interest at any stage in the food production and supply chain. The Act provides for the Agency's main organisational and accountability arrangements. In addition, it provides powers to establish a scheme for the notification of the results of tests for food-borne diseases.

OVERVIEW OF THE ACT

6. The main body of the Act is arranged as follows:

- *The Food Standards Agency* (sections 1–5), concerns the establishment of the Agency, its main objective and its main organisational arrangements including the establishment of advisory committees (more detailed provisions are contained in Schedules 1 and 2);
- *General functions in relation to food* (sections 6–8), confers on the Agency responsibility for developing food policy and advising Ministers and other public authorities, for advising consumers and other interested parties and for keeping abreast of developments relevant to its remit;
- *General functions in relation to animal feedingstuffs* (section 9) supplements the Agency's functions in relation to animal feed;
- *Observations with a view to acquiring information* (sections 10–11) gives the Agency functions in relation to surveillance and provides powers to enable it to carry them out;
- *Monitoring of enforcement action* (sections 12–16) gives the Agency a function of monitoring food and feedingstuffs law enforcement and provides powers to enable it to carry it out;
- *Other functions of the Agency* (sections 17–21) describes the Secretary of State and the devolved authorities' powers to delegate the making of emergency orders to the Agency, the Agency's power to publish its advice, its functions under other Acts and supplementary functions (detailed functions under the Food Safety Act 1990 and other primary legislation are provided for in Schedule 3);
- *General provisions relating to the functions of the Agency* (sections 22–25), concerns certain considerations which the Agency must observe in carrying out its functions; provides for directions by Ministers and the devolved authorities should the Agency fail to perform its duties, and allows for modification of enactments to allow disclosure of information to the Agency and publication by it;
- *Miscellaneous provisions* (sections 26–35), sets out the functions no longer to be exercised by the Minister of Agriculture, Fisheries and Food, and the Department of Agriculture for Northern Ireland and makes various provisions for consultation with other parts of Government or the devolved administrations on aspects of food safety. It also allows secondary legislation to apply to animal feedingstuffs provisions equivalent to those of the Food Safety Act 1990, and corresponding Northern Ireland legislation and makes provisions for the modification of the constitution of the Agency, in the light of experience with devolution, or in the event of Scotland or Northern Ireland exercising their right to withdraw from the Agency or any of its functions;
- *Final provisions* (sections 36–43), defines various terms used in the Act, makes provision in relation to the financing of the Agency (accounts and audit provisions are in Schedule 4), applies the provisions of the Act to the Crown and amends or repeals legislation as a consequence of the main provisions of the Act (details are set out in the associated Schedules 5 and 6).

[The Commentary on the Sections in the Explanatory Notes are reproduced here after each relevant section of the Act.]

The Food Standards Agency

1 The Food Standards Agency

(1) There shall be a body to be called the Food Standards Agency or, in Welsh, yr Asiantaeth Safonau Bwyd (referred to in this Act as 'the Agency') for the purpose of carrying out the functions conferred on it by or under this Act.

(2) The main objective of the Agency in carrying out its functions is to protect public health from risks which may arise in connection with the consumption of food (including risks caused by the way in which it is produced or supplied) and otherwise to protect the interests of consumers in relation to food.

(3) The functions of the Agency are performed on behalf of the Crown.

This section establishes the Food Standards Agency and sets its main objective. More details concerning the constitution of the Agency can be found in Schedule 1.

Subsection (1) establishes the Agency for the purpose of carrying out the functions that are provided for in the rest of the Act. These functions provide the framework in which the Agency will operate. The way in which they will be carried out is limited by the requirements that are set down in the subsequent provisions, in particular sections 22 and 23. These provide for the Agency to carry out its functions in accordance with a statement of objectives and practices that has been approved by the appropriate authorities (as described in section 2 below). Section 23 furthermore requires that the Agency must act in a proportionate manner by taking account of risks, costs and benefits, as well as of any advice it receives from its advisory committees.

Subsection (2) defines the main objective of the Agency. Food safety is central to this objective, but the subsection also embraces the Agency's role in relation to nutrition and diet, and protecting the wider food-related interests of consumers – sometimes referred to as food standards. This would cover in particular such matters as the labelling and composition of food (section 36(2) clarifies that the expression 'interests of consumers in relation to food', used in section 1 and at various places in the Act, includes matters related to the labelling, marking, presenting or advertising of food, and the descriptions which may be applied to food). This subsection does not imply that the Agency has any wider powers or functions than those provided by the rest of the Act, but sets the context in which the Agency's powers must be used.

Subsection (3) establishes the Agency as a Crown body. It will be a non-Ministerial government department.

---

2 Appointment of members etc

(1) The Agency shall consist of a chairman and deputy chairman and not less than eight or more than twelve members, of whom—

  (a) one member shall be appointed by the National Assembly for Wales;
  (b) two members shall be appointed by the Scottish Ministers;
  (c) one member shall be appointed by the Department of Health and Social Services for Northern Ireland; and
  (d) the others shall be appointed by the Secretary of State.

(2) The chairman and deputy chairman shall be appointed by the appropriate authorities acting jointly and, before appointing a person as one of the other members of the Agency the authority making the appointment shall consult the other appropriate authorities.

(3) Before appointing a person as chairman, deputy chairman or member of the Agency, the authorities or authority making the appointment shall—

(a)   have regard to the desirability of securing that a variety of skills and experience is available among the members of the Agency (including experience in matters related to food safety or other interests of consumers in relation to food); and

(b)   consider whether any person it is proposed to appoint has any financial or other interest which is likely to prejudice the exercise of his duties.

(4) Schedule 1 (constitution etc of the Agency) has effect.

This deals with the membership of the Agency and the procedures for appointing people to serve.

Subsection (1) provides for the Agency to have a Chairman, Deputy Chairman and 8–12 other members, of whom one will be appointed by the National Assembly for Wales, two by the Scottish Ministers, and one by the Department of Health and Social Services for Northern Ireland. The rest will be appointed by the Secretary of State for Health.

Subsection (2) specifies that the appointment of the Chairman and Deputy Chairman will be made jointly by the Secretary of State and his counterparts in the 'appropriate authorities' for Scotland, Wales and Northern Ireland. The 'appropriate authorities' are defined in section 36 of the Act and are:

- the Secretary of State: in practice, for the purposes of the Food Standards Agency, this will be the Secretary of State for Health;
- in Scotland, the Scottish Ministers: this is a collective term for the members of the Scottish Executive of the devolved administration. Again, for practical purposes, the Scottish Minister with responsibility for health is expected to take the lead:
- in Wales, the National Assembly for Wales. Under the Government of Wales Act 1998, powers are vested in the National Assembly as a whole. In practice, those with responsibility for health matters would be expected to lead on the Agency in Wales;
- in Northern Ireland, the Department of Health and Social Services: in Northern Ireland, powers are vested in departments, acting on behalf of Ministers, or after the Northern Ireland Act 1998 is brought into force, the Northern Ireland Executive.

Subsection (2) requires the authorities to consult each other before making appointments.

Subsection (3) provides for the authorities, in making appointments, to try to secure a reasonable balance of relevant skills and experience in the Agency's membership. The members will not be appointed to be representative of any particular interest or sector. *Subsection (3)(b)* requires the appropriate authorities to consider whether the person's financial or other interests – for example shares in a major food manufacturer – are likely to compromise his or her position as a member of the Agency. This does not necessarily mean that any such interests will automatically disqualify a person from appointment as a member. Under paragraph 9 of Schedule 1, the Agency will be obliged to establish and publish a register of the private interests of members: although the Act does not specifically require it, the Agency's procedural rules would be expected to prevent a member with an interest in a particular matter from taking part in discussions on it.

---

3   Appointment of chief executive and directors

(1) A chief executive shall be appointed for the Agency.

(2) The chief executive shall be responsible for (among other things) securing that the activities of the Agency are carried out efficiently and effectively.

(3) The first appointment under subsection (1) shall be made by the appropriate authorities acting jointly; and subsequent appointments shall be made by the Agency, subject to the approval of each of those authorities.

(4) Directors shall be appointed for Wales, for Scotland and for Northern Ireland, each of whom shall be responsible under the chief executive for (among other things) securing that the activities of the Agency in Wales, Scotland or Northern Ireland (as the case may be) are carried out efficiently and effectively.

(5) The first appointment under subsection (4) for Wales, for Scotland and for Northern Ireland shall be made by the appropriate authority for that part of the United Kingdom; and subsequent appointments shall be made by the Agency, subject to the approval of that authority.

(6) The chief executive and the directors appointed under subsection (4) shall hold and vacate office in accordance with the terms of their appointments.

Subsection (2) gives the Agency's Chief Executive particular responsibility to ensure that the Agency is run efficiently and effectively. He or she will be responsible to the Agency's members for the day to day running of the Agency itself and will also be the Agency's accounting officer (the officer responsible to Parliament for the way in which the Agency spends its money). Under *subsection (3)* the first Chief Executive is to be appointed jointly by the appropriate authorities, because the members of the Agency are unlikely all to be appointed when this appointment is made. Subsequent appointments will be a matter for the Agency, with the approval of the appropriate authorities.

The separate directors for Scotland, Wales and Northern Ireland are appointed under *subsection (4)*. Each will head an executive body with responsibility for the operation of the Agency in the relevant part of the UK and will report to the Chief Executive. By analogy with the Chief Executive, the first appointment of the directors under *subsection (5)* will be made by the appropriate authority in Scotland, Wales or Northern Ireland, with subsequent appointments by the Agency with the authority's approval.

4   Annual and other reports

(1) The Agency shall prepare a report on its activities and performance during each financial year.

(2) The Agency shall, as soon as possible after the end of each financial year, lay its report for that year before Parliament, the National Assembly for Wales, the Scottish Parliament and the Northern Ireland Assembly.

(3) The Agency may from time to time lay other reports before any of those bodies.

The Agency will be required to lay an annual report on its activities and performance before Parliament and before the Scottish Parliament, the National Assembly for Wales and the Northern Ireland Assembly. It may also make other reports to them.

5   Advisory committees

(1) There shall be established an advisory committee for Wales, an advisory committee for Scotland and an advisory committee for Northern Ireland for the purpose of giving advice or information to the Agency about matters connected with its functions (including in particular matters affecting or otherwise relating to Wales, Scotland or Northern Ireland, as the case may be).

(2) The Secretary of State may, after consulting the Agency, direct that an advisory committee for, or for any region of, England shall be established for the purpose of giving advice or information to the Agency about matters connected with its functions (including in particular matters affecting or otherwise relating to the area for which the committee is established).

(3) The Agency may, after consulting the appropriate authorities, establish other advisory committees for the purpose of giving advice or information to the Agency about matters connected with its functions.

(4) Schedule 2 (which contains supplementary provisions about advisory committees) has effect.

The purpose of the committees established by *subsection (1)* of this section will be to provide a focus for Scottish, Welsh and Northern Ireland interests in food safety and standards. They will be set up with a defined remit that will reflect the responsibilities of the UK Agency. Their membership will reflect the range of interests on food safety and standards issues in Scotland, Wales and Northern Ireland. The Agency is obliged under section 23 to take their advice into account when carrying out its functions or advising Ministers or the appropriate authorities.

Subsection (2) enables the Secretary of State to establish an advisory committee for England, or English regions, with a similar purpose to those for Scotland, Wales and Northern Ireland. This provision has been included in case the Secretary of State feels such comittees may be needed in future – in particular for the English regions. There is no current intention to establish such committees.

Subsection (3) empowers the Agency to establish other specialist advisory committees if it so wishes. Further details on advisory committees, including provisions for the transfer of existing committees to the Agency and the creation of joint committees, are contained in Schedule 2.

General functions in relation to food

6   Development of food policy and provision of advice, etc to public authorities

(1) The Agency has the function of—

(a)   developing policies (or assisting in the development by any public authority of policies) relating to matters connected with food safety or other interests of consumers in relation to food; and

(b)   providing advice, information or assistance in respect of such matters to any public authority.

(2) A Minister of the Crown or government department, the National Assembly for Wales, the Scottish Ministers or a Northern Ireland Department may request the Agency to exercise its powers under this section in relation to any matter.

(3) It is the duty of the Agency, so far as is reasonably practicable, to comply with any such request.

This section gives the Agency the function of providing advice, information and assistance, including on matters relating to the development of policy on food safety and related matters, to any public authority (which would include, for example, local authorities or agencies of government). So far as Ministers, government departments and their equivalents in the devolved authorities are concerned, the Agency will have a duty to provide such advice, information and assistance on request, unless it is not reasonably practicable for it to do so (for example, because the resource costs of providing any particular item of information would be disproportionate).

The advice, information and assistance which the Agency has the function of providing could for example include making recommendations to Ministers on the need for new primary legislation or proposing and drafting secondary legislation in order to improve food safety and standards. Another important aspect of the Agency's function of assisting Ministers will be to represent the UK at official level in relevant EU and other international forums.

It is intended that the Agency as a UK body will be the primary source of policy advice in relation to food safety and associated areas to the Government as a whole, and to the devolved authorities. Most of the relevant expertise available to the Government and those authorities in the area of food safety and standards will therefore reside with the Agency and will not be duplicated within other government departments. The Agency will also be able to advise on the development of policies by other government departments on matters that are relevant to the Agency's own area of responsibility, for example advice to the Minister of Agriculture, Fisheries and Food on activities on the farm which may have an impact on food hygiene; or on relevant consumer protection matters to the Department of Trade and Industry.

7 Provision of advice, information and assistance to other persons

(1) The Agency has the function of—

    (a) providing advice and information to the general public (or any section of the public) in respect of matters connected with food safety or other interests of consumers in relation to food;

    (b) providing advice, information or assistance in respect of such matters to any person who is not a public authority.

(2) The function under subsection (1)(a) shall be carried out (without prejudice to any other relevant objectives) with a view to ensuring that members of the public are kept adequately informed about and advised in respect of matters which the Agency considers significantly affect their capacity to make informed decisions about food.

This section deals with the provision of advice, information and assistance to the general public or to individuals and bodies who are not public authorities.

The section allows for information and advice to be given to either the general public as a whole or to individuals or particular sections of it such as groups representative of food industry sectors. Among other things, the Agency will be able, for example, to:

- run information campaigns on issues of current interest or importance;
- publish scientific data arising from research or surveillance and advise on its interpretation;
- publish information on enforcement activities, such as the existing BSE/meat enforcement publications;
- produce leaflets on food hygiene, labelling etc.;
- run a consumer helpline;
- issue advice for people with food allergies;
- pass on information about developments in food science to the public as a whole and to particular groups such as food producers;
- produce guidance on food safety matters for the food industry;
- issue food hazard warnings, alerting the public to particular problems.

8 Acquisition and review of information

(1) The Agency has the function of obtaining, compiling and keeping under review information about matters connected with food safety and other interests of consumers in relation to food.

(2) That function includes (among other things)—

    (a) monitoring developments in science, technology and other fields of knowledge relating to the matters mentioned in subsection (1);

    (b) carrying out, commissioning or co-ordinating research on those matters.

(3) That function shall (without prejudice to any other relevant objectives) be carried out with a view to ensuring that the Agency has sufficient information to enable it to take informed decisions and to carry out its other functions effectively.

This section concerns the Agency's function of keeping itself properly informed in order to carry out its other functions.

Under *Subsection (2)(a)*, the Agency will keep abreast of new developments in discharging this general function.

Subsection (2)(b) provides for the Agency to develop its scientific understanding by undertaking, commissioning or coordinating research. Current research and development projects within the remit of the Agency funded by the

Ministry of Agriculture, Fisheries and Food and any relevant research funded by other departments (such as the Department of Health) will be transferred to the Agency at the outset.

Subsection (3) makes it clear that the purpose of the Agency's information-gathering activities, including the carrying out of observations (see section 10 below), is to enable it to carry out its general functions in an informed and effective way.

General functions in relation to animal feedingstuffs

9   General functions in relation to animal feedingstuffs

(1) The Agency has the same general functions in relation to matters connected with the safety of animal feedingstuffs and other interests of users of animal feedingstuffs as it has under sections 6(1), 7(1) and 8 in relation to matters connected with food safety and other interests of consumers in relation to food.

(2) Section 6(2) and (3) apply in relation to the Agency's powers under this section corresponding to those under section 6(1).

(3) Section 7(2), in its application to the Agency's function under this section corresponding to that under section 7(1)(a), applies with the substitution, for the words 'members of the public' and 'food', of the words 'users of animal feedingstuffs' and 'animal feedingstuffs'.

(4) In this section 'Safety of animal feedingstuffs' means the safety of animal feedingstuffs in relation to risks to animal health which may arise in connection with their consumption.

This section provides that the Agency has the same functions of giving policy and other advice to public authorities, advice and information to the public and other bodies, and on the acquisition of information, in relation to animal feedingstuffs.

The Agency will have wide-ranging responsibilities in the area of animal feedingstuffs. These include, for example, EU controls governing the safety, composition and labelling of animal feeds. The main reason for giving the Agency responsibility in this area is because of the possible implications of animal feedingstuffs for the safety of human consumers eating meat and animal products. This is already encompassed by the Agency's main objective in section 1 and its advice and information functions in sections 6–8, which apply to food safety and other interests of consumers in relation to food. However, in carrying out its responsibilities on animal feed, the Agency will also incidentally deal with matters which are not directly about food safety or the interests of consumers of food. For example, most of the relevant EU and domestic provisions also apply to pet foods, and responsibility for these cannot readily be separated from responsibility for animal feeds. Similarly there are provisions which relate to protecting the interests of the purchasers of animal feeds, or ensuring that the safety or health of the animal itself is not damaged. Although these matters are secondary to the Agency's primary purpose in relation to human health, the Agency needs to be able to have the legal basis to undertake these functions and this section provides it.

Prior to this Act, feedingstuffs were regulated by means of regulations under the Food Safety Act 1990, the Agriculture Act 1970 and the European Communities Act 1972, and by Orders made under the Animal Health Act 1981. Under the Act, the Minister of Agriculture, Fisheries and Food will cease to have responsibility for regulations under the 1990 Act, but will remain responsible for the 1970 and 1981 Acts. Both the Secretary of State and the Minister of Agriculture, Fisheries and Food can make feed-related regulations under the European Communities Act 1972. The Agency will be able to give advice to both Ministers on the need for legislation under all these Acts as it sees appropriate. However, orders under the Animal Health Act in relation to feed are usually used to control feed borne diseases of animals, where MAFF's veterinary expertise is very important. Thus MAFF will retain the primary policy making role in relation to these. Arrangements will be put in place to ensure that MAFF and the Agency do not duplicate work in this area. MAFF and the Agency will co-operate closely to ensure that both bodies consult each other on feedingstuffs matters affecting human and animal health (see also section 28 in relation to cooperation on zoonoses).

Observations with a view to acquiring information

10   Power to carry out observations

(1) The Agency may, for the purpose of carrying out its function under section 8 or its corresponding function under section 9, carry out observations (or arrange with other persons for observations to be carried out on its behalf) with a view to obtaining information about—

(a) any aspect of the production or supply of food or food sources; or
(b) any aspect of the production, supply or use of animal feedingstuffs.

(2) Without prejudice to the generality of subsection (1), the information that may be sought through such observations includes information about—

(a) food premises, food businesses or commercial operations being carried out with respect to food, food sources or contact materials;
(b) agricultural premises, agricultural businesses or agricultural activities;
(c) premises, businesses or operations involved in fish farming; or
(d) premises, businesses or operations involved in the production, supply or use of animal feedingstuffs.

(3) In this section—

'agricultural activity' has the same meaning as in the Agriculture Act 1947 or, in Northern Ireland, the Agriculture Act (Northern Ireland) 1949;

'agricultural business' has the same meaning as in section 1 of the Farm Land and Rural Development Act 1988 or, in Northern Ireland, Article 3 of the Farm Business (Northern Ireland) Order 1988;

'agricultural premises' means any premises used for the purposes of an agricultural business; and

'fish farming' means the breeding, rearing or keeping of fish or shellfish (which includes any kind of crustacean or mollusc).

This section and section 11 set out specific powers that will help the Agency to fulfil its general function of obtaining and keeping under review any information relevant to its work. 'Observations' describes the gathering of information on food safety and related matters through undertaking surveillance programmes or by other appropriate means for this purpose. The Agency will, if necessary, be able to conduct such work at any point in the food production and supply chain and anywhere else where there might be implications for food safety and related matters. For example, the Agency will be able to undertake observations on farms.

The two sections give the Agency specific powers necessary to obtain information, either directly or through an authorised person acting on its behalf. These powers replace previous more limited powers contained in section 25 of the Food Safety Act 1990 and corresponding Northern Ireland legislation, which allow Ministers to make orders concerning the provision of information and the taking of samples of food, substances used in the preparation of food and contact materials. These new provisions expand the previous powers to allow the Agency to carry out its proposed role in monitoring activities at earlier stages of food production and without the need for further secondary legislation; to allow authorised persons to make observations; and to require disclosure of certain relevant records relating to employees.

Examples of the types of observations that the Agency might carry out are surveillance programmes to investigate the presence of pathogens that could carry risks for human health levels; or of a particular contaminant, such as lead, in certain types of foodstuffs; or surveys of hygiene practices in a certain type of food business.

It should be noted that the powers in these sections relate to the gathering of information of a general and representative nature and not to the investigation of individual complaints or failures for which the enforcement powers in the Food Safety Act 1990 and corresponding Northern Ireland legislation and other powers will continue to be used by enforcement authorities. Since the observations made under this section are not intended for enforcement purposes there is no requirement that these powers be used to gather evidence in accordance with the kind of safeguards contained in the Police and Criminal Evidence Act 1984, and thus any information obtained could not in general be used directly for the purposes of food law enforcement. Where apparent problems were identified in the course of a surveillance exercise, the information gathered would normally be passed to the relevant enforcement authorities who would then take a decision on the need for further investigation.

11 Power of entry for persons carrying out observations

(1) The Agency may authorise any individual (whether a member of its staff or otherwise) to exercise the powers specified in subsection (4) for the purpose of carrying out any observations under section 10 specified in the authorisation.

(2) No authorisation under this section shall be issued except in pursuance of a decision taken by the Agency itself or by a committee, sub-committee or member of the Agency acting on behalf of the Agency.

(3) An authorisation under this section shall be in writing and may be given subject to any limitations or conditions specified in the authorisation (including conditions relating to hygiene precautions to be taken while exercising powers in pursuance of the authorisation).

(4) An authorised person may, if it appears to him necessary to do so for the purpose of carrying out the observations specified in his authorisation—

   (a) enter any premises at any reasonable hour;
   (b) take samples of any articles or substances found on any premises;
   (c) take samples from any food source found on any premises;
   (d) inspect and copy any records found on any premises which relate to a business which is the subject of the observations (and, if they are kept in computerised form, require them to be made available in a legible form);
   (e) require any person carrying on such a business to provide him with such facilities, such records or information and such other assistance as he may reasonably request;

but in this subsection 'premises' does not include a private dwelling-house.

(5) An authorised person shall on request—

   (a) produce his authorisation before exercising any powers under subsection (4); and
   (b) provide a document identifying any sample taken, or documents copied, under those powers.

(6) The references in subsection (4)(d) and (e) to records include any records which—

   (a) relate to the health of any person who is or has been employed in the business concerned; and
   (b) were created for the purpose of assessing, or are kept for the purpose of recording, matters affecting his suitability for working in the production or supply of food or food sources (including any risks to public health which may arise if he comes into contact with any food or food source).

(7) If an authorised person who enters any premises by virtue of this section discloses to any person any information obtained on the premises with regard to any trade secret he is, unless the disclosure is made in the performance of his duty, guilty of an offence and liable on summary conviction to a fine not exceeding level 5 on the standard scale.

(8) A person who—

(a) intentionally obstructs a person exercising powers under subsection (4)(a), (b), (c) or (d);

(b) fails without reasonable excuse to comply with any requirement imposed under subsection (4)(e); or

(c) in purported compliance with such a requirement furnishes information which he knows to be false or misleading in any material particular or recklessly furnishes information which is false or misleading in any material particular;

is guilty of an offence and liable on summary conviction to a fine not exceeding level 5 on the standard scale.

(9) In this section 'authorised person' means a person authorised under this section.

Subsection (1) provides for observations to be undertaken on the Agency's behalf, by an authorised person, where the Agency is satisfied that they are qualified to do the work. The authorisation for powers of entry to be used must specify the nature of the observations to be carried out. *Subsection (2)* requires that the decision to grant any authorisation to exercise powers of entry must be taken by the Agency itself, or a committee, subcommittee or individual member, and not by members of the Agency's staff.

Subsections (3) to *(5)* describe the powers to enter premises, take samples and inspect records, and the conditions under which they must be exercised. The authorisation to exercise powers of entry may include limitations, including requiring any authorised person entering premises to follow any necessary food safety precautions. Samples may include samples from food sources which are defined in the Food Safety Act 1990 as any growing crop or live animal, bird or fish from which food is intended to be derived. Under subsection (5), the authorised person is required to provide a receipt on request for any sample taken or document copied.

Subsection (6) provides for access to health records of people employed in food production, but only where that information is relevant to food safety. For example, under certain of the food hygiene directives, employers are required to obtain medical certificates assessing their employees' suitability, on health grounds, to be employed in the handling of food, so as to ensure they do not constitute a general risk to public health. This provision would not, however, allow the Agency general access to an individual's personal health records.

Subsection (7) makes it an offence for any authorised individual to disclose any information he or she has obtained during the course of carrying out observations about any trade secret, other than in the course of his or her duty. This provision does not in any way restrict the provision of any information to the Agency, or affect the Agency's own powers to publish information. It deals with the kind of situation where an authorised person entering premises as part of a duty to carry out observations obtains commercially confidential information and then, acting in a private capacity, passes that information on, for example, to a commercial rival of the business. As such it parallels section 32(7) of the Food Safety Act 1990 and corresponding Northern Ireland legislation.

Subsection (8): this provision is similar to that contained in the Food Safety Act 1990 and corresponding Northern Ireland legislation. The current (November 1999) maximum value of a level 5 fine is £5,000.

Monitoring of enforcement action

12   Monitoring of enforcement action

(1) The Agency has the function of monitoring the performance of enforcement authorities in enforcing relevant legislation.

(2) That function includes, in particular, setting standards of performance (whether for enforcement authorities generally or for particular authorities) in relation to the enforcement of any relevant legislation.

(3) Each annual report of the Agency shall contain a report on its activities during the year in enforcing any relevant legislation for which it is the enforcement authority and its performance in respect of—

(a) any standards under subsection (2) that apply to those activities; and

(b) any objectives relating to those activities that are specified in the statement of objectives and practices under section 22.

(4) The Agency may make a report to any other enforcement authority on their performance in enforcing any relevant legislation; and such a report may include guidance as to action which the Agency considers would improve that performance.

(5) The Agency may direct an authority to which such a report has been made—

(a) to arrange for the publication in such manner as may be specified in the direction of, or of specified informtion relating to, the report; and

(b) within such period as may be so specified to notify the Agency of what action they have taken or propose to take in response to the report.

This section empowers the Agency to monitor, set standards for and audit the performance of enforcement authorities (which are defined in section 15) in carrying out food law enforcement.

Subsection (2) gives the Agency power to set standards against which to monitor performance. Normally, these would be set in respect of enforcement authorities generally, although the power extends to the setting of standards for individual authorities, should this be necessary.

Under *subsection (3)* the Agency must publish (as part of its annual report) information about its own performance as an enforcement authority corresponding to the information it would obtain about other authorities. At present, for the most part, this would relate to its role in enforcing the provisions of the various meat hygiene regulations through the Meat Hygiene Service (which will become part of the Agency) and in the enforcement of dairy hygiene regulations. The information published must include details on the Agency's performance in relation to any standards it has set to apply to its own enforcement activities which might, for example, be contained in a code of practice or equivalent; and any particular objectives it has set in its section 22 statement of objectives and practices. During consideration in the House of Lords, the Government gave a commitment that these would include objectives relating to the principles of better regulation.

The general publication of audit reports by the Agency is dealt with in section 19.

It is envisaged that a reasonable period of time would be provided for an enforcement authority to report back under *subsection (5)(b)* on its response to a report on its performance that was issued under *subsection (4)*. This would take account of the need for local authorities to consider their response in the course of their usual committee cycle.

13 Power to request information relating to enforcement action

(1) For the purpose of carrying out its function under section 12 in relation to any enforcement authority the Agency may require a person mentioned in subsection (2)—

(a) to provide the Agency with any information which it has reasonable cause to believe that person is able to give, or

(b) to make available to the Agency for inspection any records which it has reasonable cause to believe are held by that person or otherwise within his control (and, if they are kept in computerised form, to make them available in a legible form).

(2) A requirement under subsection (1) may be imposed on—

(a) the enforcement authority or any member, officer or employee of the authority, or

(b) a person subject to any duty under relevant legislation (being a duty enforceable by an enforcement authority) or any officer or employee of such a person.

(3) The Agency may copy any records made available to it in pursuance of a requirement under subsection (1)(b).

This section and section 14 provide the specific powers necessary for the Agency or an authorised person to carry out the monitoring role provided for in section 12. Section 41 of the Food Safety Act 1990 makes provision for Ministers to require reports and returns, but does not allow for audit visits or the provision of detailed returns, statistics and supporting documentation, nor does it provide for Ministers to set performance targets in relation to enforcement. Part IV of the Agriculture Act 1970 contains no powers comparable to section 41 of the Food Safety Act 1990. The majority of the powers contained in these sections are therefore new.

Subsection (1) empowers the Agency to require any information that may be relevant to its assessment of an enforcement authority's performance. As provided for in *subsection (2)*, this requirement would apply to anyone representing, working for or acting on behalf of that authority.

---

14   Power of entry for persons monitoring enforcement action

(1) The Agency may authorise any individual (whether a member of its staff or otherwise) to exercise the powers specified in subsection (4) for the purpose of carrying out its function under section 12 in relation to any enforcement authority.

(2) No authorisation under this section shall be issued except in pursuance of a decision taken by the Agency itself or by a committee, sub-committee or member of the Agency acting on behalf of the Agency.

(3) An authorisation under this section shall be in writing and may be given subject to any limitations or conditions specified in the authorisation (including conditions relating to hygienic precautions to be taken while exercising powers in pursuance of the authorisation).

(4) An authorised person may—

(a) enter any premises mentioned in subsection (5) at any reasonable hour in order to inspect the premises or anything which may be found on them;

(b) take samples of any articles or substances found on such premises;

(c) inspect and copy any records found on such premises (and, if they are kept in computerised form, require them to be made available in a legible form);

(d) require any person present on such premises to provide him with such facilities, such records or information and such other assitance as he may reasonably request.

(5) The premises which may be entered by an authorised person are—

(a) any premises occupied by the enforcement authority;

(b) any laboratory or similar premises at which work related to the enforcement of any relevant legislation has been carried out for the enforcement authority; and

(c) any other premises (not being a private dwelling-house) which the authorised person has reasonable cause to believe are premises in respect of which the enforcement powers of the enforcement authority are (or have been) exercisable.

(6) The power to enter premises conferred on an authorised person includes power to take with him any other person he may consider appropriate.

(7) An authorised person shall on request—

(a) produce his authorisation before exercising any powers under subsection (4); and

(b) provide a document identifying any sample taken, or documents copied, under those powers.

(8) If a person who enters any premises by virtue of this section discloses to any person any information obtained on the premises with regard to any trade secret he is, unless the disclosure is made in the performance of his duty, guilty of an offence and liable on summary conviction to a fine not exceeding level 5 on the standard scale.

(9) Where—

(a) the enforcement authority in relation to any provisions of the Food Safety Act 1990 (in this Act referred to as 'the 1990 Act') or orders or regulations made under it is (by virtue of section 6(3) or (4) of that Act) a Minister of the Crown, the National Assembly for Wales, the Scottish Ministers or the Agency, or

(b) the enforcement authority in relation to any provisions of the Food Safety (Northern Ireland) Order 1991 (in this Act referred to as 'the 1991 Order') or orders or regulations made under it is (by virtue of Article 26(1A), (1B), (2), (3) or (3A) of that Order) a Northern Ireland Department or the Agency,

this section applies to that authority (in relation to its performance in enforcing those provisions) with the omission of subsection (5)(a).

(10) In this section 'authorised person' means a person authorised under this section.

Subsection (1) provides for the Agency to authorise the use of powers of entry in connection with its enforcement monitoring function. Under *subsection (2)* the decision to grant any authorisation must be given by the Agency itself, or a committee or subcommittee or individual member, and not by the Agency's staff.

Subsection (3) provides that the authorisation may include limitations, including requiring any authorised person entering premises to follow any necessary food safety precautions. It is expected that in authorising powers of entry, the Agency will require that any reasonable food safety precautions required on the premises should be followed.

Subsection (4) provides an authorised person with powers to enter and inspect individual premises in order to carry out monitoring work. This gives access to records and data held by the enforcement authority, anyone acting on its behalf, or where enforcement powers are exercisable and also provides for the taking of samples.

Subsection (5) specifies the types of premises that may be entered under the previous subsection. Besides offices and other premises used by the enforcement authority, this would include any laboratories that provide it with services relevant to its enforcement activity (this would include both in-house and independent laboratories). The Agency would not be expected to publish details of the performance of the laboratories themselves; nor would its monitoring powers impinge on any service provided by the laboratories to private customers. The third category of premises subject to these powers covers any in which food law enforcement may be carried out (i.e. food shops, food manufacturers, slaughterhouses etc.).

Subsection (6) provides a power for an authorised person when entering premises to be accompanied by another person. This is needed, for example, to provide for an official of the European Commission engaged in a routine audit of member states' enforcement of the provisions of EC food law to accompany the Agency's authorised officer.

Subsection (7) requires that the authorised person must provide a receipt on request for any sample taken or document copied.

Subsection (8) provides for an offence for the same purpose as that described in section 11(7) above but also covering a person accompanying an authorised person under subsection (6).

Subsection (9) adapts the provisions of this section to monitoring of enforcement activity of the Agency itself or of Ministers or the devolved authorities (for example the enforcement of meat hygiene legislation). The power of entry to premises occupied by the enforcement authority is excluded as it would be unnecessary to give a power to the Agency to authorise a person to enter its own premises.

---

15   Meaning of 'enforcement authority' and related expressions

(1) In sections 12 to 14 'relevant legislation' means—

(a)   the provisions of the 1990 Act and regulations or orders made under it;

(b)   the provisions of the 1991 Order and regulations or orders made under it; and

(c)   the provisions of Part IV of the Agriculture Act 1970 and regulations made under that Part of that Act, so far as relating to matters connected with animal feedingstuffs.

(2) In those sections 'enforcement authority' means—

(a)   in the case of provisions of the 1990 Act or regulations or orders made under it, the authority by whom they are to be enforced (including a Minister of the Crown, the National Assembly for Wales, the Scottish Ministers or the Agency itself if, by virtue of section 6(3) or (4) of the 1990 Act, that authority is the enforcement authority in relation to those provisions);

(b)   in the case of provisions of the 1991 Order and regulations or orders made under it, the authority by whom they are to be enforced (including a Northern Ireland Department or the Agency itself if, by virtue of the Order, it is the enforcement authority in relation to those provisions); and

(c)   in the case of provisions of Part IV of the Agriculture Act 1970 (or regulations made under it), an authority mentioned in section 67 of that Act;

and 'enforcement', in relation to relevant legislation, includes the execution of any provisions of that legislation.

(3) Any reference in those sections (however expressed) to the performance of an enforcement authority in enforcing any relevant legislation includes a reference to the capacity of that authority to enforce it.

Subsection (1) defines the legislation covered by the enforcement monitoring powers.

Subsection (2) defines an enforcement authority for the purposes of the above provisions. The bodies responsible for enforcing or executing the provision of the Food Safety Act 1990 or legislation made under it are normally, unless otherwise specified, 'food authorities'. They are defined in the Act as normally being local authorities (metropolitan borough, district or county councils in England and Wales; island or district councils in Scotland) or, where appropriate, port health authorities. In some cases, by virtue of section 6(4) of the 1990 Act, Ministers themselves, or, following this Act, the Agency, may also be specified as enforcement authorities for particular regulations. Under the corresponding Northern Ireland legislation, the enforcement authorities are district councils or the Department of Agriculture. Under Part IV of the Agriculture Act 1970, 'enforcement authorities' are county, metropolitan district and London borough councils, and the Port of London Health Authority in England; and county and county borough councils in Wales.

---

16   Offences relating to sections 13 and 14

(1) A person who—

(a)   intentionally obstructs a person exercising powers under section 14(4)(a), (b) or (c);

(b)   fails without reasonable excuse to comply with any requirement imposed under section 13(1) or section 14(4)(d); or

(c) in purported compliance with such a requirement furnishes information which he knows to be false or misleading in any material particular or recklessly furnishes information which is false or misleading in any material particular;

is guilty of an offence.

(2) A person guilty of an offence under this section is liable on summary conviction to a fine not exceeding level 5 on the standard scale.

This section makes it an offence for anyone to obstruct the Agency's authorised officer from exercising power of entry or knowingly to provide false or misleading information or to withhold information required under sections 13 and 14. The current (November 1999) maximum value of a level 5 fine is £5,000.

Other functions of the Agency

17 Delegation of powers to make emergency orders

(1) Arrangements may be made between the Secretary of State and the Agency authorising the Agency to exercise on behalf of the Secretary of State the power to make orders under—

(a) section 1(1) of the Food and Environment Protection Act 1985 (emergency orders); and

(b) section 13(1) of the 1990 Act (emergency control orders).

(2) The authority given by any such arrangements is subject to any limitations and conditions provided for in the arrangements.

(3) Where by virtue of any such arrangements the Agency is authorised to exercise a power, anything done or omitted to be done by the Agency in the exercise or purported exercise of the power shall be treated as done or omitted by the Secretary of State.

(4) Nothing in any such arrangements prevents the Secretary of State exercising any power.

(5) This section applies with the necessary modifications—

(a) to any power mentioned in subsection (1) so far as it is exercisable by the National Assembly for Wales or the Scottish Ministers, and

(b) to the power of a Northern Ireland Department to make orders under section 1(1) of the Food and Environment Protection Act 1985 or Article 12(1) of the 1991 Order,

as it applies to a power exercisable by the Secretary of State.

Under sections 1 and 2 of the Food and Environment Protection Act 1985 and section 13 of the Food Safety Act 1990 the Secretary of State may make emergency orders in response to circumstances or incidents which pose a threat to public health in relation to food. The Secretary of State will retain these powers, and in addition the Agency may be empowered by him to make emergency orders itself on his behalf. This power does not give the Agency the ability to make legislation itself in other areas, and in practice it is envisaged that the Agency will only make orders in emergency situations where the Secretary of State is not available.

Subsection (3) makes it clear that it is the Secretary of State who is ultimately answerable for emergency legislation made by the Agency on his behalf, and that anything done by the Agency is in law done by the Secretary of State.

Responsibility for orders under the two Acts is devolved to the appropriate authorities in Scotland and Wales, and in Northern Ireland is exercised by departments under equivalent legislation. *Subsection (5)* provides these authorities with the power to delegate their powers to make emergency orders under the relevant legislation to the Agency within their own competence.

18   Functions under other enactments

(1) Schedule 3 (which contains provisions conferring functions under certain enactments on the Agency) has effect.

(2) Any amendment made by Schedule 3 which extends to Scotland is to be taken as a pre-commencement enactment for the purposes of the Scotland Act 1998.

This section introduces Schedule 3, concerning amendments to other enactments which confer functions on the Agency.

Much of the legislation which is amended by Schedule 3 has been devolved to Scotland. This means that many functions of Ministers of the Crown (i.e. the Secretary of State and Minister of Agriculture, Fisheries and Food) under the legislation have transferred to Scottish Ministers, and Parliament's role in relation to secondary legislation to the Scottish Parliament.

However, the provisions of the Scotland Act 1998, and orders made under it which give effect to the transfer, do not generally amend the text of Acts of Parliament to show what has been done. Thus when this Act amends Acts which have been subject to devolution, it does not attempt to alter the text of those Acts to reflect post-devolution responsibilities. Instead, the amendments are deemed to date from before the enactment of the Scotland Act, so that the provisions of that Act automatically transfer functions to the relevant parties in Scotland. This ensures that all the powers under the Scotland Act to make further provisions flowing from devolution are available.

19   Publication etc by the Agency of advice and information

(1) The Agency may, subject to the following provisions of this section, publish in such manner as it thinks fit—

  (a) any advice given under section 6, 7 or 9 (including advice given in pursuance of a request under section 6(2));
  (b) any information obtained through observations under section 10 or monitoring under section 12; and
  (c) any other information in its possession (whatever its source).

(2) The exercise of that power is subject to the requirements of the Data Protection Act 1998.

(3) That power may not be exercised if the publication by the Agency of the advice or information in question—

  (a) is prohibited by an enactment;
  (b) is incompatible with any Community obligation; or
  (c) would constitute or be punishable as a contempt of court.

(4) Before deciding to exercise that power, the Agency must consider whether the public interest in the publication of the advice or information in question is outweighed by any considerations of confidentiality attaching to it.

(5) Where the advice or information relates to the performance of enforcement authorities, or particular enforcement authorities, in enforcing relevant legislation, subsection (4) applies only so far as the advice or information relates to a person other than—

(a) an enforcement authority, or

(b) a member, officer or employee of an enforcement authority acting in his capacity as such.

(6) Expressions used in subsection (5) and defined in section 15 have the same meaning as in that section.

(7) Except as mentioned above, the power under subsection (1) is exercisable free from any prohibition on publication that would apply apart from this section.

(8) In this section 'enactment' means an enactment contained in, or in subordinate legislation made under, any Act, Act of the Scottish Parliament or Northern Ireland legislation.

(9) The Agency may also disclose to another public authority any advice or information mentioned in subsection (1); and the other provisions of this section apply in relation to disclosure under this subsection as they apply in relation to publication under that subsection.

This section empowers the Agency to publish advice given by it in accordance with its general functions under sections 6 (development of food policy and provision of advice, etc. to public authorities) and 7 (provision of advice, information and assistance to other persons) or information obtained by it as a result of its observations or enforcement monitoring (sections 10 and 12). It also enables the Agency to publish any other information it holds.

The Agency's express ability to publish any of its advice to Ministers will be an important factor in its influence and independence: although Ministers would not be obliged to accept the Agency's advice, they would normally be expected to explain their reasons for not doing so.

It is envisaged that the Agency will normally wish to publish much of its advice and information. There are however certain limited circumstances in which publication would be inappropriate. For example, the provisions of the Data Protection Act 1998 will continue to apply in relation to personal information (*subsection (2)*). *Subsection (3)* also makes clear that the Agency's power to publish information does not automatically override prohibitions on publication in existing legislation or EU obligations that prohibit the publication of certain kinds of information. Section 25 nevertheless empowers the Secretary of State and the devolved authorities to make orders relaxing or lifting statutory prohibitions where these prevent the Agency from carrying out its functions effectively or from publishing information that is clearly in the public interest.

Subsection (4) provides that in deciding to publish any advice or information, the Agency will first have to consider whether the public interest in disclosure (for example, in terms of promoting openness or in making people aware of health risks) is outweighed by confidentiality considerations (such as personal privacy or commercial confidence).

Subsection (5) provides that the duty to take account of any consideration of confidentiality under *subsection (4)* does not apply to information relating to the performance of enforcement authorities or people acting on behalf of enforcement authorities. However, in respect of information on, for example, the activities of a business that was obtained by the Agency while monitoring a local authority's enforcement work, the test in subsection (4) would apply.

Subsection (7) makes clear that the Agency's power to publish is limited only by those duties and considerations that are set down in subsections (2), (3) and (4).

Subsection (9) provides for the Agency to disclose information to another public authority, subject to the same considerations as set out in this section. Therefore, for example, the Agency could pass on confidential information to enforcement authorities to assist them in carrying out their enforcement functions.

---

20 Power to issue guidance on control of food-borne diseases

(1) The Agency may issue general guidance to local authorities or other public authorities on matters connected with the management of outbreaks or suspected outbreaks of food-borne disease.

(2) Guidance issued under this section must identify the authority or authorities to which it is addressed.

(3) The Agency shall publish any guidance issued under this section in such manner as it thinks fit.

(4) Any authority to whom guidance under this section is issued shall have regard to the guidance in carrying out any functions to which the guidance relates.

(5) In this section 'food-borne disease' means a disease of humans which is capable of being caused by the consumption of infected or otherwise contaminated food.

(6) This section has effect without prejudice to any other powers of the Agency.

This section expands on the Agency's general function to give advice, information and assistance to provide it with the specific function of providing guidance to local authorities and other public authorities, including health authorities, on the management and control of outbreaks of food-borne illness (for example, salmonella, E.coli 0157, or campylobacter). Such guidance might, for example, include guidance on tracing the food-related source of any outbreak, or on the speed with which action needs to be taken to limit the spread of food poisoning.

---

21 Supplementary powers

(1) The Agency has power to do anything which is calculated to facilitate, or is conducive or incidental to, the exercise of its functions.

(2) Without prejudice to the generality of subsection (1), that power includes power—

    (a) to carry on educational or training activities;
    (b) to give financial or other support to activities carried on by others;
    (c) to acquire or dispose of any property or rights;
    (d) to institute criminal proceedings in England and Wales and in Northern Ireland.

(3) The Agency may make charges for facilities or services provided by it at the request of any person.

This section gives the Agency power to take action which will help it to discharge its functions (subject to other provisions in the Act which constrain the manner in which the Agency may act). This section, although very general, does not give the Agency any power to act outside the area of its functions.

Subsection (2) makes clear that the Agency's powers include the ability to provide education or training. Specific reference is also made to the provision of financial support, the acquisition or disposal of property and the institution of criminal proceedings (in England, Wales and Northern Ireland — prosecutions in Scotland are the sole responsibility of the Procurator Fiscal). Other relevant action might include entering into contracts.

Subsection (3) allows the Agency to charge for any facilities or services it provides at the request of any person. Such charges would be made in accordance with the usual Government guidance on fees and charges.

General provisions relating to the functions of the Agency

22 Statement of general objectives and practices

(1) The Agency shall prepare and publish a statement of general objectives it intends to pursue, and general practices it intends to adopt, in carrying out its functions.

(2) The statement shall include the following among the Agency's general objectives, namely—

(a) securing that its activities are the subject of consultation with, or with representatives of, those affected and, where appropriate, with members of the public;

(b) promoting links with any of the following authorities with responsibilities affecting food safety or other interests of consumers in relation to food, namely—

    (i) government departments, local authorities and other public authorities;

    (ii) the National Assembly for Wales (and its staff) and Assembly Secretaries, the Scottish Administration and Northern Ireland Departments;

with a view to securing that the Agency is consulted informally from time to time about the general manner in which any such responsibilities are discharged;

(c) securing that records of its decisions, and the information on which they are based, are kept and made available with a view to enabling members of the public to make informed judgments about the way in which it is carrying out its functions,

and any other objectives (which may include more specific objectives relating to anything mentioned in paragraphs (a) to (c)) which are notified to the Agency by the appropriate authorities acting jointly.

(3) Nothing in subsection (2) prevents the inclusion in the statement of more specific objectives relating to anything mentioned in that subsection.

(4) The statement shall be submitted in draft to the appropriate authorities for their approval before it is published.

(5) The appropriate authorities acting jointly may approve the draft statement submitted to them with or without modifications (but they must consult the Agency before making any modifications).

(6) As soon as practicable after a statement is approved under subsection (5), the Agency shall—

(a) lay a copy of the statement as so approved before Parliament, the National Assembly for Wales, the Scottish Parliament and the Northern Ireland Assembly; and

(b) publish that statement in such manner as the appropriate authorities acting jointly may approve.

(7) The first statement under this section shall be submitted to the appropriate authorities within the period of three months beginning with the date of the first meeting of the Agency.

(8) The Agency may revise its current statement under this section; and subsections (2) to (6) apply to a revised statement as they apply to the first statement.

This section requires the Agency to prepare and publish a statement of its general objectives and practices. The statement must be approved by the appropriate authorities. The statement will be formulated within the general framework of the Agency's main objective, in section 1(2).

Subsection (2) specifies that, among any other general objectives it wishes to include in the statement, the Agency must address three in particular. These relate to

- consulting with interested parties on the Agency's activities,
- facilitating proper consultation between the Agency and other Departments of Government, local authorities and other public authorities on matters of mutual interest, and
- ensuring that the Agency's activities and decisions are open and transparent to the public.

It also provides for the appropriate authorities acting jointly to ask for the inclusion of particular objectives in the Statement. *Subsections (4), (5)* and *(6)* require that the statement should be approved by the Secretary of State and the devolved authorities, acting jointly, and published. The Secretary of State and the other appropriate authorities may amend the draft proposed by the Agency, but must consult the Agency before doing so. The final version of the approved statement must be laid before Parliament, the National Assembly for Wales and the Northern Ireland Assembly.

---

23   Consideration of objectives, risks, costs and benefits, etc

(1) In carrying out its functions the Agency shall pay due regard to the statement of objectives and practices under section 22.

(2) The Agency, in considering whether or not to exercise any power, or the manner in which to exercise any power, shall take into account (among other things)—

   (a)   the nature and magnitude of any risks to public health, or other risks, which are relevant to the decision (including any uncertainty as to the adequacy or reliability of the available information);

   (b)   the likely costs and benefits of the exercise or non-exercise of the power or its exercise in any manner which the Agency is considering; and

   (c)   any relevant advice or information given to it by an advisory committee (whether or not given at the Agency's request).

(3) The duty under subsection (2)—

   (a)   does not apply to the extent that it is unreasonable or impracticable for it to do so in view of the nature or purpose of the power or in the circumstances of the particular case; and

   (b)   does not affect the obligation of the Agency to discharge any other duties imposed on it.

This section requires the Agency, in carrying out its functions, to have due regard to its statement of general objectives and practices (section 22) and take account of relevant advice from advisory committees and certain other considerations, as follows.

Subsection (2) requires the Agency to take account in its decision-making process of:

   a)   the nature and magnitude of risks which the action under consideration is designed to address. Risk to health is highlighted as of particular importance but other risks in relation to consumer protection (for example where labelling may mislead consumers) may also be relevant. The Agency is also required to take account of any uncertainty in the evidence. For example, where it is taking decisions in relation to a risk which is potentially very serious, but about which there is very little evidence, the Agency is likely to want to take a precautionary approach; and

   b)   the likely costs and benefits associated with the course of action under consideration. This would mean that the Agency must balance obvious compliance costs, as well as matters such as restriction of consumer choice, against the benefits of reduced risk to health etc. arising from any action.

Subsection (3) provides that the duty under the section does not apply where it is unreasonable or impracticable. For example, some of the Agency's actions may raise no concerns about risk, or an analysis of costs and benefits may not be appropriate. Decisions on appointments would be examples of this kind.

---

24   Directions relating to breach of duty or to international obligations

(1) If it appears to the Secretary of State that there has been a serious failure by the Agency—

   (a)   to comply with section 23(1) or (2), or

(b) to perform any other duty which he considers should have been performed by it,

he may give the Agency such directions as he may consider appropriate for remedying that failure.

(2) The power under subsection (1) may also be exercised—

(a) so far as it is exercisable in relation to Wales, by the National Assembly for Wales;
(b) by the Scottish Ministers (in so far as it is exercisable by them within devolved competence or by virtue of an Order in Council made under section 63 of the Scotland Act 1998); and
(c) so far as it is exercisable in relation to Northern Ireland, by the Department of Health and Social Services for Northern Ireland.

(3) Directions under subsection (1) must include a statement summarising the reasons for giving them.

(4) The Secretary of State may give the Agency such directions as he considers appropriate for the implementation of—

(a) any obligations of the United Kingdom under the Community Treaties, or
(b) any international agreement to which the United Kingdom is a party.

(5) The power under subsection (4) may also be exercised—

(a) by the National Assembly for Wales (in relation to implementation for which it is responsible);
(b) by the Scottish Ministers (in relation to implementation within devolved competence or for which they have responsibility by virtue of an Order in Council under section 63 of the Scotland Act 1998); and
(c) by the Department of Health and Social Services for Northern Ireland (in relation to implementation for which a Northern Ireland Department is responsible).

(6) An authority proposing to give directions under this section shall consult the Agency and the other appropriate authorities before doing so.

(7) If the Agency fails to comply with any directions under this section, the authority giving the directions may give effect to them (and for that purpose may exercise any power of the Agency).

(8) If the Agency fails to comply with directions under subsection (1), the Secretary of State may, with the agreement of the other appropriate authorities, remove all the members of the Agency from office (and, until new appointments are made, may carry out the Agency's functions himself or appoint any other person or persons to do so).

(9) Any directions given under this section shall be published in such manner as the authority giving them considers appropriate for the purpose of bringing the matters to which they relate to the attention of persons likely to be affected by them.

(10) In this section 'devolved competence' has the same meaning as in the Scotland Act 1998.

This section permits the Secretary of State (*subsection (1)*) to give the Agency directions in cases where it appears to him that the Agency has failed to fulfil the duty to comply with its statement of objectives and practices, take account of the advice of advisory committees, or consider risks, costs and benefits; or where it has failed in any other duty that he considers it should have performed. The power of direction relates only to serious failures by the Agency.

Subsection (2) gives similar powers of direction to the devolved authorities to the extent that it is within their devolved competence and to the Northern Ireland Department. This means that they will generally be able to direct in relation to the Agency's activities in Scotland, Wales and Northern Ireland, as appropriate.

Subsection (3) provides that any direction given in accordance with subsection (1) must contain a statement summarising the reasons for giving the direction.

Subsection (4) allows the Secretary of State to give the Agency directions to do anything the UK is obliged to do under EU or international law. These are reserve powers, for use if the Agency has not already taken steps to fulfil the UK's obligations.

This power to issue directions is also vested in the devolved authorities or Northern Ireland department (see *subsection (5)*) where the directions relate to the implementation of EU or other international obligations which is the responsiblity of that authority (in general, this will be the case for matters within devolved competence).

Subsection (6) requires that an authority proposing to give directions must consult the Agency and the other appropriate authorities before doing so.

If the Agency fails to follow directions given under subsection (1), the Secretary of State or the other appropriate authority may give effect to them, or the Secretary of State may take the steps outlined in *subsection (8)* with the agreement of the other appropriate authorities. Such powers, however, would only be used in the last resort and where normal processes of dialogue had failed to secure the necessary changes.

25   Power to modify enactments about disclosure of information

(1) If it appears to the Secretary of State that an enactment prohibits the disclosure of any information and is capable of having either of the efforts mentioned in subsection (5) he may by order make provision for the purpose of removing or relaxing the prohibition so far as it is capable of having that effect.

(2) If it appears to the Scottish Ministers that an enactment prohibits the disclosure of any information and is capable of having either of the effects mentioned in subsection (5) the Scottish Ministers may by order make provision for the purpose of removing or relaxing the prohibition so far as it is capable of having that effect.

(3) The power under subsection (2) may not be exercised to make provision which would not be within the legislative competence of the Scottish Parliament.

(4) If it appears to the First Minister and deputy First Minister acting jointly that any enactment dealing with transferred matters (within the meaning of section 4(1) of the Northern Ireland Act 1998) prohibits the disclosure of any information and is capable of having either of the effects mentioned in subsection (5) they may by order make provision for the purpose of removing or relaxing the prohibition so far as it is capable of having that effect.

(5) The effects mentioned in subsections (1), (2) and (4) are that the enactment in question—

  (a) prevents the disclosure to the Agency of information that would facilitate the carrying out of the Agency's functions; or
  (b) prevents the publication by the Agency of information in circumstances where the power under section 19 would otherwise be exercisable.

(6) An order under this section may—

  (a) make provision as to circumstances in which information which is subject to the prohibition in question may, or may not, be disclosed to the Agency or, as the case may be, published by the Agency; and

(b)   if it makes provision enabling the disclosure of information to the Agency, make provision restricting the purposes for which such information may be used (including restrictions on the subsequent disclosure of the information by the Agency).

(7)   This section applies in relation to a rule of law as it applies in relation to an enactment, but with the omission of—

(a)   subsection (5)(b) and any reference to the effect mentioned in subsection (5)(b); and
(b)   in subsection (6)(a), the words from 'or, as' to the end.

(8)   In this section 'enactment' means an enactment contained in any Act (other than this Act) or Northern Ireland legislation passed or made before or in the same Session as this Act.

This section enables the Secretary of State to make orders for the purpose of relaxing or overriding any prohibitions on disclosure of information contained in other legislation that would otherwise prevent the Agency from obtaining or publishing information in carrying out its functions under the Act. While section 19 requires the Agency to observe statutory bars on disclosure in exercising its power to publish, this section provides a means for dealing with those that would unnecessarily limit the Agency's ability to carry out its functions effectively. Some specific bars to disclosure are already dealt with directly in this Act (for example, by over-riding the limitation on disclosure of information about veterinary medicines in the Medicines Act 1968). This section provides the power to respond to any further barriers to disclosure identified in the light of experience.

Subsection (1) provides the basic order-making power.

A parallel enabling power exercisable by Scottish Ministers is provided in *subsection (2)*. *Subsection (3)* prevents Scottish Ministers from exercising their parallel powers in relation to legislation that lies outside their devolved competence. *Subsection (4)* makes similar provision for Northern Ireland.

Subsection (5) specifies the circumstances in which the enabling powers may be used to modify legislation i.e. where the legislation prevents the disclosure of information relevant to the Agency's functions, or prevent the Agency from publishing some information which would otherwise be published in accordance with section 19.

Subsection (7) applies this section (with appropriate modifications) to allow the removal or modification of common law rules.

Miscellaneous provisions

26 Statutory functions ceasing to be exercisable by Minister of Agriculture, Fisheries and Food and Department of Agriculture for Northern Ireland

(1)   The functions of the Minister of Agriculture, Fisheries and Food under—

(a)   Part I of the Food and Environment Protection Act 1985;
(b)   the 1990 Act; and
(c)   the Radioactive Substances Act 1993,

shall cease to be exercisable by that Minister.

(2)   The functions of the Department of Agriculture for Northern Ireland under—

(a)   Part I of the Food and Environment Protection Act 1985; and
(b)   Part II of the 1991 Order (except Article 8(7), 10(5) to (7), 11(5) to (10), 18(1), 22 and 25(2)(e) and Schedule 1),

shall cease to be exercisable by that Department.

(3) Subsections (1) and (2) do not affect enforcement functions under directions or subordinate legislation under the enactments mentioned in those subsections (or any power under those enactments to confer such functions in directions or subordinate legislation).

Under this Act, the Minister of Agriculture, Fisheries and Food will cease to have any statutory functions in relation to most matters within the Agency's remit.

This section removes that Minister's statutory responsibilities in relation to emergencies which are likely to create a hazard to human health through the contamination of food stuffs (under Part I of the Food and Environment Protection Act 1985); food safety and standards (under the Food Safety Act 1990); and radioactive substances and waste (under the Radioactive Substances Act 1993). Similar provision is made for Northern Ireland in relation to certain functions of the Department of Agriculture.

The detailed transfer of responsibilities to the Secretary of State for Health and devolved authorities and/or the Agency is dealt with in Schedules 3 and 5.

---

27 Notification of tests for food-borne disease

(1) Regulations may make provision for requiring the notification of information about tests on samples taken from individuals (whether living or dead) for the presence of—

   (a) organisms of a description specified in the regulations; or
   (b) any substances produced by or in response to the presence of organisms of a description so specified.

(2) A description of organisms may be specified in the regulations only if it appears to the authority making the regulations that those organisms or any substances produced by them—

   (a) are capable of causing disease in humans; and
   (b) are commonly transmitted to humans through the consumption of food.

(3) The power to make the regulations is exercisable for the purpose of facilitating the carrying out of functions of the Agency or any other public authority which relates to the protection of public health.

(4) The regulations shall, as respects each specified description of organisms—

   (a) specify the information to be notified about them and the form and manner in which it is to be notified;
   (b) make provision for identifying the person by whom that information is to be notified; and
   (c) specify the person to whom that information is to be notified;

but the regulations may not require a person to notify information which is not in his possession, or otherwise available to him, by virtue of his position.

(5) The regulations may—

   (a) make provision as to the tests about which information is to be notified;
   (b) require or permit the person specified under subsection (4)(c) to disclose any information to any other person or to publish it;
   (c) restrict the purposes for which any information may be used (whether by the person so specified or by any other person);

(d) make provision with a view to ensuring that patient confidentiality is preserved;

(e) create exceptions from any provision of the regulations;

(f) create summary offences, subject to the limitation that no such offence shall be punishable with imprisonment or a fine exceeding level 5 on the standard scale.

(6) Before making regulations under this section the authority making them shall consult the Agency and such organisations as appear to the authority to be representative of interests likely to be substantially affected by the regulations.

(7) Any consultation undertaken before the commencement of subsection (6) shall be as effective, for the purposes of that subsection, as if undertaken after that commencement.

(8) The power to make regulations under this section is exercisable—

(a) as respects tests carried out in England, by the Secretary of State;

(b) as respects tests carried out in Wales, by the National Assembly for Wales;

(c) as respects tests carried out in Scotland, by the Scottish Ministers; and

(d) as respects tests carried out in Northern Ireland, by the Department of Health and Social Services for Northern Ireland.

This section enables the Secretary of State for Health and his equivalents in the devolved administrations to make regulations to set up a notification scheme for the results of laboratory tests for food borne organisms. This means that if a laboratory finds evidence that indicates a person may have been exposed to certain pathogens (which will be specified in any regulations) that are capable of causing illness and are commonly transmitted through food, they will be required to report it to the central authorities ('commonly' here means that when the disease occurs it is often food-borne; it does not mean the disease itself has to be common). This information will improve data collection on types of food-borne disease. It will enable the Agency better to understand patterns of the incidence and prevalence of food borne disease. The pathogens initially expected to be covered by a notification scheme are salmonella, E.coli 0157 and campylobacter.

Subsection (3) allows the scheme to be set up to assist the work both of the Agency and of other bodies with public health responsibilities, such as the Department of Health and the Public Health Laboratory Service.

Subsection (4) describes provisions which must be included in any regulations, which include the type and form of notification required for each organism specified, and to whom it is to be notified. *Subsection (5)* sets out further detail which may be included in regulations. The regulations may create an offence of failure to notify. The regulations may set the maximum fine for this offence at any level up to 5 on the standard scale (currently £5,000).

Under *subsection (6)*, the Health Departments must consult representatives of interested parties before making any regulations.

---

28 Arrangements for sharing information about food-borne zoonoses

(1) The Agency and each authority to which this section applies with responsibility for any matter connected with food-borne zoonoses shall make arrangements with a view to securing (so far as reasonably practicable) that any information relating to food-borne zoonoses in the possession of either of them is furnished or made available to the other.

(2) The authorities to which this section applies are Ministers of the Crown, the National Assembly for Wales, Scottish Ministers and Northern Ireland Departments.

(3) Arrangements under this section may also include arrangements for co-ordinating the activities of the Agency and the authority concerned in relation to matters connected with food-borne zoonoses.

(4) Arrangements under this section shall be kept under review by the Agency and the authority concerned.

(5) In this section 'food-borne zoonosis' means any disease of, or organism carried by, animals which constitutes a risk to the health of humans through the consumption of, or contact with, food.

This section makes it a duty of the Minister of Agriculture, Fisheries and Food (or any other Minister of the Crown whose responsibilities include matters related to foodborne zoonoses) and the devolved authorities or Northern Ireland Department on the one hand and the Agency on the other to make administrative arrangements for sharing relevant information on food-borne zoonoses (as defined in *subsection (5)*: this would include, for example, salmonella, campylobacter and E.coli).

---

29   Consultation on veterinary products

(1) The Minister of Agriculture, Fisheries and Food, and each Secretary of State having responsibility for any matters connected with the regulation of veterinary products, shall consult the Agency from time to time about the general policy he proposes to pursue in carrying out his functions in relation to those matters.

(2) In this section 'veterinary products' means—

   (a) veterinary drugs, as defined in section 132(1) of the Medicines Act 1968;
   (b) veterinary medicinal products, as defined in Article 1(2) of Council Directive 81/851/EEC (including products manufactured from homeopathic stock);
   (c) medicated feedingstuffs, as defined in Article 1(2) of Council Directive 81/85/EEC;
   (d) zootechnical products, as defined in regulation 2(1) of the Feedingstuffs (Zootechnical Products) Regulations 1999.

(3) The Minister or the Secretary of State concerned may disclose any information to the Agency (including information obtained by or furnished to him in pursuance of any enactment) relating to matters connected with the regulation of veterinary products.

(4) This section applies to the Department of Health and Social Services for Northern Ireland and the Department of Agriculture for Northern Ireland as it applies to the Minister of Agriculture, Fisheries and Food.

Subsection (1) requires that Ministers who have responsibility for regulating veterinary products (principally, the Minister of Agriculture, Fisheries and Food acting through the Veterinary Medicines Directorate, an executive agency of MAFF) must consult the Agency on general policy matters relating to this work.

Subsection (3) allows the Secretary of State and the Minister to disclose to the Agency any information they have on matters connected with veterinary products, even if it was obtained by them pursuant to any enactment. In particular, this means that they can override the general restriction in the Medicines Act 1968 and secondary legislation based on it on disclosures of information relating to veterinary products (provided, for example, by businesses in connection with a licence application).

The further disclosure or publication of the information provided to the Agency under this sub-section is not prohibited by any statutory provision, and thus, subject to section 19(3) of the Act, the Agency may publish it or disclose it to other public authorities.

Subsection (4) applies this section to Northern Ireland.

---

30   Animal feedingstuffs: Great Britain

(1) The Ministers may, for the purpose of regulating any animal feedingstuff or anything done to or in relation to, or with a view to the production of, any animal feedingstuff, make an order under this section.

(2) An order under this section is one which applies, or makes provision corresponding to, any provisions of the 1990 Act (including any power to make subordinate legislation or to give directions), with or without modifications.

(3) Such an order may be made by reference to the 1990 Act as it stands immediately before this Act is passed or as it stands following any amendment or repeal made by this Act.

(4) Such an order under this section may make provision with a view to protecting animal health, protecting human health or for any other purpose which appears to the Minister to be appropriate.

(5) The provision which may be made in an order under this section by virtue of section 37(1)(a) includes provision amending or repealing any enactment or subordinate legislation.

(6) Before making such an order, the Ministers shall—

   (a)   consult such organisations as appear to them to be representative of interests likely to be substantially affected by the order; and

   (b)   have regard to any advice given by the Agency.

(7) Any consultation undertaken before the commencement of subsection (6) shall be as effective, for the purposes of that subsection, as if undertaken after that commencement; and any consultation undertaken by the Agency may be treated by the Ministers as being as effective for those purposes as if it had been undertaken by them.

(8) In this section 'the Ministers' means—

   (a)   in the case of an order extending to England and Wales, the Secretary of State and the Minister of Agriculture, Fisheries and Food, acting jointly;

   (b)   in the case of an order extending to Scotland, the Scottish Ministers.

The Agency has a general function of providing advice and information to Ministers in relation to animal feed. This is provided by sections 6 and 7 (by virtue of the effect feedingstuffs can have on food safety), and by section 9 in relation to the general safety of animal feed and the interests of users of feed.

At present, feedingstuffs are regulated under Part IV of the Agriculture Act 1970, and by regulations and Orders made under that Act, the European Communities Act 1972 and the Animal Health Act 1981.

This section allows Ministers to establish by order new provisions for the regulation of feed, based on the Food Safety Act 1990. Such an order, which would have the effect of updating the primary powers available for the regulation of feedingstuffs, could cover areas such as the composition, processing, treatment, manufacturing conditions and labelling of feedingstuffs.

The order would probably establish a general requirement for the safety of feedingstuffs (similar to the 'food safety requirements' set out in section 8 of the Food Safety Act 1990), and allow further subordinate legislation to deal with more detailed requirements.

An order under this section can make incidental amendments and repeals to existing legislation – in practice, it would probably repeal Part IV of the Agriculture Act as it applies to feed. The application of Part IV to fertilisers would be unaffected.

The control of feedingstuffs is fully devolved to Scotland, and thus the order-making power is conferred on Scottish Ministers in relation to Scotland.

Subsection (1) enables the Ministers to regulate feedingstuffs along the lines described above.

Subsection (2) provides that an order made under these powers can be used to apply to animal feedingstuffs provisions which match those contained in the Food Safety Act 1990, so that food and feed may be dealt with in a similar manner. It will also allow EC requirements to be readily transposed into UK provisions under a single set of powers. This will give a more coherent body of legislation than at present where provisions are implemented under both the Agriculture Act 1970 and the European Communities Act 1972.

Subsection (3) provides that the power can also be used in relation to provisions of the Food Safety Act 1990, as amended by the Food Standards Act.

Subsection (4)(a) provides for orders made under this section to address the needs of animal health or human health and is necessary because the scope of the powers in this Act would not otherwise extend to animal health.

Subsection (8) provides for the order to be made jointly by the Secretary of State and the Minister of Agriculture, Fisheries and Food for England and Wales, and by the Scottish Ministers for Scotland. Orders made under this section must be subject to the affirmative resolution procedure – i.e. approved in draft by each House of Parliament or by the Scottish Parliament as appropriate before being made (as required by section 37).

A general definition of 'animal feedingstuffs' is given in section 37, although this may be refined in any orders to cover specific areas. Section 37 also provides that the order can repeal or amend existing legislation as necessary.

31   Animal feedingstuffs: Northern Ireland

(1) The Department of Agriculture for Northern Ireland and the Department of Health and Social Services for Northern Ireland acting jointly shall have the same power to make provision by order for Northern Ireland by reference to the 1991 Order as the Ministers have by virtue of section 30 to make provision by order for England and Wales or Scotland by reference to the 1990 Act.

(2) Subsections (6) and (7) of section 30 apply in relation to an order under this section as they apply to an order under this section as they apply to an order under that section.

This section makes provision parallel to that in section 30 in relation to Northern Ireland.

32   Modification of certain provisions of this Act

(1) Her Majesty may by Order in Council make such provision as She considers appropriate for modifying—

   (a) the functions exercisable under this Act by any of the appropriate authorities (including functions exercisable jointly by two or more of them);
   (b) the powers under this Act of either House of Parliament, the Scottish Parliament or the Northern Ireland Assembly; or
   (c) the constitution of the Agency.

(2) Without prejudice to the generality of subsection (1), provision made under paragraph (a) or (b) of that subsection may—

   (a) confer on any one or more of the appropriate authorities functions (including powers to make subordinate legislation) which relate to anything connected with the Agency or its activities;

(b)   confer powers on either House of Parliament, the Scottish Parliament or the Northern Ireland Assembly.

(3) Where provision is made under subsection (1)(a) or (b), the provision which may be made in the Order by virtue of section 37(1)(a) includes provision modifying functions of, or conferring functions on, the Agency or any other person in connection with any one or more of the appropriate authorities or with any body mentioned in subsection (1)(b).

(4) For the purposes of subsection (1)(c) the reference to the constitution of the Agency is a reference to the subject-matter of sections 2 to 5 and 39(7) (together with Schedules 1, 2 and 4).

(5) The provision which may be made by an Order under this section does not include provision modifying this section or section 33 (except that where provision is made under subsection (1)(c) the Order may make consequential amendments to subsection (4)).

(6) No recommendation shall be made to Her Majesty in Council to make an Order under this section unless the Agency has been consulted.

This section provides powers to modify the provisions of the Act and is intended to deal with circumstances where the need for change arises from experience of operating a UK body in the area of food safety and standards, where responsibility has been devolved.

The Agency is being established with powers in relation to policy areas which have been wholly devolved to Scotland, Wales and Northern Ireland, and is therefore appropriate that it should be the shared responsibility of the three devolved authorities and the UK Government (which also in effect represents the English interest). Its establishment coincides with the coming into operation of devolved authorities and legislatures in Scotland and Wales and there is therefore inevitably a degree of uncertainty about how they will choose to exercise their devolved powers in this area. Devolution in Northern Ireland has not yet come into effect in November 1999. Although Scottish Ministers and the Scottish Parliament and the National Assembly for Wales were consulted formally on the principle of a UK Agency, it is possible that experience will show a need for some adjustment to the constitution of the UK body. As such, alterations to the constitution of the Agency could in principle concern all four of the authorities and it is therefore necessary to have procedures whereby all four bodies are associated with such changes. This section and section 33 provide for such arrangements. They follow the model established in sections 89 and 90 of the Scotland Act 1998 which are concerned with the adaptation and transfer of property for cross-border public authorities.

Subsection (1) provides for modification to be made to the Food Standards Act by Order in Council where it is necessary to amend functions exercised by the appropriate authorities (i.e. the Secretary of State and the devolved administrations), Parliament, the Scottish Parliament or the Northern Ireland Assembly, or to amend the provisions on the establishment and constitution of the Agency (in particular sections 2 to 5 and Schedules 1, 2 and 4). For example it might, in the light of experience, be necessary to change the arrangments for the Scottish, Welsh and Northern Ireland advisory committees as established by section 5, or to change the number of members of the Agency or the experience which between them they must have.

The Order in Council route is chosen because it is clear that for the Agency to fuction successfully as a UK body it will depend on co-operation between the four authorities. Thus any amendments to its constitution, or the relationship between the different authorities in the UK, will need to be jointly agreed in each part of the UK. The Order in Council procedure is the most appropriate procedure for allowing each legislature formally to consider and consent to such changes.

Subsection (2) elaborates on the matters which can be included in an Order in Council made under this provision.

Subsection (6) provides for the Agency to be consulted before any amendments are made.

It should be noted that while section 32 provides a procedure for altering the Agency's constitution, it would not prevent Parliament making changes by a further Act. To the extent it is within their competence under the Scotland and Northern Ireland Acts, the Scottish Parliament and Northern Ireland Assembly will also be able to make changes to the arrangements in the Act using Acts passed by them.

---

33   Consequences of Agency losing certain functions

(1) This section applies if—

- (a) the Scottish Parliament passes an Act providing for any functions of the Agency to be no longer exercisable in or as regards Scotland; or
- (b) the Northern Ireland Assembly passes an Act providing for any functions of the Agency to be no longer exercisable in or as regards Northern Ireland.

(2) Her Majesty may by Order in Council make provision—

- (a) modifying this or any other Act as She considers necessary or expedient in consequence of the functions concerned being no longer exercisable by the Agency in or as regards Scotland or Northern Ireland;
- (b) for the transfer of any property, rights and interests of the Agency falling within subsection (3);
- (c) for any person to have such rights or interests in relation to any property, rights or interests falling within subsection (3) as She considers appropriate (whether in connection with a transfer or otherwise); or
- (d) for the transfer of any liabilities of the Agency falling within subsection (4).

(3) Property, rights and interests fall within this subsection if they belong to the Agency and appear to Her Majesty—

- (a) to be held or used wholly or partly for or in connection with the exercise of any of the functions concerned, or
- (b) not to be within paragraph (a) but, when last held or used for or in connection with the exercise of any function, to have been so held or used for or in connection with the exercise of any of the functions concerned.

(4) Liabilities of the Agency fall within this subsection if they appear to Her Majesty to have been incurred wholly or partly for or in connection with the exercise of any of the functions concerned.

(5) An Order under this section may make provision for the delegation of powers to determine anything required to be determined for the purposes of provision made under subsection (2)(b), (c) or (d).

(6) No recommendation shall be made to Her Majesty in Council to make an Order under this section unless the Agency has been consulted.

Although the Food Standards Agency is being established as a UK body, the Scottish Parliament and the Northern Ireland Assembly may, within their competence, withdraw from the UK arrangements or any part of them, by means of an Act of the Scottish Parliament or Northern Ireland Assembly. This section provides for amendments to the Food Standards Act to be made to deal with the consequences for the Agency of any such decision. As with section 32, the Order in Council route is chosen since it provides a suitable procedure for use in all four legislatures. This section does not apply to the National Assembly for Wales which does not have primary legislative powers.

Subsection (1) provides that this section has effect where the Scottish Parliament or Northern Ireland Assembly pass an Act which has the effect of withdrawing from any of the functions of the Agency. For example, the Scottish Parliament might in future decide that it wished to set up a separate agency for Scotland, or that it wished some other body to carry out some of the Agency's functions, such as enforcement monitoring, without withdrawing Scotland from the Agency completely.

Subsection (2) goes on to specify the provisions which may be included in an Order in Council to make any consequential adjustments to the Agency. These include provisions to deal with the transfer of any property, rights and liabilities. The effect of the sub-section, read with *subsections (3)* and *(4)*, is to allow the Order to transfer property and liabilities which were used (or arose) in relation to the functions which the Agency is to cease to have, to be transferred to whatever body appears appropriate.

34   Duty to take account of functions of the Food Safety Promotion Board

(1)   The Agency must—

(a)   take account of the activities of the Food Safety Promotion Board in determining what action to take for the purpose of carrying out its functions; and

(b)   consult that Board from time to time with a view to ensuring so far as is practicable that the activities of the Agency do not unnecessarily duplicate the activities of the Board.

(2)   Nothing in this Act affects the functions of the Food Safety Promotion Board.

Under the North/South Cooperation (Implementation Bodies) (Northern Ireland) Order 1999, made on 10 March following the Agreement between the Government of Great Britain and Northern Ireland of 8 March in implementation of the Belfast Agreement, the Food Safety Promotion Board (FSPB) will be established as an all-Ireland implementation body. Its functions include promotion of food safety, research into food safety, communication of food alerts and surveillance of food-borne diseases. The FSPB Order will come into force on the appointed day when devolution takes place in Northern Ireland under the Northern Ireland Act 1998. This section provides for the Agency to cooperate with the FSPB in Northern Ireland, so as to ensure that it does not duplicate the activities of the FSPB.

35   Devolution in Scotland and Northern Ireland

(1) For the purposes of—

(a)   section 23(2)(b) of the Scotland Act 1998 (power of Scottish Parliament to require persons outside Scotland to attend to give evidence or produce documents); and

(b)   section 70(6) of the Act (accounts prepared by cross-border bodies),

the Agency shall be treated as a cross-border public authority (within the meaning of that Act).

(2) It is not outside the legislative competence of the Scottish Parliament, by virtue of the reservation of matters relating to the constitution mentioned in paragraph 1 of Schedule 5 to that Act, to remove, alter or confer relevant functions of the Agency which are exercisable in or as regards Scotland.

(3) Nothing in subsection (2) affects any legislative competence of the Scottish Parliament apart from this section.

(4) Relevant functions of the Agency in relation to Northern Ireland shall be regarded as functions of a Minister of the Crown for the purposes of paragraph 1(a) of Schedule 2 to the Northern Ireland Act 1998 (excepted matters).

(5) In this section 'relevant functions of the Agency' means functions relating to, or to matters connected with—

(a)   food safety or other interests of consumers in relation to food; or

(b)   the safety of animal feedingstuffs or other interests of users of animal feedingstuffs.

Section 35 deals with various matters relating to Scotland and Northern Ireland.

Subsection (1)(a) concerns the power of the Scottish Parliament to call witnesses. Under section 23 of the Scotland Act 1998, the Scottish Parliament has a general power to call witnesses on any subject within the responsibility of members of the Scottish Executive. However, persons outside Scotland can be required to attend and give evidence only in relation to the discharge of functions of the Scottish Administration, of Scottish public authorities or cross-border public authorities (as defined in the Scotland Act). Since the Agency is not a Scottish authority or cross-border public authority, without the provision in section 35(1)(a), the Parliament would have no power to call witnesses from outside Scotland in relation to its activities.

Subsection (1)(b) concerns the Agency's accounts. Section 70(6) of the Scotland Act prevents Scottish legislation imposing a requirement to prepare accounts on cross-border public authorities, where other legislation already requires them to prepare accounts to be examined either by the Auditor General for Scotland or the Comptroller and Auditor General. Section 35(1)(b) deems the Agency to be a cross-border public authority for the purposes of section 70(6), so the prohibition on Scottish legislation duplicating accounting requirements will apply in relation to the Agency. As a UK non-Ministerial department, the Agency will be subject to audit by the National Audit Office. Schedule 4 sets out the detailed accounts and audit arrangements for the Agency.

Subsection (2) clarifies that it is within the legislative competence of the Scottish Parliament to remove, alter or confer relevant functions (as defined by *subsection (5)*, i.e. matters within the Agency's general remit) of the Agency within its own jurisdiction. The reservation in paragraph 1 of Schedule 5 to the Scotland Act, which reserves to the UK Government matters relating to the constitution does not apply even though the Agency is constituted as a UK Crown body.

Subsection (3) makes clear that the legislative competence of the Scottish Parliament is not affected in any other way by this section.

Subsection (4) similarly provides for the relevant functions of the Agency in Northern Ireland to be recognised as falling within the competence of the devolved authority in Northern Ireland. The Agency's relevant functions in relation to Northern Ireland are to be regarded as functions of a Minister of the Crown and therefore not included as excepted matters by virtue of being part of the Crown.

Final provisions

36   Interpretation

(1) In this Act—

'Agency' means the Food Standards Agency;

'Animal feedingstuff' means feedingstuff for any description of animals, including any nutritional supplement or other similar substance which is not administered through oral feeding;

'appropriate authorities' means the Secretary of State, the National Assembly for Wales, the Scottish Ministers and the Department of Health and Social Services for Northern Ireland;

'Food Safety Promotion Board' means the body of that name established by the agreement establishing implementation bodies done at Dublin on 8th March 1999 between the Government of the United Kingdom and the Government of Ireland;

'the 1990 Act' means the Food Safety Act 1990; and

'the 1991 Order' means the Food Safety (Northern Ireland) Order 1991.

(2) Any reference in this Act to 'the appropriate authority', in relation to Wales, Scotland or Northern Ireland, is a reference to the National Assembly for Wales, the Scottish

Ministers or the Department of Health and Social Services for Northern Ireland (as the case may be).

(3) In this Act the expression 'interests of consumers in relation to food' includes (without prejudice to the generality of that expression) interests in relation to the labelling, marking, presenting or advertising of food, and the descriptions which may be applied to food.

(4) Expressions used—

(a)   as regards England and Wales and Scotland, in this Act and in the 1990 Act, or

(b)   as regards Northern Ireland, in this Act and the 1991 Order,

have, unless the context otherwise requires, the same meaning in this Act as in that Act or that Order (except that in this Act 'animal' includes any bird or fish).

(5) The purposes which may be specified in an order under section 1(3) of the 1990 Act (meaning of the term 'premises' to include, for specified purposes, ships or aircraft of a description specified by order), or under the corresponding provisions of Article 2(2) of the 1991 Order, include purposes relating to provisions of this Act.

This contains definitions of terms used in the Act.

Subsection (3) provides a gloss to the phrase 'interests of consumers of food'. The definition makes clear that matters such as labelling are included within the scope of this term. The saving in brackets 'without prejudice to the generality of that expression' makes clear that the term is not limited solely to the matters mentioned in the definition.

Powers of entry in the Act are related to 'premises'. *Subsection (5)* provides that if the definition of 'premises' in the Food Safety Act 1990 is extended by an Order under section 1(3) or the corresponding Northern Ireland provision of that Act to include ships and aircraft of a specified description, this extended definition may also be applied to functions under this Act.

It is important to read this Act in conjunction with the Food Safety Act 1990 since that Act defines many important concepts, including 'food' itself.

---

37   Subordinate legislation

(1) Subordinate legislation under section 25, 27, 30, 31, 32 and 33—

(a)   may contain such supplementary, incidental, consequential, transitional or saving provision as the person making it considers necessary or expedient;

(b)   may make different provision for different purposes.

(2) Any power under this Act to make an order or regulations is exercisable—

(a)   in the case of an order or regulations made by the First Minister and deputy First Minister or a Northern Ireland Department, by statutory rule for the purposes of the Statutory Rules (Northern Ireland) Order 1979; and

(b)   in any other case, by statutory instrument.

(3) No order under section 25, 30 or 31 shall be made unless a draft of it has been laid before and approved by resolution of—

(a)   each House of Parliament, if it is made by the Secretary of State or the Minister of Agriculture, Fisheries and Food;

(b)   the Scottish Parliament, if it is made by the Scottish Ministers;

(c)   the Northern Ireland Assembly, if it is made by the First Minister and deputy First Minister or by a Northern Ireland Department.

(4) A statutory instrument made under section 27 or 42 is subject to annulment in pursuance of a resolution of—

(a)   either House of Parliament, if it is made by the Secretary of State;

(b)   the Scottish Parliament, if it is made by the Scottish Ministers;

and a statutory rule made under that section is subject to negative resolution within the meaning of section 41(6) of the Interpretation Act (Northern Ireland) 1954.

(5) No recommendation shall be made to Her Majesty to make an Order in Council under section 32 or 33 unless a draft of the Order has been laid before and approved by resolution of each House of Parliament, the National Assembly for Wales, the Scottish Parliament and the Northern Ireland Assembly.

This section groups together the general provisions relating to the manner in which the powers in the Act to make subordinate legislation may be used. These are the powers:

- to modify statutory bars on disclosure of information to the Agency (in section 25);
- to establish a notification system for food borne diseases (in section 27);
- to apply the Food Safety Act 1990 or the corresponding Northern Ireland legislation to feedingstuffs (in sections 30 and 31); and
- to make Orders in Council relating to the constitution of the Agency and the consequences of the Scottish Parliament or Northern Ireland Assembly removing functions from the Agency (in sections 32 and 33).

---

38   Crown application

(1) This Act binds the Crown (but does not affect Her Majesty in her private capacity).

(2) Subsection (1)—

(a)   does not require subordinate legislation made under this Act to bind the Crown; and

(b)   is to be interpreted as if section 38(3) of the Crown Proceedings Act 1947 (references to Her Majesty in her private capacity) were contained in this Act.

(3) If the Secretary of State certifies that it appears to him requisite or expedient in the interests of national security that the powers of entry conferred by sections 11 and 14 should not be exercisable in relation to any premises specified in the certificate, being premises held or used by or on behalf of the Crown, those powers shall not be exercisable in relation to those premises.

This section applies the requirements and powers contained in the Act (including powers of entry) to activities and premises carried out or used by or on behalf of the Crown (but does not apply to the Queen in her private capacity). This reflects the provisions of the Food Safety Act 1990, which is applied to the Crown by section 54 of that Act.

Subsection (3) permits the Secretary of State to certify that powers of entry should not be exercised in relation to specified premises of national security importance, such as defence establishments.

---

39   Financial provisions

(1) There shall be paid out of money provided by Parliament—

(a)   any expenditure incurred by a Minister of the Crown by virtue of this Act;

(b) any increase attributable to this Act in the sums payable out of money so provided under any other Act.

(2) Any expenditure incurred by the Agency shall be paid out of money provided by Parliament unless it is met from money paid or appropriated under subsection (3) (or from money which the Agency is authorised by virtue of any relevant provision to apply for the purpose).

(3) Sums may be—

(a) paid by the National Assembly for Wales;
(b) paid out of the Scottish Consolidated Fund; or
(c) appropriated by Act of the Northern Ireland Assembly,

for the purpose of meeting any of the expenditure of the Agency.

(4) Any sums received by the Agency, other than—

(a) money provided by Parliament or paid or appropriated under subsection (3);
(b) receipts which are, by virtue of provision made by or under any enactment, payable—
   (i)   to the National Assembly for Wales;
   (ii) into the Scottish Consolidated Fund; or
   (iii) into the Consolidated Fund of Northern Ireland,
   or which would be so payable but for any relevant provision relating to those receipts; and
(c) other receipts specified, or of a description specified, in a determination under subsection (5),

shall be paid into the Consolidated Fund.

(5) The Treasury, the National Assembly for Wales, the Scottish Ministers and the Department of Finance and Personnel for Northern Ireland acting jointly may determine that any sums received by the Agency which are specified, or of a description specified, in the determination shall (instead of being payable into the Consolidated Fund by virtue of subsection (4)) be payable to the National Assembly for Wales, into the Scottish Consolidated Fund or into the Consolidated Fund of Northern Ireland, subject to any relevant provision relating to such sums.

(6) A determination under subsection (5) may be revoked or amended by a further determination.

(7) Schedule 4 (accounts and audit) has effect.

(8) In this section—

'enactment' means an enactment contained in an Act, an Act of the Scottish Parliament or in Northern Ireland legislation;

'relevant provision' means—
   (a) provision made by or under any Act as to the disposal of or accounting for sums payable to the National Assembly for Wales;
   (b) provision made by or under the Scotland Act 1998 or any Act of the Scottish Parliament as to the disposal of or accounting for sums payable into the Scottish Consolidated Fund; and

(c) provision made by or under any Act or any Northern Ireland legislation as to the disposal of or accounting for sums payable into the Consolidated Fund of Northern Ireland.

This section provides for the financing of the Agency. Because the Agency is a UK body operating in a devolved area, it is to be funded not only from money provided by Parliament, but also from the Scottish Parliament, the National Assembly for Wales and the Northern Ireland Assembly. In practice, as a general rule, it is envisaged that the costs of the Agency's main headquarters and staff and its activities in England, will be met by money provided by Parliament, and the costs of its executive bodies in Scotland, Wales and Northern Ireland, and of activities carried out on the ground in those parts of the UK, will be funded by them. The section ensures that devolved legislatures as well as Parliament can make the contributions to the expenditure of the Agency, and deals with the treatment of the Agency's receipts (both from statutory charges – in practice this is likely to be mostly charges for the Meat Hygiene Service – and miscellaneous income such as charges for documents produced by the Agency).

Subsection (1) contains provisions authorising payment by Parliament of increases in Ministerial expenditure and spending under other Acts by virtue of the Act.

Subsection (2) provides for Parliament to meet the expenditure of the Agency, other than that part which is provided by the devolved authorities. It should be noted that the Agency (as a Government Department) will be funded directly by Parliamentary 'Vote', rather than by means of a grant paid by a Minister.

Subsection (3) provides the legal authority to the devolved administrations to pay money to the Agency and removes any doubt as to whether this would be within their devolved competence.

Subsection (4) deals with the Agency's receipts, in particular receipts from the performance of statutory functions, such as charges for meat hygiene enforcement. Under existing legislation, such receipts are normally paid into the Consolidated Fund, though (subject to certain criteria being satsified) the Treasury may direct that it can be 'appropriated in aid' to the Department or body concerned. This subsection clarifies that receipts are payable into the Consolidated Fund, unless they are

- actually provided by Parliament (and sums appropriated in aid count as this);
- received by the Agency from the Scottish, Welsh and Northern Ireland administrations;
- payable to the National Assembly for Wales or into the Consolidated Funds for Scotland or Northern Ireland, as the case may be, by virtue of a provision in legislation; or
- determined to be payable to Wales, Scotland or Northern Ireland under subsection (5), explained below.

The Agency is also likely to have other minor non-statutory receipts, such as income from charges for consultancy or other services provided on request. *Subsection (5)* deals with this by providing a mechanism for the Treasury and the devolved administrations, acting jointly, to determine that receipts be payable to the Scottish or Northern Ireland Consolidated Fund, or the National Assembly for Wales (rather than to the Consolidated Fund) as appropriate according to the nature of the receipt.

It should be noted that in general, sums received by the Agency, whether under Statutory Charges or from miscellaneous fees, are likely to be of the type it will be allowed to retain as appropriations or negative public expenditure. Thus the payments into the various funds described above will be nominal payments, for accounting purposes only.

---

40   Minor and consequential amendments and repeals

(1) Schedule 5 (minor and consequential amendments) has effect.

(2) Any amendment made by Schedule 5 which extends to Scotland is to be taken as a pre-commencement enactment for the purposes of the Scotland Act 1998.

(3) The National Assembly for Wales (Transfer of Functions) Order 1999 shall have effect, in relation to any Act mentioned in Schedule 1 to the Order, as if any provision of this Act amending that Act was in force immediately before the Order came into force.

(4) The enactments mentioned in Schedule 6 are repealed to the extent specified.

(5) Her Majesty may by Order in Council direct that any amendment or repeal by this Act of any provision in the 1990 Act shall extend to any of the Channel Islands with such modifications (if any) as may be specified in the Order.

As in section 18 (see note), amendments to existing Acts made by Schedule 5 are to be treated as pre-commencement enactments for the purposes of the Scotland Act 1998.

Subsection (3) ensures that the National Assembly for Wales (Transfer of Functions) Order 1999, which transfers functions under various Acts to the National Assembly for Wales, takes account of any amendments to those Acts made by this Act. The amendments made by this Act are therefore treated as if made prior to the Order coming into force.

41   Transfer of property, rights and liabilities to the Agency

(1) The Secretary of State may make one or more schemes for the transfer to the Agency of such property, rights and liabilities of a Minister of the Crown (in this section referred to as 'the transferor') as appear to him appropriate having regard to the functions conferred on the Agency by provision made by or under this Act, the 1990 Act or the 1991 Order.

(2) The power conferred by subsection (1) may also be exercised by the National Assembly for Wales, the Scottish Ministers or a Northern Ireland Department in relation to their property, rights and liabilities.

(3) A transfer scheme—

   (a)   may provide for the transfer of property, rights and liabilities that would not otherwise be capable of being transferred or assigned;
   (b)   may define property, rights and liabilities by specifying or describing them or by referring to all of the property, rights and liabilities comprised in a specified part of the undertaking of the transferor (or partly in one way and partly in the other);
   (c)   may provide for the creation—
      (i)   in favour of the transferor, or of the Agency, of interests in, or rights over, property to be transferred or, as the case may be, retained by the transferor; or
      (ii)   of new rights and liabilities as between the Agency and the transferor;
   (d)   may require the transferor or the Agency to take any steps necessary to secure that the transfer of any foreign property, rights or liabilities is effective under the relevant foreign law; and
   (e)   may make such incidental, supplemental and consequential provision as the authority making it considers appropriate.

(4) On the date appointed by a transfer scheme the property, rights and liabilities which are the subject of the scheme shall, by virtue of this subsection, become property, rights and liabilities of the Agency (and any other provisions of the scheme shall take effect).

(5) The authority making a transfer scheme may, at any time before the date so appointed, modify the scheme.

This section provides a transitional power to enable the Secretary of State or devolved authorities to make arrangements to transfer property, rights and liabilities to the Agency. This power is expected to be used, for example, at the time of the Agency's establishment to transfer uncompleted research contracts or relevant intellectual property rights.

42   Power to make transitional provision etc

(1) The Secretary of State may by regulations make such transitional and consequential provisions and such savings as he considers necessary or expedient in preparation for, or in connection with, or in consequence of—

   (a)   the coming into force of any provision of this Act; or
   (b)   the operation of any enactment repealed or amended by a provision of this Act during any period when the repeal or amendment is not wholly in force.

(2) Such regulations may make modifications of any enactment (including an enactment contained in this Act).

(3) The power to make regulations under this section is also exercisable—

   (a)   by the Scottish Ministers, in relation to provision that would be within the legislative competence of the Scottish Parliament to make;
   (b)   by the First Minister and deputy First Minister acting jointly, in relation to provision dealing with transferred matters (within the meaning of section 4(1) of the Northern Ireland Act 1998).

Subsections (1) and *(2)* provide for the Secretary of State to make regulations to deal with any transitional or consequential changes to legislation needed as a result of this Act.

Subsection (3) makes similar provision for Scotland and Northern Ireland.

---

43   Short title, commencement and extent

(1) This Act may be cited as the Food Standards Act 1999.

(2) This Act (apart from this section and paragraph 6(2) and (5) of Schedule 5) shall come into force on such day as the Secretary of State may by order appoint; and different days may be appointed for different purposes.

(3) The provisions of this Act shall be treated for the purposes of section 58 of the 1990 Act (territorial waters and the continental shelf) as if they were contained in that Act.

(4) Until the day appointed under section 3(1) of the Northern Ireland Act 1998, this Act has effect with the substitution—

   (a)   for references to the First Minister and deputy First Minister acting jointly, of references to a Northern Ireland Department;
   (b)   for references to an Act of the Northern Ireland Assembly, of references to a Measure of the Northern Ireland Assembly; and
   (c)   for references to transferred matters within the meaning of section 4(1) of the Northern Ireland Act 1998, of references to transferred matters within the meaning of section 43(2) of the Northern Ireland Constitution Act 1973;
   (d)   for references to paragraph 1(a) of Schedule 2 to the Northern Ireland Act 1998, of references to paragraph 1(a) of Schedule 2 to the Northern Ireland Constitution Act 1973.

(5) This Act extends to Scotland and Northern Ireland.

Subsection (3) deems this Act to be part of the Food Safety Act 1990 for the purposes of section 58 of the 1990 Act. Section 58 has two effects.

First, in relation to territorial waters (i.e. inland waters and the sea, generally out to 12 miles), it deems the authority responsible for any food premises (for example on gas rigs or other fixed structures) to be the same as that on the adjoining land. This provision also determines whether a structure lies in England, Scotland or Wales.

Secondly, section 58 allows the Food Safety Act to be extended by Order to structures outside territorial waters, but within areas which are British for oil and gas exploration purposes. No such Order has yet been made, but were it to be made, then the Agency would, by virtue of this section, obtain appropriate powers in relation to the carrying out of surveys and monitoring of the work of enforcement authorities at installations in the British sector.

Subsection (4) makes transitional modifications until a day is appointed for the coming into operation of parts II and III of the Northern Ireland Act 1998.

SCHEDULES

SCHEDULE 1   Section 2(4)

Constitution etc of the Agency

Status

1 The Agency is a body corporate.

Tenure of office of members of the Agency

2(1) A person appointed as chairman or deputy chairman or as one of the other members shall hold and vacate office in accordance with the terms of his appointment and, on ceasing to hold that office, is eligible for re-appointment.

(2) The terms of appointment of the chairman, deputy chairman and other members shall be determined by the appropriate authorities acting jointly.

3(1) The person holding office as chairman or deputy chairman—

  (a) may resign his office by giving notice to any of the appropriate authorities (and on doing so ceases to be a member of the Agency); and
  (b) may be removed from office by the appropriate authorities acting jointly if they are satisfied that he is eligible to be removed under paragraph 4.

(2) A member other than the chairman or deputy chairman—

  (a) may resign his office by giving notice to the authority by which he was appointed; and
  (b) may be removed from office by that authority if it is satisfied that he is eligible to be removed under paragraph 4.

4 A person may be removed from office as chairman, deputy chairman or other member only if—

  (a) he has been adjudged bankrupt, has had his estate sequestrated or has made a composition or arrangement with, or granted a trust deed for, his creditors; or
  (b) he is failing to carry out the duties of his office or is otherwise unable or unfit to carry out those duties.

Remuneration, pensions, etc of members of the Agency

5(1) The Agency shall pay its members such remuneration, and such travelling and other allowances, as may be determined by the appropriate authorities acting jointly.

(2) The Agency shall, if so required by the appropriate authorities acting jointly—

   (a) pay such pensions, allowances or gratuities as may be determined by the appropriate authorities acting jointly,

   (b) make such payments as may be so determined towards provision for the payment of pensions, allowances or gratuities, or

   (c) provide and maintain such schemes (whether contributory or not) as may be so determined for the payment of pensions, allowances or gratuities,

to or in respect of persons who are or have been members.

6 If, when a person ceases to hold office as a member, the appropriate authorities acting jointly determine that there are special circumstances which make it right that he should receive compensation, the Agency shall pay to him a sum by way of compensation of such amount as may be so determined.

Disqualification

7(1) In Part II of Schedule 1 to the House of Commons Disqualification Act 1975 (bodies whose members are disqualified) there shall be inserted at the appropriate place the words 'The Food Standards Agency'.

(2) In Part II of Schedule 1 to the Northern Ireland Assembly Disqualification Act 1975 (bodies whose members are disqualified) there shall be inserted at the appropriate place the words 'The Food Standards Agency'.

Staff

8(1)   The Agency may, with the approval of the Minister for the Civil Service as to numbers and terms and conditions of service, appoint such staff as it may determine.

(2) Sub-paragraph (1) is subject to section 3 in the case of the chief executive and the directors for Wales, Scotland and Northern Ireland.

Proceedings etc

9(1) The Agency may regulate its own procedure (including quorum) and shall, in particular, establish and maintain a system for the declaration and registration of private interests of its members.

(2) The entries recorded in the register of members' interests shall be published by the Agency.

10 The validity of any proceedings of the Agency is not affected by a vacancy amongst its members or by a defect in the appointment of a member.

11 A document purporting to be—

   (a) duly executed under the seal of the Agency, or

   (b) signed on behalf of the Agency,

shall be received in evidence and shall, unless the contrary is proved, be taken to be so executed or signed.

Delegation of powers

12(1) Anything authorised or required to be done by the Agency (including the exercise of the power conferred by this paragraph) may be done by any member of the Agency who, or any committee (or sub-committee) of the Agency which, is authorised for the purpose by the Agency, whether generally or specially.

(2) Sub-paragraph (1) does not affect the rule of law by virtue of which functions of the Agency may be carried out through members of its staff.

This Schedule sets out detailed provisions on the constitution, staffing and operation of the Agency. The term 'the Agency' means the Food Standards Agency appointed in accordance with section 2.

Paragraph 2 provides that members of the Agency can be re-appointed to the Agency, including to posts they already hold or have held in the past, including those of chairman and deputy chairman.

Paragraph 4 describes the circumstances in which the appropriate authorities may dismiss a member of the Agency. They have to satisfy themselves that the person is failing to perform his duties, has been declared bankrupt, is unable to meet his debts or is otherwise unfit to carry out his functions.

Paragraph 6 covers the circumstances in which the appropriate authorities may pay compensation to a member of the Agency who ceases to hold office. It is up to the appropriate authorities to make such a decision and thereafter the Agency is under a duty to pay whatever sum of money is decided.

Paragraph 7 disqualifies members of the Agency from standing as Members of Parliament or the Northern Ireland Assembly. Disqualification from membership of the European Parliament also flows automatically from this provision. Whether members should be disqualified from the Scottish Parliament and the National Assembly for Wales is a question for those bodies.

Paragraph 8 gives the Agency a power to appoint other staff, subject to the requirement that the Minister for the Civil Service approve their numbers and terms and conditions. The staff will be civil servants.

Paragraph 9 provides for the establishment of a register of members' interests and the publication of the entries recorded in it.

Paragraph 11 is an evidential provision: it provides that any document which appears to be signed or sealed by or on behalf of the Agency is treated as having been properly signed or executed unless shown not to be.

Paragraph 12 sets out to whom the Agency may delegate. *Subparagraph (2)* preserves the rule whereby the staff of a Minister (or in this case a non-Ministerial department) may act on his/its behalf.

SCHEDULE 2   Section 5(4)

ADVISORY COMMITTEES

Advisory committees for Wales, Scotland and Northern Ireland

1(1) This paragraph applies to any advisory committee established under section 5(1).

(2) Such a committee shall consist of—

    (a) a chairman appointed by the appropriate authority from among the members of the Agency;

    (b) such other persons as may be appointed by the appropriate authority, after consulting the Agency.

(3) No more than one member appointed under sub-paragraph (2)(b) may be a member of the Agency.

(4) The basic terms of reference of a committee to which this paragraph applies are to carry out the purpose mentioned in section 5(1); but the Agency may, with the approval of the appropriate authority, supplement the terms of reference of any such committee.

(5) In this paragraph 'appropriate authority', in relation to any committee, means the appropriate authority for the part of the United Kingdom for which the committee is established.

Advisory committee or committees for England

2(1) This paragraph applies to a committee established under section 5(2).

(2) Such a committee shall consist of a chairman and such other persons as may be appointed by the Secretary of State, after consulting the Agency.

(3) No more than two persons appointed under sub-paragraph (1) may be members of the Agency.

(4) The basic terms of reference of such a committee shall be to carry out the purpose mentioned in section 5(2); but the Agency may, with the approval of the Secretary of State, supplement the terms of reference of any such committee.

Other advisory committees

3(1) The members of a committee established under section 5(3) shall consist of such persons as may be appointed by the Agency, after consulting the appropriate authorities.

(2) The members so appointed may include members of the Agency.

(3) The terms of reference of such a committee shall be such as the Agency may determine.

(4) The Agency may, after consulting the appropriate authorities, abolish a committee established under section 5(3).

Remuneration of members of advisory committees

5 The Agency may pay to the members of an advisory committee established under section 5 such remuneration or allowances in respect of expenses (or both) as the Agency may determine.

Expenditure of advisory committees

6 Any expenditure incurred by an advisory committee established under section 5 shall be defrayed by the Agency.

Transfer of existing non-statutory advisory committees

7(1) The Secretary of State or the Minister of Agriculture, Fisheries and Food may direct that any advisory committee specified in the direction shall, from such date as may be so specified, be treated as if it had been established by the Agency under section 5 and its members appointed in accordance with paragraph 3(1).

(2) A direction under this paragraph may be given only if the committee in question is maintained for the purpose of giving advice or information to any one or more public authorities on matters connected with the Agency's functions.

(3) A direction under this paragraph may not be given in relation to a committee which—

   (a)   is established on or after the day on which this paragraph comes into force; or
   (b)   is established, or is required to be established, by any enactment.

(4) Before giving a direction under this paragraph the person giving it shall consult—

   (a)   the Agency; and
   (b)   any public authority which the committee is maintained to give advice as mentioned in sub-paragraph (2).

Joint committees

8(1) Without prejudice to the generality of section 21, the Agency may join with one or more other public authorities in making arrangements for establishing a joint committee to advise the Agency and the other authority or authorities on such matters connected with their functions as they may determine.

(2) The membership, terms of reference and any remuneration or allowances for members shall be in accordance with those arrangements.

(3) The expenditure of a joint advisory committee shall be defrayed by the Agency and the other authority or authorities in accordance with those arrangements.

(4) The Agency shall consult the appropriate authorities before making any arrangements under this paragraph.

This Schedule supplements the provisions in section 5 on advisory committees. It provides for the appointment of members, terms of reference, remuneration and expenses of committees for Scotland, Wales, Northern Ireland and England, and for specialist committees.

Paragraph 7 concerns the transfer of existing non-statutory advisory committees. A number of non-statutory independent advisory committees currently exist prior to the establishment of the Agency which deal with food related matters. They include the Advisory Committee on the Microbiological Safety of Food (ACMSF), the Advisory Committee on Novel Foods and Processes (ACNFP), the Food Advisory Committee (FAC) and the Consumer Panel. Under this paragraph the Secretary of State or the Minister of Agriculture, Fisheries and Food may direct that these committees be treated as if they were established by the Agency in accordance with section 5 after consulting the Agency and any other authorities to whom the committees in question report.

Paragraph 8 provides that the Agency may establish joint committees with another authority. Current examples of joint committees include the Spongiform Encephalopathy Advisory Committee (SEAC), the Committee on the Medical Aspects of Food and Nutrition Policy (COMA), the Committee on Toxicity of Chemicals in Food, Consumer Products and the Environment (COT) and the Advisory Committee on Animal Feedingstuffs.

SCHEDULE 3   Section 18

THE AGENCY'S FUNCTIONS UNDER OTHER ENACTMENTS

As explained in the note on section 18, the amendments in Schedules 3 and 5 are to Acts passed before the devolution Acts came into force. Thus, although many powers in relation to food, the environment, and agriculture have been devolved to the Scottish Administration, the amendments still refer to the Secretary of State and Minister of Agriculture, Fisheries and Food alone and not to Scottish Ministers. However, where the relevant functions have in fact been devolved, the references to the Secretary of State are intended to take effect in relation to Scotland as if they were references to Scottish Ministers. In general this will be the automatic result of the Scotland Act, but the powers under that Act will be available to make any further changes as necessary.

PART I

FUNCTIONS UNDER THE 1990 ACT

1 This Part has effect for conferring functions under the 1990 Act on the Agency (and references to sections are to sections of the 1990 Act).

Section 6 (enforcement)

2 The Agency—

   (a) may be directed to discharge duties of food authorities under section 6(3);

   (b) may be specified as an enforcement authority for regulations or orders in pursuance of section 6(4); and

   (c) may take over the conduct of proceedings mentioned in section 6(5) either with the consent of the person who instituted them or when directed to do so by the Secretary of State.

Section 13(3) (emergency control orders)

3 The Agency may grant consent under subsection (3), and give directions under subsection (5), of section 13.

Section 40 (codes of practice)

4(1) The Agency may, after consulting the Secretary of State—

   (a) give directions to food authorities under section 40(2)(b) as to steps to be taken in order to comply with codes of practice under section 40; and

   (b) enforce any such directions.

(2) The Agency may undertake consultation with representative organisations regarding proposals for codes of practice under section 40.

Section 41 (information from food authorities)

5 The Agency may exercise the power to require returns or other information from food authorities under section 41.

Section 42 (default powers)

6 The Agency may be empowered by an order under section 42 to discharge any duty of a food authority.

Section 48 (regulations and orders)

7 The Agency may undertake consultation with representative organisations required by section 48 regarding proposals for regulations or orders under the 1990 Act.

This Part describes the functions under the Food Safety Act 1990 which will be taken over by the Agency. The amendments to that Act which give effect to this are detailed in Schedule 5.

These functions allow the Agency to act as an enforcement authority in similar circumstances to those in which the Minister of Agriculture, Fisheries and Food, the Secretaries of State for Health, Scotland and Wales can act (the option of allowing any of the Ministers to be an enforcement authority is retained). The powers of the Secretaries of State for Scotland and Wales are now exercised by Scottish Ministers and the National Assembly for Wales respectively. These provisions do not therefore create new powers. In addition, the Agency may grant consents or give directions in relation to emergency control orders (see also section 17); issue Codes of Practice and give directions for their enforcement (in both cases after consulting the Secretary of State); require returns of information from food authorities; exercise default powers; and undertake consultation on proposals for regulations and orders on behalf of the Secretary of State.

In general, the functions of the Minister of Agriculture, Fisheries and Food will be transferred to the Secretary of State for Health, although the Act retains the option for the Minister to be an enforcement authority. The Minister's current enforcement functions (for example on dairy and meat hygiene) will be transferred to the Agency by amending relevant secondary legislation.

Part II

Functions under the 1991 Order

8 This Part has effect for conferring functions under the 1991 Order on the Agency (and references to Articles are to Articles of the 1991 Order).

Article 12 (emergency control orders)

9 The Agency may grant consent under paragraph (3), and give directions under paragraph (5), of Article 12.

Article 26 (enforcement)

10 The Agency—

(a)   may be directed to discharge duties of district councils under Article 26(2);

(b)   may be specified as an authority to enforce and execute regulations or orders in pursuance of Article 26(3); and

(c)   may take over the conduct of proceedings mentioned in Article 26(4) either when directed to do so by the Department of Health and Social Services for Northern Ireland or with the consent of the district council which instituted them.

Article 39 (codes of practice)

11(1)   The Agency may, after consulting the Department of Health and Social Services for Northern Ireland—

(a)   give directions to district councils under Article 39(2)(b) as to steps to be taken in order to comply with codes of practice under Article 39; and

(b)   enforce any such directions.

(2)   The Agency may undertake consultation with representative organisations regarding proposals for codes of practice under Article 39.

Article 40 (information from district councils)

12 The Agency may exercise the power to require returns or other information from district councils under Article 40.

Article 41 (default powers)

13 The Agency may be empowered by an order under Article 41 to discharge any duty of a district council.

Article 47 (regulations and orders)

14 The Agency may undertake consultation with representative organisations required by Article 47 regarding proposals for regulations or orders under the 1991 Order.

This part makes provision parallel to that in Part I in relation to Northern Ireland.

PART III

OTHER FUNCTIONS

Medicines Act 1968 (c 67)

15(1) The Medicines Act 1968 shall be amended as follows.

(2) In section 4 (establishment of committees), after subsection (5) there shall be inserted the following subsection—

'(5A) Where a committee is established under this section for purposes including the consideration of veterinary products as defined in section 29(2) of the Food Standards Act 1999, one member of the committee shall be appointed by the Ministers establishing the committee on the nomination of the Food Standards Agency.'

(3) In section 129 (orders and regulations), after subsection (6) there shall be inserted the following subsection—

'(6A) The organisations to be consulted under subsection (6) of this section include, where any provisions of the regulations or order apply to veterinary products as defined in section 29(2) of the Food Standards Act 1999, the Food Standards Agency.'

Food and Environment Protection Act 1985 (c 48)

16(1) The Agency shall have the following functions under the Food and Environment Protection Act 1985.

(2) The Agency may exercise the following powers under section 2 (powers when emergency order has been made)—

(a) the power to give consents under subsection (1);
(b) the power to give directions or do anything else under subsection (3);
(c) the power to recover expenses under subsection (5) or (6).

(3) In section 7 (exemptions from need for licence under Part II), after subsection (3) there shall be inserted the following subsection—

(3A) A licensing authority—

(a) shall consult the Food Standards Agency as to any order the authority contemplates making under this section; and

(b) shall from time to time consult that Agency as to the general approach to be taken by the authority in relation to the granting of approvals and the imposition of conditions under subsections (2) and (3) (including the identification of circumstances in which it may be desirable for the Agency to be consulted in relation to particular cases).'

(4) In section 8 (licences under Part II), after subsection (11) there shall be inserted the following subsections—

'(11A) The matters to which a licensing authority is to have regard in exercising powers under this section include any advice or information given to that authority by the Food Standards Agency (whether of a general nature or in relation to the exercise of a power in a particular case).

(11B) A licensing authority shall from time to time consult the Food Standards Agency as to the general manner in which the authority proposes to exercise its powers under this section in cases involving any matter which may affect food safety or other interests of consumers in relation to food (including the identification of circumstances in which it may be desirable for the Agency to be consulted in relation to particular cases).'

(5) In section 16 (control of pesticides), after subsection (9) there shall be inserted the following subsection—

'(9A) The Ministers—

(a) shall consult the Food Standards Agency as to regulations which they contemplate making; and

(b) shall from time to time consult that Agency as to the general approach to be taken by them in relation to the giving, revocation or suspension of approvals and the imposition of conditions on approvals (including the identification of circumstances in which it may be desirable for the Agency to be consulted in relation to particular cases).'

(6) In Schedule 5 (the Advisory Committee), after paragraph 1 there shall be inserted the following paragraph—

'1A. The committee shall include one member appointed by the Ministers on the nomination of the Food Standards Agency.'

Environmental Protection Act 1990 (c 43)

17 In section 108(7) and section 111(7) of the Environmental Protection Act 1990 (grant of exemptions) after the words 'Secretary of State' there shall be inserted the words ', or by the Secretary of State and the Food Standards Agency acting jointly,'.

18 For section 126 of that Act (exercise of certain functions relating to genetically modified organisms jointly by Secretary of State and Minister of Agriculture, Fisheries and Food) there shall be substituted the following section—

'Mode of exercise of certain functions

126(1) Any power of the Secretary of State to make regulations under this Part (other than the power conferred by section 113 above) is exercisable, where the regulations to be made relate to any matter with which the Minister is concerned, by the Secretary of State and the Minister acting jointly.

(2) Any function of the Secretary of State under this Part (other than a power to make regulations) is exercisable, where the function is to be exercised in relation to a matter with which the Minister is concerned, by the Secretary of State and the Minister acting jointly (but subject to subsection (3) below).

(3) Any function of the Secretary of State under sections 108(8) and 110 above is exercisable, where the function is to be exercised in relation to a matter with which the Agency is concerned—

   (a) if it is a matter with which the Minister is also concerned, by the Secretary of State, the Minister and the Agency acting jointly;
   (b) otherwise, by the Secretary of State and the Agency acting jointly.

(4) Accordingly, references in this Part to the Secretary of State shall, where subsection (1), (2) or (3) above applies, be treated as references to the authorities in question acting jointly.

(5) The Agency shall be consulted before—

   (a) any regulations are made under this Part, other than under section 113 above, or
   (b) any consent is granted or varied.

(6) The reference in section 113 above to expenditure of the Secretary of State in discharging functions under this Part in relation to consents shall be taken to include a reference to the corresponding expenditure of the Minister in discharging those functions jointly with the Secretary of State.

(7) The validity of anything purporting to be done in pursuance of the exercise of a function of the Secretary of State under this Part shall not be affected by any question whether that thing fell, by virtue of this section, to be done jointly with the Minister or the Agency (or both).

(8) In this section—

"the Agency" means the Food Standards Agency; and

"the Minister" means the Minister of Agriculture, Fisheries and Food.'

Genetically Modified Organisms (Northern Ireland) Order 1991 (S.I. 1991/1714 (N.I. 19))

19 In Article 5(7) and Article 8(7) of the Genetically Modified Organisms (Northern Ireland) Order 1991 (grant of exemptions) after the word 'Department' there shall be inserted the words ', or by the Department and the Food Standards Agency acting jointly,'.

20(1) For Article 22 of that Order (exercise of certain functions relating to genetically modified organisms jointly by the Department of the Environment and the Department of Agriculture) there shall be substituted the following Article—

'Mode of exercise of certain functions

22(1) Any power of the Department to make regulations under this Order (other than the power conferred by Article 10) is exercisable, where the regulations to be made relate to any matter with which the Department of Agriculture is concerned, by the Department and the Department of Agriculture acting jointly.

(2) Any function of the Department under this Order (other than a power to make regulations) is exercisable, where the function is to be exercised in relation to a matter with which the Department of Agriculture is concerned, by the Department and the Department of Agriculture acting jointly (but subject to paragraph (3)).

(3) Any function of the Department under Article 5(8) and 7 is exercisable, where the function is to be exercised in relation to a matter with which the Food Standards Agency is concerned—

  (a) if it is a matter with which the Department of Agriculture is also concerned, by the Department, the Department of Agriculture and the Food Standards Agency acting jointly;
  (b) otherwise, by the Department and the Food Standards Agency acting jointly.

(4) Accordingly, references in this Order to the Department shall, where paragraph (1), (2) or (3) applies, be treated as references to the authorities in question acting jointly.

(5) The Food Standards Agency shall be consulted before—

  (a) any regulations are made under this Order, other than under Article 10, or
  (b) any consent is granted or varied.

(6) The reference in Article 10 to expenditure of the Department in discharging functions under this Order in relation to consents shall be taken to include a reference to the corresponding expenditure of the Department of Agriculture in discharging those functions jointly with the Department.

(7) The validity of anything purporting to be done in pursuance of the exercise of a function of the Department under this Order shall not be affected by any question whether that thing fell, by virtue of this Article, to be done jointly with the Department of Agriculture or the Food Standards Agency (or both).'

(2) In consequence of sub-paragraph (1), in the definition of 'the Department' in Article 2(2) of that Order, after the word 'means' there shall be inserted the words '(subject to Article 22)'.

Radioactive Substances Act 1993 (c 12)

21 The Agency shall have the right to be consulted in the circumstances mentioned in subsection (4A) of section 16 or subsection (2A) of section 17 of the Radioactive Substances Act 1993 (proposals for granting or varying authorisations) about the matters mentioned in paragraphs (a) and (b) of that subsection.

Paragraph 15: Section 4 of the Medicines Act 1968 provides for the establishment of committees to advise on various aspects of the licensing of medicines (including veterinary medicines). *Subparagraph (2)* amends this provision to provide for the Agency to nominate a member of any committee established under it dealing with veterinary medicinal products for appointment by the Secretary of State.

This provision will in practice apply to the Veterinary Products Committee, which considers applications for authorisation of new veterinary medicines and related products. (It should be noted that, as with the Advisory Committee on Pesticides, it is expected that the Agency will also provide an adviser to this committee and its sub-committee.)

Section 129 of the Medicines Act 1968 provides the general procedure for the making of regulations and orders under that Act. *Subparagraph (3)* amends section 129 to specify that the Agency must be consulted on any new regulations concerning veterinary drugs or medicated feedingstuffs.

Paragraph 16, subparagraphs (1) and *(2)* set out the Agency's functions in relation to emergency control orders made under the Food and Environment Protection Act 1985 (FEPA 1985), conferred by amendments to sections 2 and 3 of that Act. Consequential amendments are set out in more detail in Schedule 5.

Subparagraphs (3) to *(5)* amend Parts II and III of FEPA 1985, which relate respectively to the licensing of deposits at sea and of pesticides. The amendments introduce a requirement for the Agency to be consulted on licensing matters under Part II (dumping at sea), and a more general requirement for consultation of the Agency on matters covered by Part III (pesticides).

Powers are available under Part II of the Food and Environment Protection Act 1985 for Ministers to license the deposit of substances and articles in the sea and the loading of vessels with materials destined for incineration at sea. For these purposes, 'licensing authority' means the Minister of Agriculture, Fisheries and Food and the Secretary of State (in practice the Secretary of State for the Environment, Transport and the Regions) acting jointly in relation to England and Wales; and the Scottish Ministers in relation to Scotland. They may also make orders which specify types of operation which do not need a licence or which specify the conditions under which they may be exempt.

The purpose of such powers is primarily to protect the marine environment and to prevent interference with legitimate uses of the sea, and it is proposed that the powers should remain with Ministers as defined. However, in view of the potential effects of dumping at sea on the safety of food obtained from it, subparagraph (3) amends the powers to grant exemption from the requirement for licences to require that the Agency be consulted before any exemptions are made or conditions for exemptions set down in law.

Subparagraph (4) requires the licensing authority to consult on specific applications and on the general way in which food safety should be addressed when considering licence applications. The licensing authority is obliged to take the Agency's advice into account.

Part III of FEPA 1985 concerns the licensing of pesticides and related products for the purposes of protecting human, animal and plant health, safeguarding the environment and securing safe, efficient and humane methods of controlling pests. Primary responsibility for such licensing lies with Agriculture, Health and Environment Ministers. Section 16 of the Act relates to the requirements on Ministers to consult the Advisory Committee on Pesticides (ACP) on proposals:

- for regulations;
- for giving, revoking or suspending approvals of pesticide products;
- for conditions to which they are considering making approvals subject.

Subparagraph (5) amends this provision to require Ministers to consult the Agency as well as the ACP on proposals for regulations, and from time to time on the general policy towards pesticides approvals. These are similar to the provisions concerning veterinary products outlined in the notes to section 29 and Schedule 3, paragraph 15 above.

In practice, the amendment means that the Agency will be formally consulted by officials from the Pesticides Safety Directorate on policy advice that they intend to submit to Ministers on any of the above three matters. It will also be achieved through the provision by the Agency of an assessor to the ACP and its sub-committee (the assessor's duty is to contribute to the assessment and authorisation of pesticides). This supplements the provision in *subparagraph (6)* below.

Subparagraph (6) amends FEPA 1985 to provide for the Agency to nominate a member of the Advisory Committe on Pesticides.

Paragraphs 17 and *18* amend Part VI of the Environmental Protection Act 1990 (EPA 1990), which is concerned with preventing or minimising any damage to the environment which may result from the escape or release of genetically modified organisms (GMOs). Lead responsibility for this area of policy lies with the Secretary of State for the Environment, Transport and the Regions. However, the Secretary of State for Health could (through normal machinery of government arrangements) take part in the decision-making process where appropriate.

The amendments are designed to give the Agency a role in relation to regulations controlling the import, acquisition, release or marketing of any GMO and related matters. Paragraph 17 provides a new option allowing such regulations to specify that the Agency may act jointly with the Secretary of State in addition to the Secretary of State acting alone in considering any exemptions from the risk assessment or notification requirements for the matters mentioned above (section 108(7)) and exempting from the consent requirements relating to the same actions (section 111(7)).

Paragraph 18 modifies section 126 of the EPA 1990, which provides more generally for regulations under Part VI to be made jointly by the Secretary of State and the Minister of Agriculture, Fisheries and Food, where the regulations concern any matter with which the latter is concerned. The amendment made by this section does not alter this requirement, since MAFF will retain an interest in the economic and environmental implications of GMOs for the farming and food industries after the Agency comes into being.

It does however introduce mechanisms to ensure that the Agency can exercise the same degree of influence as MAFF does now. In particular, the Agency must be consulted before any regulations on the deliberate release of GMOs are made where these relate to matters with which the Agency is concerned.

The amendment to section 126 would have the following effect.

- *Subsection (1)* of this new section continues the Minister of Agriculture, Fisheries and Food's role in relation to regulations under Part VI of the EPA 1990. It does however exclude him from the power to make regulations relating to fees and charges under section 113 of that Act (but see subsection (6) below).
- *Subsection (2)* preserves the Minister of Agriculture, Fisheries and Food's role in all the functions under Part VI (other than the power to make regulations, which is dealt with under subparagraph (1) above).
- *Subsection (3)* applies in relation to the powers (other than powers to make regulations):
  - under section 108(8), to require certain persons to apply for authorisation to release, market, import or acquire GMOs;
  - under section 110, to prohibit certain persons from releasing, marketing, importing or acquiring GMOs if it is believed they risk damaging the environment.
- The effect of the amendment is that these powers must now be exercised jointly by the Secretary of State, the Agency, in relation to matters connected with food safety and other interests of consumers in relation to food, and the Minister of Agriculture, Fisheries and Food where he is also concerned with the matter in question.
- *Subsection (5)* introduces a new requirement for the Agency to be consulted:
  - before any regulations under Part VI of EPA 1990 are made, other than regulations relating to fees and charges under section 113;
  - before any consent relating to deliberate releases is issued (under section 111) or the conditions and limitations on the granting of a consent are varied (under section 112).
- *Subsection (6)* requires the Secretary of State to take account of costs incurred by the Minister of Agriculture, Fisheries and Food and the Agency in drawing up charging scheme under section 113 of the EPA 1990.
- *Subsection (7)* qualifies the subsections of this section that deal with joint action and consultation. Essentially, it provides that any regulatory power or function exercised under this subsection is not rendered invalid if there is subsequently any question as to whether it should have been done (or not done) jointly with the Minister of Agriculture, Fisheries and Food or the Agency (or both), rather than by the Secretary of State acting alone.

Paragraphs 19 and *20* amend the Genetically Modified Organisms (Northern Ireland) Order 1991 to make corresponding provision for Northern Ireland to that made by the amendments to the Environment Protection Act 1990 in paragraphs 17 and 18.

Paragraph 21 sets out the Agency's right to be consulted on authorisations to dispose of radioactive waste. The detailed amendments to the Radioactive Substances Act 1993 are made in Schedule 5.

SCHEDULE 4   Section 39(7)

ACCOUNTS AND AUDIT

1 For the purposes of this Schedule—

'relevant authorities' means the Treasury, the National Assembly for Wales, the Scottish Ministers and the Department of Finance and Personnel for Northern Ireland;

'relevant bodies' means the House of Commons, the National Assembly for Wales, the Scottish Parliament and the Northern Ireland Assembly;

'the Department' means the Department of Finance and Personnel for Northern Ireland.

Appropriation accounts

2(1) Where any appropriation accounts of the Agency or report of the Comptroller and Auditor General on such accounts are laid before the House of Commons under the Exchequer and Audit Departments Act 1866, the Comptroller and Auditor General shall send copies to the relevant authorities for Wales, Scotland and Northern Ireland.

(2) The Scottish Ministers shall present documents received under this paragraph to the Scottish Parliament and the Department shall present such documents to the Northern Ireland Assembly.

Accounts of Agency relating to sums paid or appropriated under s 39(3)

3(1) The Agency shall prepare separate accounts for each year of its expenditure in relation to each of the following descriptions of sums, that is to say—

(a) the sums paid by the National Assembly for Wales under section 39(3)(a);
(b) the sums paid out of the Scottish Consolidated Fund under section 39(3)(b); or
(c) sums appropriated by Act of the Northern Ireland Assembly under section 39(3)(c).

(2) Any sum received by the Agency which it applies by virtue of any relevant provision (within the meaning of section 39) shall be regarded as falling within paragraph (a), (b) or (c) of sub-paragraph (1), as the case may require.

(3) Accounts required under this paragraph relating to sums of any description mentioned in sub-paragraph (1)—

(a) shall be prepared in such form, and
(b) shall be sent to the Comptroller and Auditor General, and to the relevant authority for the accounts, before such time,

as the relevant authority for the accounts may direct after consulting the Agency and the other relevant authorities.

(4) The Comptroller and Auditor General shall examine any accounts sent to him under sub-paragraph (3) on behalf of the National Assembly for Wales, the Scottish Parliament or the Northern Ireland Assembly (according to the description of sums to which the accounts relate).

(5) In carrying out his examination of any such accounts the Comptroller and Auditor General shall, among other things, satisfy himself that the money expended by the Agency has been applied to the purpose or purposes for which the sums in question were intended to provide.

(6) When the Comptroller and Auditor General has certified and reported on any accounts under this section, he shall—

(a) send the accounts and report to the relevant authority for the accounts; and
(b) send copies to the other relevant authorities.

(7) The Treasury shall present documents received under sub-paragraph (6) to the House of Commons, the Scottish Ministers shall present such documents to the Scottish Parliament and the Department shall present such documents to the Northern Ireland Assembly.

(8) In this paragraph 'the relevant authority for the accounts' is—

(a) in the case of accounts relating to sums within sub-paragraph (1)(a), the National Assembly for Wales;

(b) in the case of accounts relating to sums within sub-paragraph (1)(b), the Scottish Ministers; and

(c) in the case of accounts relating to sums within sub-paragraph (1)(c), the Department.

Consolidated accounts

4(1) The Agency shall prepare consolidated accounts for each financial year showing its income and expenditure and its overall state of affairs for that year.

(2) Accounts under this paragraph shall—

(a) be prepared in such form (and include such documents), and

(b) be sent to the Comptroller and Auditor General and to the Treasury before such time,

as the Treasury may direct after consulting the Agency and the other relevant authorities.

(3) The Comptroller and Auditor General shall examine any accounts sent to him under sub-paragraph (2) on behalf of the House of Commons.

(4) When any such accounts have been certified and reported on by the Comptroller and Auditor General, he shall—

(a) send the certified accounts and the report to the Treasury who shall lay them before the House of Commons; and

(b) send copies of those documents to the other relevant authorities.

(5) The Scottish Ministers shall present documents received under sub-paragraph (4) to the Scottish Parliament and the Department shall present such documents to the Northern Ireland Assembly.

Accounts under s 5 of the Exchequer and Audit Departments Act 1921

5(1) Any functions of the Treasury under section 5 of the Exchequer and Audit Departments Act 1921 shall, subject to sub-paragraph (2), be exercisable in relation to the Agency with the consent of the other relevant authorities and after consulting the Agency.

(2) The consent of a relevant authority is not required if the operations concerned do not include operations carried out in or in relation to the jurisdiction for which it is the relevant authority.

(3) If a direction under section 5 of that Act is given in respect of the Agency, that section shall have effect as if any reference to Parliament or the House of Commons included a reference to each of the other relevant bodies, other than the relevant body for any jurisdiction referred to in sub-paragraph (2).

Functions of Comptroller under s 9 of the National Audit Act 1983

6(1) The power of the Comptroller and Auditor General to make reports to the House of Commons under section 9 of the National Audit Act 1983 includes power, in relation to any examination of the Agency under section 6 of that Act, to make reports to any of the other relevant bodies.

(2) If the Comptroller and Auditor General makes a report to one or more of the relevant bodies under section 9 of that Act in relation to such an examination, he shall lay a copy of the report before each of the other relevant bodies.

This Schedule sets out the arrangements for the Agency's accounts and audit.

As a UK Government department, the Agency will automatically be subject to the requirements of the Exchequer and Audit Departments Acts, under which it is required to produce appropriation accounts for Parliament in respect of monies voted to it by Parliament, which are audited by the Comptroller and Auditor General. However, section 39 of the Act provides for the Agency to receive money not only from Parliament but also from the Scottish Parliament, National Assembly for Wales, and Northern Ireland Assembly. The Agency must be able to account to those bodies for the expenditure of the money provided by them, and as this is not covered by existing legislation, specific provision is made here. In addition, section 35 states that the Agency is to be treated as a cross border public authority for the purposes of section 70(6) of the Scotland Act 1998. This means that the arrangements for accounting to the Scottish Parliament may not be made in Scottish legislation, and therefore provisions are included here for accounts to be made to the Scottish Parliament.

Paragraph 1 defines the relevant authorities and bodies with an interest in the Agency's accounts (ie the devolved administrations and the Treasury, and the devolved legislatures and the House of Commons).

Paragraph 2 states that copies of the appropriation accounts, which the Agency is already required to produce for Parliament by virtue of the Exchequer and Audit Departments Act 1866, must be sent to the relevant authorities for Wales, Scotland and Northern Ireland, who will present them to the Scottish Parliament and the Northern Ireland Assembly as the case may be. This is so that they are informed of the overall financial position of the Agency – final scrutiny of the appropriation accounts remains the task of the House of Commons, through the Public Accounts Committee.

Paragraph 3 deals with the Agency's accounts for the expenditure of the sums provided by the devolved authorities in accordance with section 39 of the Act (this includes income from statutory charges imposed in their areas). The relevant authority for each of the parts of the UK may direct the form of the accounts for their part of the UK but must first consult the Agency and the other relevant authorities. The purpose of this is to achieve consistency between the form of accounts provided to each body, thereby assisting in the preparation of the consolidated accounts (see below). The accounts will be audited on behalf of each of the devolved legislatures by the Comptroller and Auditor General. Audited accounts must be sent to the relevant authority whose money they concern, which will present them to its legislature for scrutiny. Copies of the accounts are sent to the other devolved authorities and the Treasury, and these bodies must present them to the other legislatures and the House of Commons, essentially for information.

Paragraph 4 provides for consolidated accounts to be prepared in a form directed by the Treasury after consulting the Agency and other relevant authorities, and send them to the Comptroller and Auditor General to be audited and laid before the House of Commons. The consolidated accounts will bring together into a single document all the parts of the UK Agency's accounts in order to give Parliament a view of its overall financial position. Again, copies of the accounts are sent to the devolved authorities for presentation to the devolved legislatures for information.

Paragraph 5 deals with trading accounts produced under section 5 of the Exchequer and Audit Departments Act 1921. So far as the Agency is concerned, it is envisaged that this provision will be the basis for the separate Meat Hygiene Service accounts. Since the Meat Hygiene Service will operate across GB, the Treasury is required to seek the consent of the other relevant authorities and consult the Agency before directing the form of these accounts. However, it is not necessary to seek the consent of any relevant authority not affected by the operations in question (ie Northern Ireland is not involved since the MHS does not operate in Northern Ireland).

Paragraph 6 ensures that the Comptroller and Auditor General has the power to make reports to the devolved bodies for the purposes of value for money audit under the National Audit Act 1983.

SCHEDULE 5   Section 40(1)

MINOR AND CONSEQUENTIAL AMENDMENTS

Agricultural Returns Act (Northern Ireland) 1939 (c 35) (N.I.)

1 In section 1(4) of the Agircultural Returns Act (Northern Ireland) 1939 (restriction on disclosure of returns), after paragraph (e) there shall be added the following paragraph—

'(f) to the Food Standards Agency for purposes connected with the carrying out of any of its functions.'

Agriculture Act 1947 (c 48)

2 In the proviso to section 80 of the Agriculture Act 1947 (exceptions to restriction on disclosure of information) after paragraph (d) there shall be inserted the following paragraph—

'(e) to the Food Standards Agency for purposes connected with the carrying out of any of its functions,'.

Parliamentary Commissioner Act 1967

3 In Schedule 2 to the Parliamentary Commissioner Act 1967 (departments etc subject to investigation) the following entry shall be inserted in the appropriate place—

'Food Standards Agency.'.

Trade Descriptions Act 1968 (c 29)

4(1) Section 38 of the Trade Descriptions Act 1968 (orders) shall be amended as follows.

(2) In subsection (2), the words from 'agricultural' to 'stuffs' (in the second place it appears) shall be omitted.

(3) After subsection (2) there shall be inserted the following subsections—

'(2A) Any order under the preceding provisions of this Act which relates to any agricultural, horticultural or fishery produce, whether processed or not, food, feeding stuffs or the ingredients of food or feeding stuffs shall be made by the Board of Trade acting jointly with the following Ministers, that is to say, if the order extends to England and Wales, the Secretary of State concerned with health and if it extends to Scotland or Northern Ireland, the Secretary of State concerned.

(2B) Before making an order to which subsection (2) or (2A) of this section applies the Board of Trade shall consult the Food Standards Agency.'

Agricultural Statistics Act 1979 (c 13)

5 In section 3(2) of the Agricultural Statistics Act 1979 (exceptions to restrictions on disclosure of information) after paragraph (f) there shall be inserted the following paragraph—

'(g) to the Food Standards Agency for purposes connected with the carrying out of any of its functions,'.

Food and Environment Protection Act 1985 (c 48)

6(1) The Food and Environment Protection Act 1985 shall be amended as follows.

(2) In section 1(2) (emergency orders: definition of 'designating authority') after 'Food' there shall be inserted the words 'and the Secretary of State or either of them'.

This sub-paragraph shall come into force on the passing of this Act.

(3) In section 1(2) as so amended, for the words from 'the Minister' to 'them' there shall be substituted the words 'the Secretary of State'.

(4) In section 2 (powers of designating authority when emergency order is made)—

(a) in subsection (1)—
  (i) after the words 'A designating authority' there shall be inserted the words 'or the Food Standards Agency'; and
  (ii) for the words 'the designating authority' there shall be substituted the words 'the authority giving the consent';

(b) in subsection (3)—
  (i) after the words 'A designating authority' there shall be inserted the words 'or the Food Standards Agency';
  (ii) in paragraph (a), for the words 'the designating authority' (in both places) there shall be substituted the words 'the authority giving the directions'; and
  (iii) in paragraph (b), after the words 'the designating authority' there shall be inserted the words 'or the Agency (as the case may be)'; and

(c) in subsections (5) and (6)—
  (i) after the words 'a designating authority' there shall be inserted the words 'or the Food Standards Agency';
  (ii) for the words 'the designating authority' (in the first place it appears) there shall be substituted the words 'the authority taking that action'; and
  (iii) for the words 'the designating authority' (in the second place it appears) there shall be substituted the words 'that authority'.

(5) In section 25(2) (application of Act to Northern Ireland)—

(a) before paragraph (a) there shall be inserted the following paragraph—
  '(za) in section 1(2), in the definition of "designating authority", for the words from "in relation" (in the first place they appear) to the end there is substituted "means the Department of Agriculture for Northern Ireland";'
(b) in paragraph (a), after the words 'reference' (in the first place it appears) there shall be inserted the words 'in Part III'.

This sub-paragraph shall come into force on the passing of this Act.

(6) In section 25(2) as amended by sub-paragraph (5)—

(a) for paragraph (za) there shall be substituted the following paragraph—
  '(za) in section 1(2), in the definition of "designating authority", for the words from "in relation" (in the first place they appear) to the end there is substituted "means the Department of Health and Social Services for Northern Ireland";'
(b) in paragraph (a), for the word 'paragraph' there shall be substituted the words 'paragraphs (ab) and'; and

(c) after paragraph (a) there shall be insereted the following paragraph—

'(ab) subject to paragraph (b) below, in section 16 for any reference to the Ministers or either of them there is substituted a reference to the Department of Agriculture for Northern Ireland and the Department of Health and Social Services for Northern Ireland acting jointly;'.

Food Safety Act 1990 (c 16)

7 The Food Safety Act 1990 shall be amended as follows.

8 In the following provisions—

section 1(2) and (3)
section 2(1)
section 5(4) and (6)
section 6(6)
section 13(1)
section 16(1), (2) and (4)
section 17(1) and (2)
section 18(1)
section 19(1) and (2)
section 27(2) and (5)
section 30(9)
section 31(1)
section 40(1) to (4)
section 41
section 42(1) to (4)
section 45(1) and (2)
section 47
section 48(1), (2) and (4)
section 49(2)
section 53(3)
section 57(1)
section 59(2)

for the words 'the Minister', 'the Ministers' or 'the Ministers or the Minister' there shall be substituted the words 'the Secretary of State'.

9 In section 5(1), after paragraph (c) there shall be inserted—

'(d) as respects the Isles of Scilly, the council of the Isles of Scilly.'

10(1) Section 6 (enforcement) shall be amended as follows.

(2) In subsection (3)—

(a) for the word 'Ministers' (in the first place it appears) there shall be substituted the words 'Secretary of State'; and

(b) for the words 'the Ministers or the Minister' there shall be substituted the words 'the Secretary of State, the Minister of Agriculture, Fisheries and Food' and after those words there shall be inserted the words 'or the Food Standards Agency'.

(3) In subsection (4)—

(a) the words 'the Ministers' shall be omitted; and

(b)　after the word 'State,' there shall be inserted the words 'the Food Standards Agency,'.

(4) In subsection (5) the words from 'and, in' to the end shall be omitted and after that subsection there shall be inserted the following subsections—

'(5A) The Secretary of State may take over the conduct of any such proceedings which have been instituted by some other person.

(5B) The Secretary of State may direct the Food Standards Agency to take over the conduct of any such proceedings which have been instituted by some other person other than the Agency.

(5C) The Food Standards Agency may take over the conduct of any such proceedings which have been instituted by some other person, but (unless the Agency has been directed to do so under subsection (5B) above) only with the consent of the person who instituted them.'

11(1) Section 13 (emergency control orders) shall be amended as follows.

(2) In subsection (3), for the words 'The Minister' there shall be substituted the words 'the Secretary of State', after those words there shall be inserted the words 'or the Food Standards Agency' and for the words 'he' there shall be substituted the words 'the authority giving the consent'.

(3) In subsection (5), for the words 'The Minister' there shall be substituted the words 'The Secretary of State', after those words there shall be inserted the words 'or the Food Standards Agency' and for the words 'him' (in both places) and 'he' there shall be substituted the words 'the authority giving the directions'.

(4) In subsection (7), for the words 'the Minister' (in the first place) there shall be substituted the words 'the Secretary of State', after those words there shall be inserted the words 'or the Food Standards Agency' and for the words 'the Minister' (in the second place) and 'him' there shall be substituted the words 'that authority'.

12 In section 17 (enforcement of Community provisions)—

(a)　in subsection (1), for the word 'them' there shall be substituted the word 'him'; and
(b)　in subsection (2), for the words 'their' and 'they consider' there shall be substituted respectively the words 'his' and 'he considers'.

13 In section 18(2) (special provisions for particular foods) for the words 'The Ministers' (in the first place), 'the Ministers consider' and 'the Minister's' there shall be substituted respectively the words 'The Secretary of State', 'the Secretary of State considers' and 'the Secretary of State's'.

14 In section 19(2) (registration and licensing of food premises), for the word 'them' there shall be substituted the word 'him'.

15 Section 25 (orders for facilitating the exercise of functions) shall cease to have effect.

16 After section 36 (offences by bodies corporate) there shall be inserted the following section—

'Offences by Scottish partnerships

36A Where an offence under this Act which has been committed by a Scottish partnership is proved to have been committed with the consent or connivance of, or to be attributable to any neglect on the part of, a partner, he, as well as the partnership shall be deemed to be guilty of that offence and liable to be proceeded against and punished accordingly.'

17(1) Section 40 (codes of practice for food authorities) shall be amended as follows.

(2) After subsection (1) there shall be inserted the following subsection—

'(1A) The Food Standards Agency may, after consulting the Secretary of State, give a food authority a direction requiring them to take any specified steps in order to comply with a code under this section.'

(3) In subsection (2)(b) for the words from 'by' to 'and' there shall be substituted the words 'under this section and'.

(4) In subsection (3), for the words 'subsection (2)(b)' and 'the Ministers or the Minister' (or if the amendment in paragraph 8 has been made, the words 'the Secretary of State') there shall be substituted respectively the words 'subsection (1A)' and 'the Food Standards Agency'.

(5) After subsection (3) there shall be inserted—

'(3A) The Food Standards Agency shall consult the Secretary of State before making an application under subsection (3) above.'

(6) In subsection (4), the words after 'shall' shall be renumbered as paragraph (a) and at the end there shall be added the words '; and

(b) have regard to any relevant advice given by the Food Standards Agency'.

(7) After subsection (4) there shall be inserted the following subsection—

'(4A) If it appears to the Secretary of State that the Food Standards Agency has undertaken any consultation with an organisation that he is required to consult under subsection (4) above, the Secretary of State may treat that consultation as being as effective for the purposes of that subsection as if undertaken by him.'

18 In section 41 (power to require returns and other information from food authorities)—

(a) before the words 'such reports' there shall be inserted the words 'or to the Food Standards Agency'; and
(b) after the words 'him' and 'he' there shall be inserted the words 'or it'.

19 In section 42 (default powers), in subsection (1), after the words 'another food authority' there shall be inserted the words 'or the Food Standards Agency'.

20 In section 45(1) (power to impose charges for things done, by Ministers under the 1990 Act), after the words 'done' there shall be inserted the words 'or to be done'.

21 In section 48 (regulations and orders), after subsection (4) there shall be inserted the following subsections—

'(4A) Before making any regulations or order under this Act, the Secretary of State shall have regard to any relevant advice given by the Food Standards Agency.

(4B) If it appears to the Secretary of State that the Food Standards Agency has undertaken any consultation with an organisation that he is required to consult under subsection (4) above, the Secretary of State may treat that consultation as being as effective for the purposes of that subsection as if undertaken by him.'

22(1) Section 57(1) (application of Act to Isles of Scilly subject to modifications) shall cease to have effect.

(2) The repeal of section 57(1) does not affect Article 20(2) of the Food Safety Act 1990 (Consequential Modifications) (England and Wales) Order 1990 (amendments of the Isles of Scilly (Functions) Order 1979).

23 After paragraph 6 of Schedule 1 (provisions which may be included in regulations under section 16) there shall be inserted the following paragraph—

'*Production of food sources*

6A Provision for prohibiting or regulating—

(a) the possession, sale or offer, exposure or advertisement for sale of any specified substance, or any substance of any specified class, with a view to its use in connection with the production of any food source;
(b) the use of any specified substance, or any substance of any specified class, in connection with the production of any food source;
(c) the carrying out of any other activity in connection with, or in a manner likely to affect, the production of any food source.'

24 In paragraph 7(2) of Schedule 1 (provisions which may be included in regulations relating to food safety or consumer protection), after the word 'falls' there shall be inserted the words '(or is likely to fall)'.

25(1) Paragraph 7 of Schedule 4 (saving from repeal of section 15 of the Food Act 1984 for certain existing byelaws) shall cease to have effect.

(2) Accordingly, any byelaws which were made (or which have effect as if made) under that section 15 and which have continued in force by virtue of that paragraph are revoked.

Food Safety (Northern Ireland) Order 1991 (S.I. 1991/762 (N.I. 7))

26 The Food Safety (Northern Ireland) Order 1991 shall be amended as follows.

27 In the following provisions—

Article 8(8)
Article 11(10)
Article 12(1)
Article 15(1)(f) and (4)
Article 16(1) and (2)
Article 17(2)(a)
Article 18(2)
Article 39(1), (2), (3) and (4)
Article 41(1), (2) and (3)
Article 44(2)
Article 47(1), (2) and (3)
Article 51(2),

for the words 'the Department concerned' or 'that Department' there shall be substituted the words 'the Department'.

28 In the following provisions—

> Article 8(7) and (9)(b)
> Article 10(5) to (7)
> Article 11(5) to (10)
> Article 18(1)
> Article 22
> Article 33(1)(b)
> Article 37(1)
> Article 42(2)(b)
> Article 44(1) and (3)
> Article 45
> Article 49(2)
> Schedule 1,

after the words 'or, as the case may be,' there shall be inserted the words 'the Food Standards Agency or'.

29 In Article 2(2) (interpretation)—

(a) in the definition of 'authorised officer'—
  (i) after paragraph (b) there shall be inserted the following paragraph—
  '(bb)in the case of functions conferred on the Food Standards Agency, a person who is generally or is specially authorised in writing by the Food Standards Agency for the purposes of this Order;'; and
  (ii) in paragraph (c), for the words 'the Department concerned' in both places where they occur there shall be substituted the words 'the Department, the Department of Agriculture or the Food Standards Agency';
(b) in the definitions of 'order' and 'regulations' for the words 'the Department concerned' there shall be substituted the words 'the Department'.

30(1) Article 12 (emergency control orders) shall be amended as follows.

(2) In paragraph (3), for the words 'The Department concerned' there shall be substituted the words 'The Department', after those words there shall be inserted the words 'or the Food Standards Agency' and for the words 'that Department' there shall be substituted the words 'the authority giving the consent'.

(3) In paragraph (5), for the words 'The Department concerned' there shall be substituted the words 'The Department', after those words there shall be inserted the words 'or the Food Standards Agency' and for the words 'that Department' in each place where they occur there shall be substituted the words 'the authority giving the directions'.

(4) In paragraph (7), for the words 'the Department concerned' there shall be substituted the words 'The Department', after those words there shall be inserted the words 'or the Food Standards Agency' and for the words 'that Department' in both places where they occur there shall be substituted the words 'that authority'.

31 Article 24 (orders for facilitating the exercise of functions) shall cease to have effect.

32 In Article 25 (regulations and orders: supplementary provisions), in paragraph (2)(e), after the words 'district council' there shall be inserted the words ', the Food Standards Agency'.

33(1) Article 26 (enforcement) shall be amended as follows.

(2) In paragraph (1), for the words 'paragraph (1A)' there shall be substituted the words 'paragraphs (1A) and (1B)'.

(3) After paragraph (1A) there shall be inserted the following paragraph—

(1B) The Food Standards Agency shall enforce and execute such provisions of this Order as may be specified by order.'.

(4) In paragraph (2)—

(a) for the words 'Department concerned' there shall be substituted the word 'Department'; and

(b) for the words 'that Department' in both places where they occur there shall be substituted the words 'the Department, the Department of Agriculture or the Food Standards Agency'.

(5) After paragraph (3) there shall be inserted the following paragraph—

(3A) Regulations or orders under paragraph (3) may specify the Food Standards Agency as an authority to enforce and execute them and references in that paragraph to any authority concerned include references to the Food Standards Agency.'.

(6) In paragraph (4)—

(a) for the words 'Department concerned' there shall be substituted the word 'Department'; and

(b) after the words 'district council' there shall be inserted the words 'or may direct the Food Standards Agency to do so'.

(7) After paragraph (4) there shall be inserted the following paragraph—

'(4A) The Food Standards Agency may take over the conduct of any such proceedings but (unless the Agency has been directed to do so under paragraph (4)) only with the consent of the district council which instituted them.'.

34 In Article 27 (appointment of public and other analysts), paragraph (6)(a) shall cease to have effect.

35(1) Article 31 (analysis, etc of samples by authorised officer of the Department of Agriculture) shall be amended as follows.

(2) After paragraph (1) there shall be inserted the following paragraph—

(1A) An authorised officer of the Food Standards Agency who has procured a sample under Article 29 may—

(a) if he considers that the sample should be analysed by a public analyst or a food analyst, submit it to be so analysed;

(b) if he considers that the sample should be examined by a food examiner, submit it to be so examined,

and for the purposes of this paragraph reference in Article 27(1) and (6) to functions conferred on district councils or to the functions of the Department of Agriculture include references to functions of the Food Standards Agency.'.

(3) In paragraph (2), after the words 'paragraph (1)' (in the first place they occur) there shall be inserted the words 'or (1A)'.

(4) In paragraph (3)—

(a) in the definition of 'the requisite qualifications', for the words 'Department of Agriculture' there shall be substituted the word 'Department'; and

(b) in the definition of 'sample', after the words 'Department of Agriculture' there shall be inserted the words 'or the Food Standards Agency'.

36(1) Article 39 (codes of practice) shall be amended as follows.

(2) After paragraph (1) there shall be inserted the following paragraph—

'(1A) The Food Standards Agency may, after consulting the Department, give a district council, a direction requiring the council to take any specified steps in order to comply with a code under this Article.'.

(3) In paragraph (2)(b) for the words from 'by' to 'and' there shall be substituted the words 'under this Article and'.

(4) In paragraph (3), for the words 'paragraph (2)(b)' and 'the Department concerned' ('the Department' if the amendment in paragraph 27 has been made) there shall be substituted respectively the words 'paragraph (1A)' and 'the Food Standards Agency'.

(5) After paragraph (3) there shall be inserted the following paragraph—

'(3A) The Food Standards Agency shall consult the Department before making an application under paragraph (3).'

(6) In paragraph (4), the words after 'shall' shall be renumbered as sub-paragraph (a) and at the end there shall be added the words '; and

(b) have regard to any relevant advice given by the Food Standards Agency'.

(7) After paragraph (4) there shall be inserted the following paragraph—

(4A) If it appears to the Department that the Food Standards Agency has undertaken any consultation with an organisation that the Department is required to consult under paragraph (4), the Department may treat that consultation as being as effective for the purposes of that paragraph as if undertaken by the Department.'.

37 In Article 40 (power to require returns), after the word 'Department' in each place where it occurs there shall be inserted the words 'or the Food Standards Agency'.

38 In Article 41 (default powers), in paragraph (1), after the word 'empower' there shall be inserted the words 'the Food Standards Agency or'.

39 In Article 44 (power to impose charges for things done by district councils or Department of Agriculture under the Order), in paragraph (1)—

(a) after the word 'done' there shall be inserted the words 'or to be done'; and

(b) after the words 'those councils' there shall be inserted the words 'or the Food Standards Agency'.

40 In Article 47 (regulations and orders), after paragraph (3) there shall be inserted the following paragraphs—

'(3A) Before making any regulations or order under this Order, the Department shall have regard to any relevant advice given by the Food Standards Agency.

(3B) If it appears to the Department that the Food Standards Agency has undertaken any consultation with an organisation that the Department is required to consult under paragraph (3), the Department may treat that consultation as being as effective for the purposes of that paragraph as if undertaken by the Department.'.

41(1) Schedule 1 (provisions which may be included in regulations relating to food safety or consumer protection) shall be amended as follows.

(2) In paragraph 2(2), after the words 'district councils' there shall be inserted the words 'or the Food Standards Agency'.

(3) In paragraph 3 (2), after the words 'Department of Agriculture' and 'Department' (in each place) there shall be inserted the words 'or the Food Standards Agency'.

(4) After paragraph 6 there shall be inserted the following paragraph—

'Production of food sources

6A Provision for prohibiting or regulating—

(a) the possession, sale or offer, exposure or advertisement for sale of any specified substance, or any substance of any specified class, with a view to its use in connection with the production of any food source;

(b) the use of any specified substance, or any substance of any specified class, in connection with the production of any food source;

(c) the carrying out of any other activity in connection with, or in a manner likely to affect, the production of any food source.'.

(5) In paragraph 7(2), after the word 'falls' there shall be inserted the words '(or is likely to fall)'.

42(1) Paragraph 5 of Schedule 3 (saving from repeal of Article 17 of the Food (Northern Ireland) Order 1989 for certain existing byelaws) shall cease to have effect.

(2) Accordingly any byelaws which were made (or which have effect as if made) under that Article and which have continued in force by virtue of that paragraph are revoked.

Radioactive Substances Act 1993 (c 12)

43(1) The Radioactive Substances Act 1993 shall be amended as follows.

(2) In section 16 (grant or authorisations)—

(a) in subsection (4A)(a), for the words 'relevant Minister' there shall be substituted the words 'Food Standards Agency';

(b) in subsection (4A)(b) for the words 'relevant Minister' and 'that Minister' there shall be substituted respectively the words 'Food Standards Agency' and 'that Agency'; and

(c) subsection (11) shall be omitted.

(3) In section 17 (revocation and variation of authorisations)—

(a) in subsection (2A)(a), for the words 'relevant Minister' there shall be substituted the words 'Food Standards Agency';

(b) in subsection (2A)(b), for the words 'relevant Minister' and 'that Minister' there shall be substituted respectively the words 'Food Standards Agency' and 'that Agency'; and

(c) subsection (5) shall be omitted.

(4) Sections 23(4A) and 24(4A) (certain functions exercisable jointly with the Minister of Agriculture, Fisheries and Food) shall be omitted.

(5) In section 25 (power of Secretary of State to restrict knowledge of applications etc)—

(a) in subsection (3A), for the words 'the relevant Minister' and 'that Minister' there shall be substituted the words 'the Food Standards Agency'; and

(b) subsection (5) shall be omitted.

(6) Sections 26(5A) and 27(7A) (certain functions exercisable jointly with the Minister of Agriculture, Fisheries and Food) shall be omitted.

Environment Act 1995 (c 25)

44(1) Section 42 of the Environment Act 1995 (approval of charging schemes) shall be amended as follows.

(2) In subsection (3)(b)—

(a) in sub-paragraph (i) for the words 'Minister' and 'his' there shall be substituted respectively the words 'Food Standards Agency' and 'its'; and

(b) sub-paragraph (ii) shall be omitted.

(3) In subsection (4)—

(a) for the words 'Minister's or the Secretary of State's' there shall be substituted the words 'Food Standards Agency's';

(b) in paragraph (b), for the words from 'the Minister' to 'be' there shall be substituted the words 'or the Food Standards Agency'.

(4) In subsection (7), the words from 'and, if' to the end shall cease to have effect.

(5) In subsection (9)—

(a) for paragraphs (a) and (b) there shall be substituted the words 'such of the costs and expenses incurred by the Food Standards Agency as fall within subsection (3) above'; and

(b) for the words from 'to the Secretary' to the end there shall be substituted the words 'to the Food Standards Agency'.

(6) In subsection (10), for the words from 'paragraph (a) or' to the end there shall be substituted the words 'that subsection shall be determined by the Secretary of State.'

Government of Wales Act 1998 (c 38)

45 In Schedule 5 to the Government of Wales Act 1998 there shall be inserted—

'Food Standards Agency.
Food Standards Agency advisory committee for Wales.'.

This Schedule makes minor amendments to other legislation which are a consequence of the creation and new responsibilities of the Agency, and also to provide for the functions of the Agency provided in Schedule 3.

Paragraphs 1 and 2 amend the relevant legislation on agricultural statistics that applies in Northern Ireland and Scotland, and has the same purpose as *paragraph 5* (see below).

Paragraph 3 amends the Parliamentary Commissioner Act 1967 by adding the Food Standards Agency to the list of bodies subject to the jurisdiction of the Parliamentary Commissioner for Administration.

Paragraph 4 amends the Trades Descriptions Act 1968. Orders made under that Act concerning food or feedingstuffs will in future be made jointly by the President of the Board of Trade, the Secretary of State for Health (rather than the Minister of Agriculture, Fisheries and Food), and the Scottish, Welsh and Northern Ireland Ministers if appropriate. The Agency will also be consulted. In practice, this provision is likely to be used only rarely since these provisions are largely duplicated by powers in the Food Safety Act 1990 and the Agriculture Act 1970.

Paragraph 5 provides that information on agricultural holding obtained for the purposes of compiling the agricultural and horticultural census in England and Wales may, at the discretion of the Minister of Agriculture, Fisheries and Food, be disclosed to the Agency for purposes connected with carrying out its functions. This would allow the Agency, as a non-Ministerial government department, to be treated in the same way as Ministerial government departments, to which disclosure is currently possible under section 3(1) of the Agricultural Statistics Act 1979.

The Agency would use information obtained in this way to assist it in planning food safety surveys on farms (in preparing for a survey of the presence of salmonella in poultry, for example, it would need to know where poultry breeding took place). The information would also assist the Agency in considering applications for industrial discharge authorisations, on which it will be a statutory consultee, as well as in dealing with emergency contamination incidents. In practice, the Agency is likely to use such data infrequently and on a limited scale.

Paragraph 6 amends the Food and Environment Protection Act 1985 (FEPA 1985) Part I. It takes account of the changes already made to FEPA 1985 by the Scotland Act 1998 (Modification of Functions) Order 1999 (SI 1756), which made textual changes to facilitate the transfer of relevant functions to Scottish Ministers. As a consequence of these changes it is necessary for subparagraphs (2) and (5) to come into force on the coming into force of this Act. These preserve the role of the Secretary of State for Health in England and Wales, and the Department of Agriculture in Northern Ireland, to make emergency orders (in Scotland this function has transferred to Scottish Ministers). On coming into force of the rest of the Act, references to the Minister of Agriculture, Fisheries and Food are removed, so the functions in Part I of FEPA 1985 may only be exercised by the Secretary of State (or the Department of Health and Social Services in Northern Ireland).

Paragraphs 7, 8 and *10–21* amend the Food Safety Act 1990, removing references to the Minister of Agriculture, Fisheries and Food. They also provide for the powers described in Part I of Schedule 3 to be exercised by the Agency itself.

Paragraphs 9 and *22* concern the Isles of Scilly. Due to the slightly anomalous position of the Scilly Isles in the local government structure, the 1990 Act provided that its application to the Isles could be subject to such exceptions and modifications as Ministers may direct. In practice however, the only modification which has been necessary is to provide for the council of the Isles of Scilly to be the enforcement authority in the Isles. This has now been made explicit by amendment to s 5 of the 1990 Act (Schedule 5 paragraph 7), so s 57(1) is no longer necessary and ceases to have effect (paragraph 22).

Paragraph 10 amends section 6 (enforcement) of the Food Safety Act 1990. It provides for the Secretary of State to direct that a duty imposed on an enforcement body under the Act should instead be discharged by himself or by the Minister of Agriculture, Fisheries and Food or by the Agency. It also provides for the Agency to be one of the bodies which may be named as an enforcement body in regulations made under section 6 of the 1990 Act (it is envisaged that this power will be used for instance in relation to the Meat Hygiene Service, which will become part of the Food Standards Agency). Amendments also provide for the Secretary of State to take over a prosecution begun by another person under the Food Safety Act 1990 (this replaces a similar provision in the current Act) or for the Agency to take over such proceedings with the consent of that person or at the direction of the Secretary of State.

Paragraph 11 amends section 13 of the Food Safety Act 1990 (emergency control orders). Power to make emergency control orders transfers to the Secretary of State, although this may be delegated to the Agency under section 17 of this Act. The amendments in paragraph 9 allow either the Agency or the Secretary of State to consent to exemptions, give directions to prevent food subject to an order being used commercially, and to recover costs from persons failing to comply with an order.

Paragraph 16 concerns offences by Scottish partnerships. Section 36 of the Food Safety Act 1990 provides that, where an offence under the Act committed by a body corporate is proved to have been committed with the consent or connivance of (or be attributable to any neglect on the part of) a director, manager, secretary or similar office holder of the body, or by a person purporting to act in such a capacity, that person (as well as the body corporate) is deemed guilty of the offence. It has been held that in Scotland the words 'body corporate' include a partnership which in Scots law has an identity separate from that of the individual partners. This section adds a new Section 36A to provide that individual partners may be charged along with the partnership in respect of any offence committed under the Act.

Paragraph 17 amends section 40 of the Food Safety Act 1990 in the following ways. *Subparagraph (2)* inserts a new subsection (1A) to give the Agency power, after consulting the Secretary of State, to issue a direction to a local authority to ensure that it complies with a statutory code of practice issued under Section 40. *Subparagraph (3)* amends section 40(2)(b) to require local authorities to comply with a direction of the Agency, but the power of Ministers to direct is removed. *Subparagraph (4)* amends section 40(3) so that the Agency rather than Ministers can obtain a court order forcing a local authority to take appropriate action where it fails to comply with a direction but it must consult the Secretary of State before doing so.

Before setting charges in relation to licence applications, including those under the RSA 1993, the Environment Agencies are currently obliged to take into account the costs and expenses of the Minister of Agriculture, Fisheries and Food and certain of those of the Scottish and Welsh administrations (i.e. those performed by the Scottish and Welsh administrations which would be performed by the Minister of Agriculture, Fisheries and Food in England). The Minister's and Secretary of State's functions under the RSA 1993 are being transferred to the Agency, and, accordingly, the amendments to Environment Act 1995 made in *paragraph 44* specify that it is the Agency's costs and expenses that must be taken into account.

As the Minister of Agriculture, Fisheries and Good will no longer have responsibilities in this area *subparagraph (4)* removes the need for that Minister to approve any relevant charging proposals.

Fees charged by the Environment Agencies for licences may include an element to meet the costs incurred by the Agency. *Subparagraphs (5)* and *(6)* allow for these sums to be transferred from the Environment Agency to the Agency after collection.

Paragraph 45 amends Schedule 5 of the Government of Wales Act 1998 to add the Agency, and its advisory committee for Wales, to the list of bodies whose members and staff can be required to attend or produce documents for the National Assembly for Wales.

SCHEDULE 6   Section 40(4)

REPEALS

Reference	Title	Extent of repeal or revocation
1968 c 29	Trade Descriptions Act 1968	In section 38(2), the words from 'agricultural' to 'stuffs' (in the second place it appears).
1990 c 16	Food Safety Act 1990	Section 4. In section 6, in subsection (4)(a), the words 'the Ministers' and, in subsection (5), the words from 'and, in' to the end. Section 25. In section 26(3), the words 'or an order under section 25 above' and the words 'or order' (in both places). In section 40(4), the words 'them or'. In section 53(2), the entries for 'the Minister' and 'the Ministers'. Section 57(1). In Schedule 4, paragraph 7.

Reference	Title	Extent of repeal or revocation
S.I. 1991/762 (N.I. 7)	Food Safety (Northern Ireland) Order 1991	In Article 2(2), the definition of 'the Department concerned'. Article 24. In Article 25(3), the words 'or an order under Article 24' and in both places where they occur the words 'or order'. Article 27(6)(a). In Schedule 3, paragraph 5.
1993 c 12	Radioactive Substances Act 1993	Section 16(11). Section 17(5). Section 23(4A). Section 24(4A). Section 25(5). Section 26(5A). Section 27(7A).
1995 c 25	Environment Act 1995	In section 42, subsection (3)(b)(ii) and, in subsection (7), the words from 'and, if' to the end. In Schedule 22, paragraphs 205(10), 206(3), 211(2), 212(2) and 213(5).
S.I. 1996/1633 (N.I. 12)	Food Safety (Amendment) (Northern Ireland) Order 1996	Article 3 (1)(a). Article 7(2)(b)(i). Articles 8 and 9.

Appendix 2
List of Useful Organisations and their Websites

Australia New Zealand Food Authority at http://anzfa.gov.au
Canadian Food Inspection Agency at http://www.cria-acia.agr.ca
Codex Alimentarius Commission at http://www.fao.org/WAICENT/FAOINFO/ECONOMIC/ESN/codex/Default.htm
Department of Health (DoH) at http://www.doh.gov.uk
Directorate General XXIV on Health and Consumer Protection at http://www.europa.eu.int/comm/dg24/
Directory of European Legislation at http://europa.eu.int/eur-lex/en/lif/index.html
European Court of Human Rights (for ECHR judgments) at http://www.echr.coe.int/
European Court of Justice (for ECJ judgments) at http://www.curia.eu.int/en/index.htm
Food and Agriculture Organisation (FAO) of the United Nations at http://www.fao.org
Food Safety Authority of Ireland at http://www.fsai.ie
Food Standards Agency at http://www.foodstandards.gov.uk
Interventionist Board at http://www.ib-uk.gov.uk
Local Authorities Coordinating Body on Food and Trading Standards (LACOTS) at http://www.lacots.org.uk
Meat Hygiene Service (MHS) at http://www.foodstandards.gov.uk/meat_hygiene.htm
Ministry of Agriculture, Fisheries and Food (MAFF) at www.maff.gov.uk
United States Food and Drug Administration (FDA) at http://www.fda.gov/
World Health Organisation (WHO) at http://www.who.org

Appendix 3

Food Standards Agency – UK Headquarters

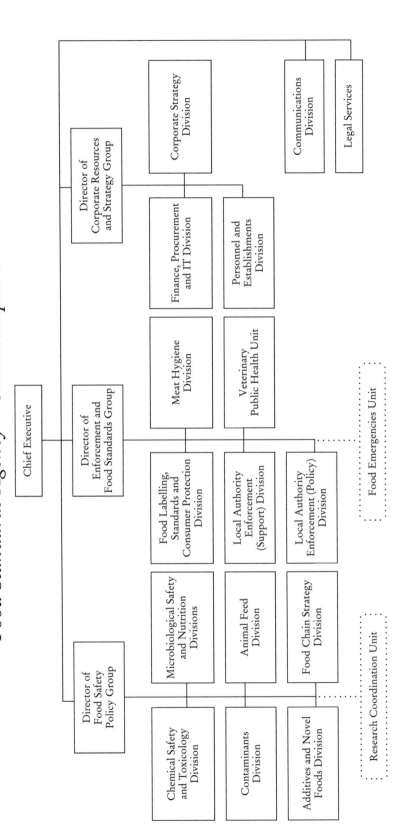

Bibliography

Andrews, C *The Enforcement of Regulatory Offences* (Sweet & Maxwell, 1998).
Bailey, SH *Cross on Principles of Local Government Law* 2nd edn (Sweet & Maxwell, 1997).
Baylis, C *Food Safety: Law and Practice* (Sweet & Maxwell, 1994).
Bell, WJ, O'Keefe, JA and Ives, R *Bell and O'Keefe's Sale of Food and Drugs* 14th edn O'Keefe, JA (ed) (Butterworths, 1968).
Better Regulatory Unit (now Regulatory Impact Unit) of the Cabinet Office *Enforcement Concordat: The Principles of Good Enforcement: Policy and Procedures* (March 1998).
Murphy, P, Stockdale, E, Birch, D *Blackstone's Criminal Practice* (Blackstone, 1999).
Butterworths' Law of Food and Drugs (Butterworths, 1980 onwards), 6 vols.
Civil Service Yearbook (Cabinet Office, HMSO, 1990–1999).
Cabinet Office Constitution Secretariat with CRP(EC)(O) *The Human Rights Act 1998* 2nd edn.
De Smith, SA, Woolf, Lord, Le Sueur, AP and Jowell, JL *Judicial Review of Administrative Action* 5th edn (Sweet & Maxwell, 1995).
Directory of Economic, Commodity and Development Organizations.
European Commission Foodstuffs Assessment Team *Results of the Evaluation of the Official Foodstuffs Control System in the UK* (30 January–3 February 1995).
European Commission Foodstuffs Assessment Team *Results of the Second Visit of Evaluation of the Official Foodstuffs Control System in the UK* (2–6 February 1998).
Food and Agriculture Organisation of the United Nations, *FAO: What it is, what it does* (1998).
Food and Agriculture Organisation of the United Nations *The Codex System: FAO, WHO and the Codex Alimentarius Commission* (1999).
Halsbury's Laws of England, Vol 8(2) *Constitutional Law and Human Rights* 4th edn (Butterworths, 1996).
Halsbury's Laws of England, Vol 18 *Food Diaries and Slaughterhouses* 4th edn (Butterworths, 1977).
Halsbury's Statutes, Vol 18 *Food* 4th edn (Butterworths, 1991).
Hedderwick, TCH *The Sale of Food and Drugs* 2nd edn (Eyre & Spottiswoode, 1900).
Hitchcock, T *Food Safety: A Practical Guide to the 1990 Act* (Fourmat, 1990).
James, Professor P *Food Standards Agency Report: An Interim Proposal* (30 April 1997).
Jennings, Sir I, Cole, GJ and Knight, C *The Law of Food and Drugs* (1938).
Jennings, Sir I and Cote, GJ *The Law of Food and Drugs* (Charles Knight, 1938).
Jukes, DJ *Food Legislation of the UK: A Concise Guide* 2nd edn (Butterworths, 1987).
LACOTS *The Home Authority Principle.*
LACOTS *About LACOTS.*
LACOTS *Scheme of Operation.*
O'Rourke, R 'Europe Adopts New Approach to Food Safety' (2000) NLJ, 18 February.
Outhwaite, W and Wheele, M *The Civil Practitioner's Guide to the Human Rights Act* (Old Bailey Press, 1999).
The Ministry of Agriculture, Fisheries and Food *About MAFF.*
Painter, AA *Butterworth's Food Law* (Butterworths, 1992).

Practitioners' Handbook of EC Law (Bar European Group, Bar Council, Trenton Publishing, 1998).

Ross, HA 'The Major Developments in UK Food Regulatory Law', paper delivered at the Food Law Group Conference, 1998.

Stone, S, Carr, AP, Richman, J, Draycott, AT *Stones Justices' Manual* (Butterworths, 1999).

Winnifrith, Sir J *The Ministry of Agriculture, Fisheries and Food* (Allen & Unwin, 1962).

World Health Organisation *About WHO* (1999).

'The Government's Measures for Success: Output and Performance Analyses' MAFF's extracts from HM Treasury Paper published 31 March 1999.

'Public Services for the Future: Modernisation, Reform, Accountability: Comprehensive Spending Review: Public Service Agreement 1999–2000' MAFF's extracts from HM Treasury Paper, Cm 4181, published December 1999.

Index

References are to paragraph numbers.